SAVING LIFE

M. Lynn Lamoreux, PhD

authorHOUSE®

AuthorHouse™
1663 Liberty Drive
Bloomington, IN 47403
www.authorhouse.com
Phone: 833-262-8899

Published by AuthorHouse 05/20/2021

ISBN: 978-1-6655-1377-7 (sc)
ISBN: 978-1-6655-1376-0 (e)

Library of Congress Control Number: 2021900830

The purpose of this book

Is to share a sustainable world view

That is biologically more true to the nature of Life

Than the failed corposystem world view that we have been taught.

This book is about achieving a viable future within the Biological system
of the Living Earth for the generations of humans yet to come,

If that is what we decide to do.

Biosystem = the system of the entire LIFE of Earth

Corposystem = The modern human social system that includes nearly all the good guys and nearly
all the bad guys; the corposystem is a subsystem of LIFE.

LIFE, written in all caps, refers to LIFE itself, the LIFE of Earth for example. The LIFE of your body.

LIFE is an emergent property of the Biosystem

It is true that human peace cannot be achieved without the dream of peace
And it is also true that human peace cannot be achieved without
A fact-based human acknowledgement of the
Biological foundations of peace that denies the fiction
of "survival of the fittest" as a core phenomenon,
And recognizes how nature really uses collaborative interactions to sustain LIFE.

Other approaches to "making peace" only end in new kinds of conflict.

This book is dedicated to:

Dr. Elizabeth (Tibby) Russell
And Dr. Mary Lyon

The PanAmerican,
Japanese, European and Asian
Pigment Cell Societies

His Holiness The Dalai Lama
and Geshe Thupten Jinpa

Father John Dear
and Pace e Bene

Beata Tsosie-Peña and
TEWA Women United

CONTENTS

PREFACE

"Really, the reason why we devote our lives and our money to . . . (basic scientific research) . . . is because we want to know the answer. . . We want to discover the way the world works. . . We want to know what this nature is that we live in, what are the rules, what are the ingredients."
(Carroll, 2015)

 My post-WWII generation had its troubles, plenty of them, but we were working hard to bring together our various cultures, with our social sciences and politics, and with the good basic science that is necessary if we are to "know the rules" of nature that can grow a sustainable world view to carry humanity forward into:

A reasonably comfortable, sustainable future, hand in hand with a healthy and productive Biosystem.

Sustainability is the ability to continue – to cycle forward in time -- forever. Or, unto the 7th generation and beyond. (Lyons & Goodman; Lyons & Moyers)

I did my bit.

On January 1, 2000, I emerged from my career as a geneticist, with some good publications and a cherished award from my peers for contributions to our common field of research, and then followed up with a co-authored book (Lamoreux *et al.*, 2010) on the subject of a lovely *naturally evolved biological system.*

It seemed like success, but outside of the field of basic scientific research, I felt like a foreigner in my own land.

What I found, as I shut down my laboratory and settled into my dream retirement on a small piece of land, with the horses and a dog and a couple of cats, was a country – my country -- actually the whole *Biosystem* (the whole system of the living Earth, see Appendix B for definitions and descriptions) as we humans need it for our survival-- in deep trouble. Trouble that seemed to me primarily the result of biological misinformation – that could be resolved, I assumed, by making available the real universal facts about how the naturally evolved system of the *LIFE of Earth*, nurturing us within itself, functions to sustain itself and us -- healthy, beautiful and bountiful.

> **Reality Number One** - *We cannot align our behaviors with the fact-based requirements for all of LIFE if we don't know what LIFE requires for its own welfare – or if we believe an alternative, unnatural or homocentric, human centered, version of the story of LIFE (Preface) See Appendix C for a list of the Realities.*

So, I sat down in my little travel trailer on my little ranch and read, researched and wrote about the universal Facts of Life.

Universal Facts apply to us and to every other part of *The Creation*. "Social facts" apply to human societies, not necessarily to the universe; and different societies may have different social facts. That's a down-side of our human reality. We are not in charge of the Universal Facts of LIFE, or of the Creator, or of *The Creation*. Problems arise when our *imprinted* social beliefs are different from the universal realities that apply to the whole of The Creation, including us.

> Universal facts are realities and processes that we cannot change because they operate throughout the entire universe, the whole of The Creation, or at least the whole of LIFE. For example, energy, entropy, information, self-assembly, natural selection, time, gravity, history as it really was.

> Our human "social facts" (Gimbel, 2015) and beliefs, on the other hand, are not universal Facts. They are beliefs or situations or answers that have been imprinted on our common consciousness, during our communal development as a naturally evolving human society. Imprinting is one of the ways that our environment communicates with us during our development (Chapter 09, LIFE codes). It is perfectly normal (Eagleman, 2017), and probably necessary. But not always perfect.

> "The rules by which we determine a social fact are internalized.
> We never think of them . . .
> sometimes the social facts are there for good reason,
> but sometimes they're not. . . . Not all social facts are desirable,
> and unless we are forced to confront and justify them,
> they will remain of their own inertia, and become worse if not challenged."
> (Gimbel, 2015)

The up-side of being human is that -- while we cannot change the laws that organize the entire universe -- we can change our human belief systems.

But it took me hardly any time to realize that very few people seem to care about the universal facts of the naturally evolved Creation – or of the biological system -- the LIFE[1] of the whole Earth Biosystem, of which we are a part.

And then my struggle began, with which I will not bore you here, to explain that the human *Fundamental Problem* (see Chapter 02 and Appendix A), our biological Problem that is at the core of most of our intractable human social, political and economic distress, is a real universal fact of LIFE that is easy to understand and largely avoidable (Diamond, 2011). I did not say easy to avoid – but avoidable, by changing our human behaviors.

The reality of our Biosystem is much more elegant than anything humans can conceive, and even so our Problem is well demonstrated (Ehrlich & Ehrlich, 1996; Goldsmith, 1981; Ripple *et al.*, 2017; Gorschkov et al., 2002; and many others quoted in this book and elsewhere). But the people would rather hear about a pretty human "social truth" that in fact cannot be squeezed into the fact-based foundations of LIFE and the naturally evolved systems of Earth. And so most people don't want to think about the universal facts; mostly we just believe the social truths.

"Why do we not want to hear about the universal facts?" I asked myself. "Apart from a few physicists, why do we prefer to believe in a story that cannot be? Or am I wrong about the science? I need to find the answers to those questions."

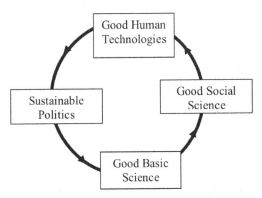

I studied many disciplines at the basic level: economics; sociology; philosophy and religion; mathematics; physics (classical, quantum, modern, chaos, information, complexity), and most important of all, Biology since I am a Biologist and the Problem is biological.

The Teaching Company (www.TheTeaching Company), was an invaluable resource, publishing basic lectures given by experts, that we can watch as many times as it takes to "get" the concepts that are understood today, and go back to if we should forget.

My goal was to learn enough about multiple relevant disciplines, based in my own specialties of genetics, evolution and ecology, so that I could fit together their basic, well-studied principles to describe some of the *emergent* patterns of LIFE, and particularly to learn how our modern human social view of LIFE differs from the reality.

I learned a lot, and it was fun learning.

> "How are the immense numbers of parts of LIFE integrated into its holistic, living, evolving, *sustainable* reality? Why do they stay together rather than fly apart because of entropy? What does the whole of LIFE require for its survival? How is that different from our modern human belief system?"

Those were my next questions.

The answers turned out to revolve around *balance* and *communication*; around maintaining the viable balance among the *systems* of the whole Biosystem as Lewin (1992) and Lloyd (2016); Heylighen *et al.*, 2010) and others describe it:

> "Life is balanced on the edge of chaos."

> And I learned how evolution does the balancing, by bringing together and integrating the laws of LIFE.

At the same time, I spent agonizing hours on Facebook responding to questions and/or statements and arguments from people who obviously were not well informed about the Living Earth environment, as well as challenges from "paid hacks" as one colleague refers to them, and presumably unpaid hacks who simply get their kicks out of creating "uproar" (Berne, 1964), rather than educating themselves and helping us all to face up to the *Facts of Life* and find our place within them. And other people who sharpened my understanding of one or another question.

Challenged by a waiter at a pub in downtown Bryan, I began a blog, Bare Bones Biology (http://FactFictionFancy.wordpress.com).

The up-side of the internet is there were occasional questions that I could not answer well enough to satisfy anyone. These helped to guide my study. Two in particular kept cropping up:

1. "How can the Biosystem be sustainable in a universe that tends toward entropy?" (see Chapter 06)
2. "If, as you claim, everything in the Biosystem is connected, from the micro-organisms to the whole ecological system, how do they connect? I am not connected to a zebra in Africa. Maybe it is connected to the grass it eats, but I am not." (see Chapters 07, 08, 09,10)

I got some answers. More than I expected. This book is an effort to organize them and share them with you as they relate to our current *fundamental human Problem*; a Problem that I thought everyone already understood because it was well studied long before the green revolution worked so hard a to prevent it. That is, *overpopulation*. (Appendix A)

But I know most people do not want to hear about that again. Therefore many of you will be happy to know that this book is NOT *primarily* about overpopulation. Rather, it is mostly about why we must believe that the balance of The Creation – biological balance -- is critical to our survival, and how it works. This view is based on:

A – Rearranging the Facts of LIFE into a world view that is more logical than than the outdated misinterpretation of the corposystem world view;

B – Adding three new insights (at least new to me):

1. Explains how and why biological (organic) energy actually uses entropy to generate the multitasking complexity that makes LIFE possible, including why our technologies cannot replace the processes of LIFE or force LIFE into a sustainable balance of our choice (Chapter 06).
2. Explains more clearly how living systems communicate with each other and why they must (Chapters 07, 09),
3. Explains why pollution diseases are likely to become our next predicable "big surprise," as climate change progresses, if we continue to focus on human wants to the exclusion of Biosystem needs (Chapter 09). Unless we tear ourselves apart first.

Whatever we believe, *ignoring any reality does not solve our problems*, as we learned well enough relative to the Covid-19 crisis. Neither does denial. We all know what became of cigarette-damage denial 40 or 50 years ago and then we know what became of climate-change denial that was hot and heavy on the web nearly twenty years ago when I began my blog. And now we know that pandemic-denial only makes the reality worse for the community as a whole system.

A few people get rich by telling the rest of us what we want to hear (nearly everyone likes to hear pretty propaganda) but real facts are much more important, because pretty propaganda fades into our memories of lost causes, while real facts eventually come around and bite the deniers (or most often their children) in the rear because, as we said above, humans cannot change the Facts of LIFE. FYI, I have made every effort to fact-check my newer world view. The corposystem has not.

Overpopulation, as critical as it is to climate change, pandemics and human survival, is just another well-established and well-studied fact, and this book will not ignore any relevant, well-understood biological fact. Or at least that is the plan.

Good books about overpopulation are readily available and extremely important (Catton, 1982; Diamond, 2011; Dowd, 2007; Gore, 2006, 20170; Gorschkov *et al.*, 2002; Heinberg and Lerch, 2010; Hopfenberg, *et al*, 2001, 2003; Martensen, 2009; Salmoney, 2004; Tiroir A Films, 2011; Wilson, 2016).

This book will not exclude awareness of our overpopulation, nor the probability that we cannot survive if we ignore or deny it and are unwilling to talk about overpopulation and deal with it, because it is BALANCE of the whole that sustains LIFE. That's why the subject of this book is *fourteen big ideas* (Chapter 10, Appendix C) that place overpopulation in the context of balanced evolution and guide us toward understanding how LIFE sustains its balance.

But, because this book takes a holistic view of LIFE, we cannot discuss any of the details at great length. The goal is to envision the over-all system of LIFE, why and how it changes in response to human pressures or any other kind of pressures. That is, how LIFE uses the Facts of LIFE to sustain itself. The answer is, it changes. It evolves.

This book is an effort to present a holistic insight that is different from what most of us have been told or taught, about how the whole cycle of LIFE sustains itself. Because:

> *Reality Number One - We cannot align our behaviors with the fact-based requirements for all of LIFE if we don't know what LIFE requires – or if we choose to believe an alternative or homocentric version of the story of LIFE. (Preface)*

Communally, we of the *corposystem* (the corposystem is our human naturally evolved corpo-political-economic-military-medical-educational-charitable social system) as a system, we are not trying to collaborate with the *Facts of LIFE*. Instead, we are trying to save ourselves from those universal facts of LIFE by looking harder and harder for ways to fight against them.

That will not work.

LIFE is bigger and more powerful than we are.

Corposystem-based versus Biosystem-based World Views – What are the Most Significant Differences?

The corposystem apparently believes it is more powerful than The Creation or the Creator, that our technologies can change nature to what we wish it were. They cannot.

Systems thinking (Chapter 04, 05, 06) (Barabasi, 2003; Meadows, 2007) applies to the Biosystem, not as mathematics or economics or politics or numbers crunching, or technology -- but as biology, because LIFE is biological -- not primarily human.

The Biosystem absolutely requires organic energy rather than technological energy such as solar or wind or hydrolic or any of those – in order for LIFE to exist (Goldsmith, 1981; West, 2017; Gorschkov *et al.*, 2002) for at least the following reasons:

1. Organic (biological, biochemical) energy recycles the matter of LIFE at the same time that it flows the biological (organic) energy through LIFE. Normal LIFE does not have trash heaps or pollution illnesses. It does not remove materials of LIFE from the cycles of LIFE.

2. Organic energy (carried by organic molecules) contains or includes the biological *information* that is needed to flow energy through the Biosystem. Our technologies cannot do that.

3. Every specific biological interaction requires a specific, complex combination of information with energy. Biological interactions are not all the same as each other, in fact they may be all different, each specifically designed for its minute or magnificent task, and we do not understand most of them.

Biological energy systems are primarily collaborative systems rather than dominational systems. Therefore the failed corposystem world view, that is based on "survival of the fittest" is primarily not a valid description of evolution, nor a valid guide to human survival (see "evolution" Appendix B and Chapters 08 and 09), and the reality is very much more complex than most or our human "big data.

The answer to the "entropy question" involves complexity, not a simple linear gradient (Chapter 06).

The necessity of communication among naturally evolved biological systems, and the probable means by which naturally evolved systems "talk to" each other are apparently not known to the corposystem (Chapters 06, 07, 09, 10).

And the saddest difference between corposystem thinking and Biosystem thinking is the split between the idealism of most basic scientists and activists, and the egoistic and greedy uses to which we all are now putting their great works. The denial of the human need for our idealism and recognition of the many ways in which we need our communities, particularly our ancient wisdom communities (religions), to help us find our way to the sustainable uses of the enormous power of our technologies.

Within the corposystem, we are smugly well educated, or proudly uneducated, but so afraid of being wrong that we would rather fight than ask questions, or even talk among ourselves about life-or-death issues. With the result that we don't understand each other, and we tend to each jump on separate bandwagons, ignoring the issues that are common to nearly all the bandwagons, with the result that our efforts tend to cancel each other out or compete against each other, and so we work against each other rather than join hands and heads around our common desire to save humanity from itself.

What we of the corposystem say is not what we really believe (which also makes discussion difficult). If we can't talk about what we want, in a realistic way, then we won't get what we really want.

What we believe we are doing – growing something better -- does not align with its reality – its cause-and-effect result, in terms of its impact on the Biosystem (Chapters 04, 05, 06, 10), because the Biosystem is not human, and we do not make the effort to learn what it really is; that is, a multitasking collaboration of naturally evolving living systems -- and what it really needs to sustain ITSELF, so that it can support us; that is, an optimally efficient, viable balance among its parts that will require, minimally, a cessation of hostile human overgrowth.

We are All Subunits of The Corposystem -- And the Biosystem

Many of us claim that God created the world and put us in it (Old and New Testaments and many other origin stories, for examples see Campbell, 1999), and of course that may or may not be a real fact, depending somewhat on our concept of God and our insight into the lovely metaphorical poetry of the origin stories.

Either way, yes or no, it is very difficult to understand why we continue to destroy the works of our Creator and instead, in our efforts to save ourselves from the natural consequences of what we have done, we worship the golden calf of our technologies; for example, designating "sacrifice zones;" essentially trash dumps where we pour our waste products into the body of The Creation, the land, water and air, and from there into the bodies of the people who live in these areas, from which the toxins ultimate recycle into the entire Biosystem; and a similar example, trying to use technologies to cure the damage that technologies have caused to the Biosystem and the people in it.

Technologies cannot maintain the efficiency required for LIFE, and they absolutely cannot flow organic energy/information through the body of LIFE.

To judge by both our words and our behaviors, we of the corposystem world view believe that our power, individually and collectively, is greater than the incomprehensible energy of The Creation/Creator that created us; that our knowledge surpasses the wisdom of our own wisdom traditions – for a few examples of wisdom traditions see (Black Elk Speaks, 1932; Easwaran, 1991; Smith, 2001; The Dalai Lama, 2010; The New Testament; The Old Testament; The Koran; The Bhagavad Gita; the many works of Joseph Campbell; and others), and of the systems of LIFE itself.

Instead, we are fighting against facts that are NOT the cause of our Problem; we are the cause of our Problem, as we apply the facts to benefit ourselves, rather than to nurture the emergence of LIFE.

> *Reality Number Two – All of LIFE is an emergent property of the Biosystem, which is a naturally evolve system that is composed of other naturally evolved systems. We humans cannot change how they evolved or how they function to sustain LIFE. Just as the growth of the human embryo requires the womb, and the mother cow feeds the calf, so do all the mothers and all the species*

require the appropriate naturally evolved environment for their survival (Preface).

We already knew all that.

Well, we might not have been in a position to appreciate the way I said it, but really we have known, in more or less primitive and metaphorical ways, since our early origins, that we evolved in and of the Biosystem.

Evolution (Appendix A; Chapters 8 and 9), the creation of a complex universe, or a star, or LIFE, or a creature, or a social system, or a world view is mostly not about bashing heads or making new bits. It's about how we use the old bits to interact communally by assembling them, or allowing them to come together in uniquely advantageous ways and then selecting those combinations that benefit the Biosystem. That is what evolution does, building on one combination after another, slowly, taking as much time as it takes to find the perfect combinations of characteristics that are able to balance LIFE against the chaotic nature of non-LIFE.

We knew that too. We already knew most of the facts that we need to save ourselves from extinction.

The solution to extinction – that is, the solution to climate change, including the pandemics, because there will be more -- is not in our technological power.

We can not overpower the Biosystem with our relatively primitive technologies.

> *The solution to our survival Problem would be, if we would do it, to find win-win behaviors and use them so that everything we do benefits both ourselves and our Biosystem – benefits ourselves BY benefiting our environment -- so that the Biosystem is able to balance itself without our pressure for more and more growth.*

This is no more impossible than travel to the moon, and probably no more expensive; it is what makes LIFE different from non-LIFE.

The Problem (see Appendix A) is *that we, the corposystem, is/are using universal facts to generate growth of what we want, rather than LIFE of the whole system that feeds us, and that is the immutable choice that we now face.*

We are making an orgy of the concept that the whole should benefit us, and that is not how evolution works. It is our job to benefit our environment if we expect to get any perks, any perks of LIFE, back from our environments.

LIFE is, after all, not a separate thing. It arises – emerges -- from a unique organizational plan consisting of matter and energy and some other things that we do not understand very well and probably more that we don't know about at all. LIFE is not a technology and LIFE cannot swallow technologies indefinitely without disorganizing the very arrangement that makes it alive, because our technologies cannot match the required efficiency of LIFE, because we cannot replicate the information that accompanies the energy of LIFE (Chapter 06) and directs the flow of energy throughout the system of LIFE.

Talking about that kind of important reality is one of our most ancient human forms of wisdom. Not talking about realities cannot save us from them. Modern wisdom cannot be wise if it declines rational discussion. Or biologically oriented community.

The purpose of this book is to start the conversation. We may be ready for it. Some people will want to skip the more complicated parts, and that is fine because the basic reality is easy to understand and simple (but not easy) to address.

> Too many people, not enough resources; too many trash dumps, not enough recycling, and we cannot fix the Problem with our technologies. Technical energy cannot replace organic energy because it cannot recycle the matter of which we are composed, and *it does not and can not contain the information that automatically directs the biological uses of organic energy (Chapter 06)*.

That is why LIFE is alive and technologies are not.

The do-able world view is what I want to share -- how to think like the real, naturally evolved system *that you are*.

What is a *System*? (See Chapters 04 and 05 and Appendix B)

> A system is a group of things, objects or characteristics that are organized so that they interact with each other (using energy, matter and information) to perform some common function. For example, I am a naturally evolved system composed of a group of organs, cells, and other structures that interact to keep me alive. My car is not a naturally evolved system, but it is a system composed of tires, engine, you know all that, which all work together to perform a common function of getting me from here to there (definition modified from Barabasi, 2003).

The subunits (parts, like the wheels, engine, etc. of a car) of *naturally evolved systems* fit together to generate *the emergent properties* of the system. The primary function of each naturally evolved system is to perpetuate its own emergent properties. An emergent property of the Biosystem is LIFE. An emergent property of the corposystem is growth. Growth for profit. (See Chapter 04 and Appendix B for a brief discussion of complex adaptive systems and their emergent properties). Every system is somewhat or a lot different from other systems, it talks to other systems using its emergent properties, and so it is useful to define and name the various systems using their emergent properties.

This is not a complicated idea. Well, maybe it is, but it is easier to think about interacting sets of systems that "talk to each other" – if our goal is to understand relationships and balance -- rather than make a list of all the details of every system – and their functions -- and try to understand how that all fits together. We really can not understand the emergent properties of a naturally evolved system by adding up the details of its structure, but we can describe and name the system according to its primary (emergent) function. As I have named the emergent property of the Biosystem – LIFE.

In this book, I will describe only a few functions – primarily fourteen interacting functions (our fourteen big ideas, see Chapter 10 and Appendix D). Only fourteen, but there are thousands or millions of ways that they interact to bring LIFE to the Biosystem. Fourteen is somewhat complicated, but is not as overwhelming as trying to figure out and understand millions of interactions. Fourteen is do-able.

Systems thinking is not a new and mysterious human discovery. It just takes looking at everything we already know from inside a different paradigm. Thinking about systems is similar to thinking about the filing system I kept track of when I was working as a secretary, many decades ago before I even knew about ecosystems. Humans have always operated within systems, and so does every other living thing and even more non-living things.

The biggest difference between the human organism and all or most of the other living systems is that humans have a uniquely analytical brain to understand with. We should use it for our benefit; and our primary benefit is LIFE (not money, not winning, and certainly not growth, which has become our biggest danger).

Each of us is a system composed of other systems (our subsystems, such as heart, lungs, feet) -- living inside an environmental system alongside many other systems (you know what your environment is – I am just putting different words to it). We are subsystems of our environmental system(s) in the same way that our organs, tissues and cells are subsystems of us. Every system of this enormous complex LIFE system is connected to the other systems by their emergent properties -- functions they perform that benefit the whole Biosystem, or at least their immediate environment.

Because of the intricately connected levels of efficiency that are required to sustain the Biosystem; and because the big fish does not normally rule in its pond, but primarily feeds off it; therefore, these relationships among the systems, subsystems and environmental systems, are more accurately viewed as collaborative, rather than dominational (Eisler, 1987; Lynn Margulis, quoted in Feldman, 2018; Janeway, 1980).

Reality Number Three —Naturally evolved LIFE systems are fundamentally collaborative, feeding information/energy back and forth and recycling matter. They are not primarily dominational. They mostly function to support themselves in ways that do not harm the whole system of LIFE, but instead support the whole (Preface).

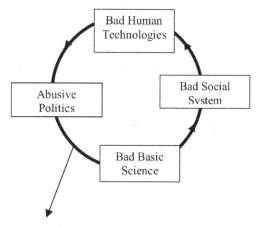

Our World Views are Systems That Direct Our Behaviors

Our *world views* are also naturally evolved systems that try (just look around at the arguments on Facebook) they try very hard to sustain themselves even against all the self-evident logic we may throw against them. Thus terms "good" and "bad" in the diagrams on these pages relate to the *sustainability* of the cycle -- NOT to human Face Book declarations, or ethics or opinions; and not to whichever organism can eat the other organisms. "Good" means sustainable; "bad" means not sustainable, relative to its own environment.

The corposystem is a naturally evolved human social system that has been vigorously working to sustain its growth ethic, even though we know, and it is intuitively obvious, that the growth ethic is the root cause of climate change because it eats up the resources, not only for humans but for all sentient beings, and then throws the discards into the trash where they cannot be biologically recycled; or it would require prodigious amounts of energy to recycle.

We have known about the imbalance of food (Brown, 2004, 2008, 2014) that is caused by human overpopulation long before our science proved it, or at least the farmers knew before the giant corporations took over management of the land some time in the 20th century. Or perhaps the giant corporations didn't care; they are not human systems (people) after all, they are systems, but not LIFE systems; they do not have a human brain with its world view; and the charter of every corporation, the charter that defines its function, requires that it **not** support the balance of LIFE, but rather the growth of money. All corporations, each in its own way, including dot orgs, function to make money by means of a growth ethic, and that behavior is not sustainable within the systems, especially the systems of LIFE. Nevertheless, our corposystem continues its growth.

The Biosystem is a living system (Lovelock, 1988; Margolis & Sagan, 1995; Wilson, 2006) that has essentially the same requirements as all of LIFE – the fertile earth, clean water, healthy air, and biological energy/information. The primary function of the Biosystem is to sustain its own emergent property of LIFE, and to do this it must balance all these resources in a way that we humans could never do. It does this with the information that is contained in the organic energy of Itself (Chapters 06 and 09).

To sustain the balance among all of its species -- its consumers, producers, everything – all the species that make up the body of the living Earth. Just in the same way that we, as human animals must maintain the balance among our subsystems (kidney, liver, gut and all that). Our physiology. To stay alive.

If the Biosystem cannot maintain its balance in the world we have created, because of our behaviors, then it must change itself (that includes but is not limited to the emergent climate and the subsystems of the Life of Earth that generate the emergent climate). That is climate change. It is obvious and self-evident, even though the corposystem has spent about the last 25 years trying to deny the word (global warming, climate change) until it is now giving in to that fact of LIFE and finding other words to deny or repress – such as overpopulation, extinction, smog, pollution diseases, or war.

Even though we knew it, all those words, all along.

Just when we humans were making such good progress toward a sustainable and compassionate lifestyle, and learning how to channel our dominational instincts into relatively productive win-win forms of behavior that support the human system and the Biosystem – both -- just then at the new century, the growth of the corposystem began to irrevocably destroy the LIFE of the Biosystem that generates our earth, air, water and organic energy, and the information of LIFE that we cannot create for ourselves.

Just exactly as a farmer who overgrazes his land is destroying his own land, also when we overgraze the Earth, we are destroying the balance that gives it LIFE, and that LIFE includes us. The Biosystem has no choice but to change – its first priority is to preserve itself, its own emergent property of LIFE -- to adapt itself to save itself. That is what LIFE does that makes it ALIVE. It adapts itself to save itself – not to save us.

That is why the deserts are expanding, the flash floods are becoming enormous while between floods the riverbeds dry up, temperature is rising, the climate is changing. And pandemics loom larger. Largely because we are causing the extinction of other organisms that made those deserts bloom and that prevent the unbalanced growth curve of the un-adapted viruses. The Life of Earth, as it was when it gave life to us – is changing to save itself from us because we, *Homo sapiens*, have changed from a few thousand individuals to a monster system now composed of more than seven billion.

Can your opinion or mine, our human world views, hold the Living Earth in orbit around the sun? No, but the universal facts of Life can and do. Can our opinions create:

> a *reasonably comfortable sustainable human presence on a healthy and fruitful Biosystem*?

No, but the real universal Facts of Life – that Sean Carroll and I and other basic scientists are trying to learn – if we would stop fighting against those realities, they could regenerate a fruitful earth amazingly quickly, if we were to yield to their superior powers and permit them to create LIFE rather than growth.

How does LIFE Sustain Itself?

And so that is what I set out to understand.

> For the future of our grandchildren, and for their home on Earth that is crumbling right under "their[2]" feet and "they" are too busy living with the "glass half full," ignoring the other half of their reality, to even think about the future.

I asked many questions; I learned a lot; somehow I thought that, if I tried hard enough, I would find people to help achieve our goal to sustain this miracle of LIFE that we share. And of course there are some. Many.

We do seem to have a common goal. Mine is:

> *To help grow a reasonably comfortable human presence within a vibrantly healthy and nourishing Life of Earth.*

But we all need more than my opinion about overpopulation. We also need to evaluate my reasons for holding that opinion – my understanding of how the Biosystem really does function, contrary to the corposystem propaganda that uses logic based on a 200-year-old inaccurate meme.

That's what I thought. We need reasons that are based on universal facts, not human opinions, because universal facts are the same for everyone and so will necessarily bring our world views closer to each other and to the reality of the Biosystem.

HOWEVER! Though there are plenty of people who want what the corposystem gives us, there are nowhere near enough who understand that what the corposystem gives us comes from and impoverishes the Biosystem. Not enough to start the discussion. And without discussion around the Problem of the balance of LIFE, even more importantly than the balance of politics, there can be no solution to either imbalance.

And the children, and especially the grandchildren we were working to save, or more likely the fact of overpopulation itself, have translated our fathers' dream of peaceful collaboration into a nightmare of violent domination; have taken the beauty and power of our dream and used it to grow a Miyazaki Mononoke Monster (Miyazaki, 1997), all the time claiming that they know more about it than my father did, or I do, or even, they apparently believe they know more how the Earth should function than nature does, or The Creator, more than the Laws of LIFE that generated this Living Earth System and have kept it alive for four or five billion years longer than we have been around.

And they turn their backs upon the complex beauty of information available from our incomparable modern sources, or from scientifically demonstrated universal facts, and claim that is all just someone's human opinion, and their opinion is better.

Do they believe that *Homo sapiens* generated the "rules" that sustain the LIFE of Earth? That we humans ARE the Creators? That we CREATED The Creation and/or we can make it work better than the Creator can?

I think some people do, and that is where our discussions can start.

In fact, that is not even "their" stated goal, or at least not the goal of their unstated behaviors, and it is with behaviors, not beliefs that we communicate with other systems.

> ***Reality Number Four*** - *Our beliefs are not important in the scheme of things except as they inform our behaviors. Our behaviors are recorded in the known and unknown history of all time; both because behaviors (interactions/energy/information) are the universal language of reality, and also because we can never undo them (Preface).*

When "they" must choose between behaviors that favor the welfare of the Biosystem – or the corposystem – "they" favor the corposystem, over the Biosystem.

Take a minute and think about that for logic. "They" actually believe, way down at the bottom of "their" world views, that "they" can save the Biosystem by "fixing" it. By aligning the Biosystem with human values or human preferences, without even bothering with that essential in-between step – giving the Biosystem what it needs for its own survival. Never hesitating to consider what it needs.

In my lifetime, I have been forced to watch most of our 20ᵗʰ century dedication fizzle and die, or morph into a biological nightmare, and swirl down the drain, along with the human ethical values and world views that supported it – or it supported.

I watched as the activist movement, the charitable sector of the economy, and then the internet, all with such glowing potential for the future of human kind, all were co-opted by the corposystem, using a range of methods from dishonest or unwise compassion through endless circular two-prong irrelevant debates, to now endless physical war that we on this side of the oceans apparently don't even see – except through the PTSD we bring home with us -- all in pursuit of money and power.

I can tell you what will happen to humans next, but I would rather not. It's no secret; no "surprise." No more of a surprise than the pandemic, which we have been expecting for a good long time. If you want to know what will happen next, look up the actual experiments on overpopulation. We have been following that script precisely, for all of my life, and blaming all the associated symptoms on something or someone else.

Overpopulation does not give us surprises; it follows a well-understood pattern, and we have known for more than 200 years what to expect from Ponzi-style growth systems. That's why there are laws against Ponzi schemes, and people sitting in prison right now for breaking those laws, even as our dominant culture is spinning its wheels trying to save its own Ponzi scheme from collapse.

That's a universal fact of history.

We are experiencing a classic overpopulation event.

That's a universal fact of biology.

We now have an entire social system, the corposystem, dedicated to Ponzi-style growth for gain, at a time when growth itself is the greatest biological danger to the future of human kind within the system of LIFE. We continue trying to support the growth with technologies; however, with no concept of the organic efficiencies required to sustain LIFE.

And, as far as I can tell, the current generation of activists is responding to the overpopulation reality by working harder, talking better, and doing worse – saying the right words, and accompanying them by behaviors that theoretically help people but in fact harm the Biosphere, which causes harm to the people -- by working even harder to get even better at squeezing more people onto our overgrazed pasture of LIFE, even though we now have the birth control technologies that my generation coveted.

Overpopulation is not the central topic of this book because we already know that, and we are doing it anyway, and we don't want to hear about it anymore. Apparently, what people really want is to know that their work is making the human condition better.

Well, it's not, and I can't change that because I can't change their behaviors. Wouldn't it be wonderful! But in fact, the human condition is getting worse, even though we are better educated and working harder at it; the economy, the educational system, war, poverty; very much worse, than it was 60 or 70 years ago when we had very few activist organizations, and when we created laws for the welfare of the people and their international human rights that we are now ignoring. Or badmouthing.

What we apparently don't understand is that the work to which we are giving our lives is not of or for the Biosystem. It is of and for the growth of the corposystem – a different naturally evolved system – trying to do what such systems do – perpetuate itself! Not save people; not save the living Earth; not change the behavior of the corposystem, but perpetuate its behavior that has caused this Problem – and not even because it wants to cause problems – it is not a person – it doesn't care.

The corposystem is a naturally evolved system that does what such systems do – they perpetuate themselves, if possible. If they survive long enough, they can become caricatures of themselves. We are.

"It's not about people at all. It's about profit. Nothing else." (Robb, 2018)

I am not worried about perpetuating the Biosystem. It will perpetuate its own emergent reality – with or without us -- as it has done following the previous great extinctions (Kolbert, 2014).

I do care about the people. We humans cannot survive without the Biosystem. Many people do not even understand this much.

We humans are amazing; we are wonderful; we are powerful; we have been given a miracle brain; we are compassionate, loving; we can think. Nevertheless, it is a universal fact that humans cannot survive without the Biosystem, the living Earth, living in the form that we require for our own survival. I believe we should use our most amazing qualities, given to us by the God of LIFE, favor for favor, to give back to LIFE. I think that's what all the major wisdom traditions say, in one way or another (The Dalai Lama, 2010).

But instead of thinking about the welfare of The Creation, what we now mostly think about is what we want –

Which is – apparently – power.

I ask --

Power to do --- what?

To help create a reasonably comfortable and sustainable human presence in a vibrantly healthy Earth system?

That is not what I see happening.

OOOOOOO

---

[1] When I use the word LIFE in all capital letters I am referring to Life itself, not to an individual living thing.

[2] When I use the word "we" in this book, I am referring to *Homo sapiens*, the human species, a naturally evolved biological system with all the responsibilities of a such a system, the first of which is to perpetuate ourselves within our environment. And I also refer to "we." You and me.

Photos by Lynn Lamoreux unless otherwise credited.
Photos of Earth are from, or modified from, NASA.

And God might well have said:
"To believe that you could master and control my Nature is proof of your idolatry.
Humble yourselves and work with, rather than against, the restorative and
regenerative dynamics of this living planet. Doing so will enable you,
over time, to restore the Garden you so foolishly defiled in your
anthropocentric hubris."
(Michael Dowd, https://youtu.be/IrkQUGUKa64)

CHAPTER 1

IT IS WHAT IT IS

 Early morning. I jump into my super-sweater and slippers, pad to the front door, and step outside, closing the door behind me, careful not to lock it, as the cold and dark on the mountain are real, implacable and dangerous.

The late night sparkles with stars such as I haven't seen since I was eight years old, when we lay on our backs on the lawn of a balmy California evening, our family, and picked out the constellations, and the sky over us was as fresh and clean as the new grass under our backs.

The Orion hero constellation has always been my favorite; for most of my life since I've been aware that he watches over me through the dark hours, whether or not I can see him. There he stands now, stalwart in the sky-space between towering Ponderosa pines. The three "stars" that make up his sheathed sword are pointed toward the Earth. My breath gleams a little in the starlight as it wafts gently toward him. I shiver back into the house as Orion fades into dawn-light, shut the door behind me, and turn on the heat, reminding myself: "It is what it is."

And that's the most important Fact of Life that I have learned. It is what It is, and It doesn't care what I want or wish for -- or what I choose to believe – because without the Laws of God and Nature, It could not exist.

I care; It is.

It is a system composed of systems, a *naturally evolved complex adaptive system* so complex and so enormous and sublime that our ordinary, less complex human minds cannot fully encompass Its reality. From the fires in the night to LIFE itself, It is what It is. We humans cannot wish It into something else, but we can learn some of the rules about how the sublime functions to maintain Itself. That learning is important to our welfare, because the Sublime is vastly bigger and more powerful than we are.

Orion is not a hero; not a system; not a unitary thing. Orion's stars appear to us as an associated constellation because, by chance, they appear to us to be lined up in a shape that has meaning. They aren't really even near to each other.

The Big Lie

Whenever I think about the difference between factual reality and our wishful fantasies, I think of Frank Sinatra and his catchy little song, "High Hopes." Frankie believed – we believed in those days — that anyone could do what Frankie did if we worked as hard as he worked. Singing about "High Hopes," about ants moving rubber tree plants. Pretty nonsense it was, and a good song.

Of course it was partly true, in a growth economy with more energy than we knew how to use well. That's why so many of us believed, and believing, many tried harder and accomplished more, echoing the song. But how many others tried harder and failed?

The family secret we are afraid to talk about, still afraid, is our failures. Our failures are just as real as our success, and perhaps more important. Imagine -- being afraid to discuss the issues of our living and dying, and instead obsessing over smart phones.

It is true that anyone could have done what Frankie did — if they had the same experiences and the same interactions with their environment and were as lucky and as clever and common-sensical — equally able, as he was, to use his own good fortune (and bad), the available factors of his environment, to his own advantage. He did have a fine voice, for one thing, and an acceptable gender, and a unique support group. So many parts of his other half — his environment — that others do not have.

But Frankie was wrong, we all were, the human dilemma today proves that point, and although Frankie probably never understood (that would be another bit of his good luck), we humans are about to see the light now, as we are gradually forced by reality to open our eyes to a corposystem wasteland. Climate change; pandemic.

We are an evolved species — uniquely privileged in our logical brain, in our ability to communicate, exchange information, and our interactions with our environment — the living earth itself — to have the Life of comparative ease and comfort that so many of us cling to today.

But we are not more powerful than the universal facts.

We are not more wise than reality.

Perhaps our comparative good fortune, *Homo sapiens* among the species of LIFE, for many of us is a reason to believe that God created humans unequal - in charge - and gave us the task of taking care of the welfare of the rest of the world. Maybe so; I wasn't there; I will not claim to know one way or the other and it does not matter in terms of resolving our biological dilemma. Because what I do know is that the LIFE of Earth survives because rules exist — Laws of Nature — that make LIFE, and the universe itself, function as they do function, and I know that on this Earth, LIFE cannot survive by destroying the balance that the Laws of LIFE created or perhaps were created to defend.

Our biggest lie tells us that we have been given dominion over — not the earth and the creatures thereon — I could imagine that — but the natural Laws that generate and sustain LIFE by balancing the myriad systems of Earth. The "forces" of gravity, strong nuclear force, and weak nuclear force, electromagnetism, and the natural laws that emerged necessarily from these forces as higher levels of organization evolved, or were caused to evolve. Life and death, natural selection, evolution, collaboration, symbiosis (Margulis and Sagan, 1995).

Who ever said, how did we come to believe, that our human opinions can somehow influence the rules – the universal functions -- how the Biosystem functions to maintain Itself; that our human technologies can save us by conquering the great unknown; by turning the works of God, and the forces and laws of nature to the unconquerable will of man? Trump maybe; but then, he is a caricature of Frankie's misunderstanding. He very obviously has not yet learned that It is what It is.

And It is bigger than we are. I fear the learning will come much harder for him, and for all of us, than it did for Frankie's mythical ant; I say that ant never did or could move the rubber tree plant. Maybe he tipped up the pot, just a little, just far enough to get under there for a good hard push; and then it fell back and squashed him dead.

It's not smart to mess with mother nature -- with the law of gravity -- and if we only look at the up-side of our technological and economic accomplishments, and ignore the down-side, our failures, the family secrets that we sweep under the carpet and forget about -- then the down-side of our accomplishments will continue to grow and grow, like that old rubber-tree plant and one day soon it will just splat down all around and squash us dead.

The true facts are:

1. My Orion constellation is not a person or a God standing over my sleeping hours.
2. Humans cannot break the immutable Laws of the Creation without negative consequences. That's why we espouse the Precautionary Principle (Chapter 09).

3

Well, of course, we already knew that, really. So I'm not hanging around waiting for Orion to save me, and neither am I planning to save myself by challenging him to a duel of swords. And I'm not interested in debating whether your mental image of Orion is better than mine. We are both wrong, because there is nothing to debate, because Orion doesn't exist, and It is what It is, we do not fully understand what It is, and our debates can never change It into anything that It is not. All of that is a waste of our life energy.

What we could be doing to save ourselves is to learn more about what LIFE is and how it functions so that we can align our behaviors with the reality. Perhaps, if we try hard enough, and if we do so in the spirit of Oren Lyons (see the references) for the benefit of the seventh generation yet to come, we might be able to save the future for our kind.

What is LIFE?

LIFE is the *emergent property* of a naturally evolved complex adaptive system, the modern Earth *Biosystem*.

The function of natural *evolution*, in relation to LIFE, is to sustain the viable balance of the Biosystem, its subsystems, and their functions, that support LIFE within the universe. Don't burn your brain over those words if they are not familiar. That's what this book is about to explain. Meantime, you can look them up in Appendix B.

The universe is not primarily an either/or debating kind of place. It is both/and, and so is LIFE. LIFE is primarily a collaborative, both/and reality. Both fire and ice; both light and dark; both life and death. Mostly, it is both energy and matter, distributed among billions of different sub-systems that co-evolved in such a way that they each in their own way support the welfare of the whole. It is composed of systems. And for that reason, there is both an up-side and a down-side to everything we do in life. For humans the lessons are mostly in the down-side, and we ignore these lessons to our peril, because the laws of nature are very effective in clearing away the "dead wood" of LIFE, if it contributes only grief and suffering to the community of systems that are created and nurtured by evolution and the other Laws of Life, the *fourteen big ideas* introduced in these pages and summarized in Appendix D.

Humans must support the welfare of the whole Biosystem just in the same way that your kidney, or your heart or lungs support the whole organism that you are, and as the organic molecules support the life of every cell. Humans and trees and lungs and kidneys and living cells, all are naturally evolved systems. They all interact in support of Life of Earth, but not all mixed up chaotically, as that phrase might suggest; in fact, incredibly tightly organized and balanced, each system making a contribution to the whole according to its specialized function and its naturally evolved relationships with the other systems, our environmental systems, our partner systems and our subsystems. Of which we are composed. We will not try to catalog all these systems, but rather we will view them holistically in terms of their interacting functions.

The parts interact among themselves according to a set of natural laws that humans have done a remarkably good (never perfect) job of understanding. All naturally evolved complex adaptive LIFE systems, so far as we know, are both unitary systems and parts of a larger system(s), and they must retain their balance in order to transmit the information that sustains the LIFE of Earth. LIFE in and of the entire Biosystem.

LIFE, the *emergent* functioning miracle of LIFE itself, is also non-human and human, and it is facts AND fantasies AND other things that are not scientific fact nor human mental fairy tales.

I remember a chilly South Carolina night, when I fell asleep by the fireplace, and dreamed that my best friend Margie was telling me about her recent experience with agape, which I later learned is a word that means brotherly love. The dream was so vivid that I telephoned Margie, in Texas, the following day, and she indeed DID have a deeply moving experience with agape.

It was lovely and real, our mutual dream, but I don't know what it was. It was not *science*. Science can't tell us the basic facts about it (regardless of what anyone claims), mostly because science is based on repeated physical measurements taken under controlled conditions. How do you control a dream? Certainly, it was not a *technology*, for reasons that are obvious. What else is there? We don't know.

We do know that we cannot control *Facts*. By definition Facts are realities we cannot control. That's why we call them facts, because that is what the word means. What we can do with facts is learn about them; and the more we know about facts, the more control we have over *how we choose to respond to them*.

Experiences are our daily, personal lives. I have strong feelings about this kind of experience that is beyond our known facts: I loved Margie for who she was, and there would be no book but for her; and I enjoy my relationship with Orion; but I have no particularly important scientific opinions about either, because:

1. There is nothing to prove and no reason to prove it; and
2. It doesn't matter, does it? It can't benefit anyone else but me.

So, that was interesting, but it changes nothing I have said above. The universe contains an immensity of things we have no idea about, including realities that are neither scientifically demonstrable facts nor fantasies, and I cannot deny this kind of experience. Nor do I want to.

What I want to do is to avoid picking fights with realities that we can demonstrate – especially fact-based or evidence based (if it is valid evidence) realities that we do know a lot about. Arguing is a waste of time when we could be, and we have the means, resolving our most urgent *human Problem*.

We know enough right now to stop destroying our earthly environment whenever we make up our minds to deal with the reality. That is what I want to do, because the reality of LIFE itself will not change for our convenience. The climate change will get worse; the pandemics will not go away; worse things will happen; because the LIFE of Earth cannot stay alive in conditions of critical imbalance. LIFE will protect itself. The most basic law of LIFE dictates that, when LIFE is out of *balance*, It will and must change Itself into something else, or die trying, and either will be a disaster for us.

We cannot long survive on the basis of feelings and personal opinions in the absence of factual reality. Nature requires more of us than knee-jerk response to our free-floating emotions, and our fact-based opinions are different from our other opinions in the sense that they apply equally to all of us. Arguing over whether or not facts are true is a waste of our wonderful *cause-and-effect* human logic when we could be studying what they mean to the Biosystem.

It is time to stop arguing over the already-demonstrated facts and start the discussions around how we need to change our behaviors in order to save ourselves, because we cannot change facts that are obviously related to reality and the common good, *which means that we could be using them to solve problems if we were not dithering around in our personal feelings and opinions to the exclusion of the reality.*

My professional opinion about the relationship between human overpopulation and climate change and the pandemic, briefly, is that they are correlated to the highest degree, and this opinion is corroborated by abundant data as well as everyday common sense that anyone can understand, with or without science, that tells us that science is not magic, it is merely human, and technology is nothing more than tool making. We are primates using rocks to break open the nuts of LIFE, but neither science nor technology can defy natural law, so we need to examine how we have come to believe that they can.

The commonsense reality tells us that nobody, not even humans, not even the laws of nature – nobody can fill up a bathtub with water to a level that is higher than its rim – and no system, human or otherwise, can eat up all the resources of its homeland environment without suffering the natural consequences of that behavior, which in the end will be starvation of one sort or another and destruction of the homeland.

Climate change has already taken us halfway there.

We cannot change the Laws of nature (our fourteen big ideas, and more). What we could change is our behaviors, but it is very important that we do NOT use corposystem guidelines, or the false corposystem mantra "survival of the fittest," to guide our behaviors. Because it is that corposystem *world view* that got us into this mess in the first place.

If we carry on as we have been, trying to control nature rather than ourselves, we will end up like Frank Sinatra's squashed ant.

OOOOOOO

Special thanks to Margie and her family and to Jo Ann.

Thanks to Mary Stuever, who reviewed Chapter 01 and set off a whole new round of writing and rewriting.

Thanks to Dot and Shodo and Larry, who reviewed almost everything, in particular Chapter 06, and some of it more than once, and set off several new rounds of writing and rewriting.

Given that we know about the Facts of Life,
(and we have known for more than 200 years
the basic science that we could be using to save ourselves),
why are we not taking action to protect our children and grand-children
from our mistaken uses of those facts?

CHAPTER 2

"TAKE CHARGE"

Doing What?

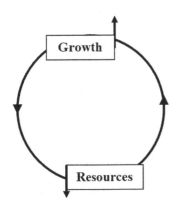

I have often wondered why we do not simply get together and reduce our human population to a viable, sustainable level. This question is essentially similar to the subject of an article in Scientific American July, 2018, page 37) entitled "The Science of Anti-Science Thinking." authored by several professors at Arizona State University, and a recent blog published in the Washington Post by Michael Morell, former Deputy Director of the CIA and Kristin Wood, a fellow at Harvard Kennedy School (dated March 27, 2020, available at https://www.washintonpost. com/opinions/2020/03/27/traged-is-that-we-knew-this-was-coming/)

Referring to the covid-19 crisis, Morel & Wood asked:

"Why do we keep doing this? . . we must overcome the tendency to under-prepare for threats that we can clearly see – as there are many more of them out there. The most obvious and most important for sure is climate change."

Yes indeed. Covid-19 is bad; don't ignore it. Sick is sick and I was, so I should know. People die. At its peak in my body, I had a conversation with my maker, and we agreed I should come back for a little more time to finish this letter to you. But Covid-19 is also a fragment of one big, bigger biological Problem that we are ignoring, and we do know that The Creation (or at least the Biosystem) IS what IT is (Chapter 01); LIFE and death and all that -- and, most importantly, we know we can't change what It is. But that we can adapt ourselves to what LIFE is, and what it requires of us, and that is how humans have survived up to recently.

But we aren't doing it. I mean, we know a lot of facts, but we aren't even trying to prepare for the upcoming minor crises, much less the looming threat of climate change that is working up to be a game-ender because we are ignoring that reality as well.

We must sit down to understand the up-side and the down-side of our relationship with our environment, the Biosystem, and work out a plan that will result in a "win-win" once again, between *Homo sapiens* and the Biosystem, and then adapt ourselves to it, and that is the theme of this chapter.

> ***Reality Number One*** - *We cannot align our behaviors with the fact-based requirements for all of LIFE if we don't know what they are – or if we believe in an alternative, unnatural or homocentric version of the story of LIFE (Preface).*

We in New Mexico have a governor who knows how to deal with reality and how to manage problems. Therefore, on day one of the official announcement of the covid-19 crisis we were instructed to practice self-isolation and social distancing, and we were told why, and our Governor set to work to help us all do that job together.

Unfortunately I missed the first part, because I was already very sick. As I am writing now, we use the car radio for a few minutes every day to keep up on the important news, but much of what we hear is the most appalling garbage, that claims to be real information from people who have evidently made no effort to understand our biological reality.

The very worst yesterday, out of Texas, was a magic pundit who "explained" our choice to us.

> "We can choose between letting a few people die in exchange for beefing up our economy for their grandchildren."

> "Good grief!" I yelled at Mira, who was snoozing in her dog seat. "We do not have that choice! Not even half of it. We are in the middle of climate change! The Earth is sick. And the economy is creating NO FUTURE, either way, not a better one. Why is he lying to us? It's his grandchildren too!"

> "We have met the enemy and he is us!" (Pogo).

We are entering the dithering phase of our response to the Covid-19 crisis – another in our escalating series of challenges as we try to deal with entry into post-carbon reality at a time when we have already over-grazed the Earth -- that has been long predicted by those who at least try to understand the needs of The Creation (Ehrlich & Ehrlich, 1996; Heinberg & Lerch, 2010; Diamond, 2011; to name only a few) as it struggles to sustain the long-term balance of its own LIFE in this over-all climate change crisis.

I do not object to death in principle, except my own of course; because without death there could be no LIFE, and I think LIFE is the most exquisitely beautiful intellectual and physical construct imaginable. Or perhaps, unimaginable for some people. I sometimes wonder how it can be real without people here to recognize it.

I do object to people messing up the discussion of the elegance of LIFE by proclaiming choices that *we do NOT have.*

In fact, our bottom-line choices have narrowed down to corposystem versus Biosystem. Between the excesses of our modern economic luxury that is based on human growth (the corposystem) -- and the entire LIFE of Earth (The Creation, the Biosystem) that requires biological balance. Like it or not, our remaining choice is between a gradual retreat into a more comfortable future -- or a catastrophic crash as the forces of evolution get rid of us. Either way, we will not HAVE an economic system if we kill the Biosystem that gives us LIFE.

Wouldn't it be better to investigate the real choices, so that we can deal with them as painlessly and compassionately as is humanly possible, rather than wait for nature to make all of our decisions for us?

Choosing how to deal with problems works very much better if we spend some time thinking about the problems before they happen, and better yet if we work together to solve them. Before it is too late.

When I use the word "we" in this book, I am referring to *Homo sapiens*, the human species, a naturally evolved biological system with all the responsibilities of a such a system (see Chapter 04), the first of which is to perpetuate ourselves within our environment. And I also refer to "we." You and me and all of us. That is what I think as I write.

The human species has always understood that our lives, our food our shelter our water and our air – earth, air, water and fire -- come from the Biosystem, not the corposystem. The corposystem cannot be anything more than a glorified delivery system, the in-between guy, like a Pizza-delivery service, because the corposystem cannot create LIFE. The Biosystem is the source of all LIFE of Earth. The corposystem has overgrazed the Biosystem, looking for food and water to deliver to us.

The corposystem cannot create food or water or air, and certainly not energy.

That is our Common Problem (see Appendix A).

The cure is not to increase the power of the corposystem; human power as we are using it is already devastating our climate and causing climate change. The cure is to stop overgrazing the Biosystem. Or at least to "DO NO MORE HARM," as the Biosystem recovers itself.

No logical person, one would think, would be making up ways to obstruct progress toward that cure, using various forms of dithering: lying, blame-placing, debate, obstruction, obfuscation; rather than discussing the options. But we do it anyhow. It's impossible in any case for human kind to "fix" the Biosystem. It's hard enough to fix our own human problems, but I should think we would try. Stop overgrazing the Biosystem. Stop trying to blame someone else. Start discussing the reality of our common human Problem.

What Can We Do?

The Biosystem Problem, that is the root cause of most modern human problems is summarized in Appendix A. I put it in the Appendix because most people have already heard about it, and in case you are tired of reading about overpopulation on line, and because the on-line versions are so often inappropriate hostile debate wars rather than positive discussions of a real Problem to be solved. This book is only indirectly about overpopulation; this book is about how the Earth survives using balance among the natural laws, or at least among our fourteen big ideas, but in fact overpopulation is the root basic cause of the imbalance, unless you prefer to say that human behaviors are the root cause, which is just saying the same thing in a different way.

So it is time to stop pretending the solution is complicated; on the contrary, it is obvious.

I did not say it is easy; I said it is obvious, but pretending it is impossible to a species that has been to the moon is ridiculous.

But if we are afraid even to talk about it – even to use the word – overpopulation – a slap in the face to the cowardly -- then of course, there is nothing that we can do together, and that is what this particular Problem will require. That we learn, probably I should say re-learn, how to think, discuss and work together, and with compassion.

Today's symptom of overpopulation is the Covid-19 pandemic; yesterday was 911; before that was the great depression and a few relatively little ones, with a number of wars and various large and small genocides between. I remember all of it from WW-II.

What can we do?

My favorite answer now, because it is succinct, straight-forward and right on topic, is from The Dalai Lama (2009), and is an excellent expression of His Holiness' emphasis on "wise compassion."

Wisdom is: "analyzing the facts and discerning the actual situation."
And then:
"If you want to get rid of painful effects, you have to get rid of their causes."

So our human solution is to analyze the Problem and eliminate the cause. More clearly, the solution to human overpopulation is to reduce the human population. How we do THAT, as compassionately as possible, is not obvious, and requires discussion.

It is not my job to solve the Problem, any more than it is your job as an individual. It is a social Problem, and solving social problems is an important function of our social systems, implementing and evaluating our decisions, using more than one brain at a time. It is what our social system, the corposystem, should be doing to help us. Instead, our corposystem is actively trying to stop the discussion of our very real Problem – to sweep the Problem under the rug in an effort to save its own self as a system based in growth.

When our social systems fail us, it is time for us to take charge, intelligently and compassionately, with a well considered common goal, at the point of blockage, and change the social systems. Discuss it, use the word. Overpopulation. If you are not doing this, then you are equally part of the Problem, whether you are president Trump or my next-door neighbor. At the same time, it is imperative that we make things better – not worse, and that is the current danger. That is what I want to talk about. How to make things better.

So far our solutions to overpopulation have ranged from killing live people using war and genocide and starvation, to simply ignoring the Problem and pretending it isn't so. I have met people who have never before heard the word overpopulation, and yet that is what is killing us. The first part of the solution is to begin the discussion. The second part is what to discuss, and what we must discuss is the fact-based reality of how LIFE sustains itself. Not the corposystem view of survival of the fittest.

That approach will not help us. In fact, none of our recent approaches was very effective. Dithering, lying, fancy memes and trick statements – they won't fix anything. Blame-placing is for cowards. So is I'm OK/You're OK (see Appendix A). I remember when we went through that phase. The fact is that some things are NOT OK. At least not for people.

And in our culture the ever-popular win/lose just recycles, over and over.

Winning is not the same thing as solving problems. I think we have, in the crises of my lifetime, amply proven that domination as a way of life will NOT achieve our goals and that survival of the fittest, interpreted as dominational, is NOT the primary function of evolution.

Fear and jealousy; fear, hatred and jealousy. Forever. That is how our modern corposystem functions, yes, but it is NOT how evolution functions to sustain the balance of LIFE. It is not how human communities evolved to function. Community. That's it. That is how humans evolved.

The proper function of a human social system is to prevent all this dithering around disinformation and unite us in the solutions. Instead, our corposystem is concerned with its own problems that are associated with the end of free energy and profits gleaned from plundering the Biosystem. Having run out of its free ride (free food), the corposystem has turned to farming, rather than nurturing, its own substance, which is we the people. Just like the beef cattle management course that I once took in Animal Husbandry. How to live off the misfortune of one's neighbor.

The aim of our corposystem world view is not to love the calf, not to nourish the grandchildren, but to profit from every phase of the process from birth to slaughter as we send the young off to war or some other occupation that the corposystem requires to sustain its core – the balance of money and growth. (Another book that is interesting in this context, and is very honest and at the same time is quite positive and a good read, is The Omnivore's Dilemma by Michael Pollan.)

That is not what this book is about. This book is about how we were embedded in the collaborative nature of the Biosystem and why the dominational growth world view of the corposystem is not compatible with the balance of LIFE.

I suggest we need to step back and take a new look at our overpopulation Problem, beginning with acknowledging that:

1. we have a Problem;
2. that the root Problem is overpopulation, with a plethora of associated symptoms that also need attention;
3. that wiser solutions than what we have been doing must be possible; we could hardly do worse;
4. that talking with each other is indeed difficult; but
5. talking good sense about something is neither lethal nor impossible. It just takes a bit of courage, collaboration, good communication and useful community.
6. even if we have to grow a new community to help us.
7. with the aim of learning how the Biosystem functions so that we can collaborate with its processes and align our behaviors and our world views with the collaborative realities of nature and universal natural law.

Collaboration, Communication, Community

But our communities, our corposystem, our country, even our neighborhoods and our religious organizations, are for the most part NOT giving us the collaborative communities that are the goal of nature (but see Helena Norberg-Hodge, 2000), or they are mostly not doing a good job. Instead of supporting us, our communities are breaking up – falling apart, dithering and fighting among themselves – not even trying to discern the actual situation.

> ***Reality Number Five A -*** *The first function of evolution of LIFE is to maintain the survival of the whole LIFE system by selecting which subsystems get to survive: that is, those that communicate well with and function collaboratively with the other systems of LIFE in support of the whole of LIFE of Earth (Chapter 02). Chapter 02.*

Why is this not happening for us? I think it is because of the second primary function of evolution:

> ***Reality Number Five B -*** *The second function of evolution, whenever the LIFE system becomes so unbalanced that it is unable to sustain itself, is to eliminate from the Biosystem the systems that cause more harm than good to the sustainable balance of their environments. Or to say another way, to stir the pot, to create more diversity, new "ideas" when the old ones aren't working anymore. (See Chapter 08). Or, if that doesn't restore a balance to the LIFE system, to get rid of the system that is causing the imbalance. That is why occasional extinctions are necessary to the balance of LIFE, so long as they do not further upset the balance Mass extinctions are harmful because they destroy their own environments. Chapter 02.*

The interactions among the fourteen processes that are our primary subject – balance, energy, entropy, evolution, genetics, etc. (Chapters 9 and 10, Appendix C) -- are built into the laws of nature. They are basic universal facts. It is the task of this book to share a glimpse into how these processes collaborate to sustain The Creation. We know enough about them, and we have the tools we need, so that we could be aligning our behaviors with the Facts of LIFE in a way that benefits both our Biosystem and ourselves.

As it is now, I think humans are causing so much harm to the whole of The Creation, or at least to the whole LIFE of Earth, that *Homo sapiens*, the species (that's us, we) are being eliminated. Extinct. Removed from the community of LIFE.

So what are we doing to respond to the Problem as it is? To change our behaviors in response to the situation we face?

Not much. In this culture it takes great courage simply to talk about it, nevermnd discussion.

And what about that obligation to our grandchildren that was mentioned somewhere above. Is it true that we would be willing to die for the grandchildren but we absolutely refuse to discuss solutions to the blight that lies over their future welfare? Why? Because it's painful to talk about? Depressing? Better to send our children and grandchildren off to war and pretend that will fix it? Use their heroism to settle our minds?

Why are we afraid to talk about overpopulation and all its associated symptoms and crises?

The Facts are Not Different

Our differences are not really about the universal facts of LIFE. We know what they are, even if most people don't know how they fit together. We all must deal with the same universal facts. Energy, for example (Chapter 06), or gravity, or the unchangeable nature of history. We all use factual reality all the time. We use it to stay alive and some people use it to generate technologies. But we do not and cannot change the facts. That is the definition of the word fact that I will use throughout this book.

> ***Reality Number Six*** - *Universal facts are realities and processes that we cannot change because they operate throughout the entire universe, for example, energy, entropy, information, self-assembly, natural selection, time that gives us history, gravity (Chapter 02, Appendix B).*

Of course, parables and metaphors also are very important human sources of information, and probably basic to our humanity. And we can make-believe anything – by descending into denial or declaring against things we would rather not believe, but human beliefs are not universal facts. They may be "social facts," as defined by Gimbel (2015), and some of them are.

> "The rules by which we determine a social fact are internalized.
> We never think of them . . .
> sometimes the social facts are there for good reason,
> but sometimes they're not. . . . Not all social facts are desirable,
> and unless we are forced to confront and justify them,
> they will remain of their own inertia,
> and become worse if not challenged."

Social facts are valid human opinions, ripe for discussion and filled with the possibility for human change. Gravity is a universal fact, no matter what we believe and even if we do not fully understand it. If it were not real, the universe would not hold together. If we don't believe it, or if we lie about it – then that's an opinion, or a scam, but the whole point of facts is that opinions cannot change facts.

> Our human social facts, are not universal Facts. They are real beliefs or situations or answers that have been imprinted on our common consciousness, during our development, as a naturally evolving human society (see Chapter 09, world views). Imprinting our worldviews is one of the ways that our environment communicates with us during our development. It is perfectly normal (Eagleman, 2017), and probably necessary. But it is not a perfect reflection of reality.

So the more we understand about the universal facts, and recognize the "social facts," and the more we discuss their implications, the better off we will be when we must deal with crises and problems, because we will be ready for them. That is the value of science. Technologies, to the contrary, are not intended (in our culture) to align our human behaviors with the facts of LIFE. The function of technologies, as we use them, is to overcome or change universal facts. It won't work.

Technologies are meant to eliminate or override natural law – to overcome natural limits to human growth (limiting factors, see Appendix B).

That can't be done. It is a temporary illusion. In the long term, it is not possible to override natural laws. That's why we call them laws. That is the difference between natural universal facts and our human social facts.

Our effort to over-ride our own biological limiting factors has reached its end and is failing now, as it must fail in the end; that is our current Problem.

Our Words May Differ, But Words do Not Change Facts

We use different words all the time to espouse the same facts and similar world views (Chapter 03; McWhorter, 2004), and we often use the same words to reflect different world views. Words can be and frequently are changed, for example by politicians (Hartmann, 2007). It's not our words that reveal our differences or similarities; it is primarily our world views that determine how we understand both the words and the facts and decide our behaviors.

When we assume that the same word (evolution for example) has the same meaning for everyone, then we begin to have our problems. For example, my guess is that president Trump and I could both use the word "evolution," in more or less the same context and there would be nothing for us to talk about because his understanding of the word and mine are so different. That is why I emphasize definitions in this book. Not because mine are right, but so -- when we do discuss facts and opinions -- we will not be talking about different things using the same words.

And, this is important.

We must discuss the realities, using reliable information. We must try our very best to fact-check our facts – those concepts that are buried so deep in our minds that we don't think about them any more but just assume that they are right.

We need to know what the realities are (Appendix C), because there is no point fighting against the basic facts and realities. Gravity is a good example. There is no point to arguing whether or not it exists. It does, whether or not we understand it, so fighting over it is a waste of time and effort.

The purpose of good basic science is to sort out the universal facts from the social facts and opinions.

Because we cannot change a universal fact, or even discuss it unless we know what it is, *but we can change a social fact and the world view that supports it*. If we need to.

Discussion

We discuss universal facts in order to learn about them, and that is mostly what this book is about; we discuss social facts for two reasons:

> First, the social facts are part of our own world view, and our world view determines our behaviors, and our behaviors, basically, are our legacy to our children and their children.

> Second, we can change our "social facts," if we get together and decide to. Together, we could find a way to take charge of our own behaviors in a way that can support the needs of the Biosystem..

Our dominational corposystem culture has taught us to debate. Debate is a formalized fight over dichotomous, often irrelevant issues; to choose who is the most powerful debater. But the best debater is not our Problem, and neither is winning. Our problem right now is that we cannot discuss our Problem.

Our dominational corposystem has NOT taught us how to discuss – to learn – to collaborate with each other for the future welfare of Humankind. We don't know the difference between learning and losing. Between co-option and communal collaboration.

In our win/lose culture, we are afraid of losing; we are afraid of each other. But in the real world outside the corposystem, in the Biosystem, learning is the norm, and for humans, collaboration is the reward.

You can read a lovely bit of a story about how collaborative discussion works in good basic science, and the joy of it, in Geoffrey West's book SCALE (2017), in section 7 of Chapter 03. Prof. West is a respected physicist, who describes his experience of learning about biology in his collaboration with basic biologists. This short section describes the collaboration as:

> "enormously productive, extraordinarily exciting, and great fun."

And the section goes on to give some important hints for developing such a collaboration that will help within basic science and other disciplines.

Of course, Prof. West already had a lot of experience with collaborations, and it isn't always fun in the learning. But in the end, communal collaboration is one of the rewards of doing good science or doing good discussion. That experience is worth the effort.

The fun is not so much in relationships between square roots and cube roots, unless perhaps you are a mathematician. The joy is in the productive human interactions; the rewards of working with other people to learn more than any one person can understand about "the true situation;" to gather and discuss new information about a subject of common interest or importance to the community; sorting out the garbage, the bad information, understanding connections; solving problems together. It is indeed fun. More fun than trying to win an argument about a fact of LIFE that in any case cannot be changed.

A similar experience was given to me by my professional associations. It has been one of the most important and rewarding parts of my entire (long) life.* That, of course, is why I try to share it with you in this book, along with the warning.

Challenge your own world view, not everyone else's. Be careful in your learning and in the people with whom you discuss it; try not to be afraid, but also to remember that some people are not trustworthy. Do not trust them. Be careful, but do not be exclusive; the whole point is to get new ideas into your own world view and then use them to benefit human kind; not to prove that someone else is wrong.

In a more negative environment, without my great good fortune in my professional companions, my peak experience might have been no fun at all. The last few chapters of Karen Armstrong's history of war (2014), FIELDS OF BLOOD, speaking of 9-1-1, point out, that for the perpetrators:

> "in such closed groups, isolated from any divergent opinion . . . 'the cause' becomes the milieu in which they live and breath."

Their cause was the destruction of themselves and others. And of course in that situation the cause – the goal -- was not worthy of their effort, which was extraordinary.

So be careful of your cause. Collaborative discussion is a powerful human tool; don't waste it on garbage goals, especially other peoples' garbage goals; find positive, like-minded partners and begin to define your common worthwhile goal, because your goal, if you succeed, will be the phenotype (defining world view/emergent reality) of the system that will grow from your efforts. If you don't have such a goal, you can share mine:

> To help grow a self-sufficient, reasonably comfortable human culture within a healthy, vibrant and richly productive Biosystem.

If you really want to help solve our human Problem, more than you want to dither around in a world of dichotomous, irrelevant arguments, then you do not go into your discussions armed for war. You begin by challenging your own world views. Don't bother trying to change other people unless they are a threat to the positive community; they probably aren't changeable anyhow, and you will waste your time.

I have changed my "scientific" corposystem world view over the years of writing this book and challenging my own opinions. Now I challenge you to challenge yours and share your results, beginning with trusted friends.

So Again, What Can We Do?

What we must do if we want to have a voice in the future of *Homo sapiens* is learn to ask good questions about our Problem, and then discuss, rather than debate or fight over, all potential answers and solutions, good or bad. What you, in your family, your church, your community can contribute to solution of our crises is to grow an environment in which opening minds can learn to discuss real problems with wise compassion.

Why Aren't We Doing It?

The corposystem is not wrong in its facts; that is, its honestly obtained data mostly are not wrong. What is wrong (that is, unsustainable) is the corposystem world view -- its interpretation of the data.

The religious or scientific interpretations of how LIFE functions to sustain itself – are not wrong, whether it be Christian or Buddhist or National Science Foundation or something else; nor are the ideals of the humanities, if we apply our beautiful ideas to humans and do not try to believe that our human "social facts" apply universally. They do not. Only universal facts apply universally.

Reductionism as a way to do basic science or technology is not wrong, and neither is holism; linear thinking is not wrong, and neither is a yin/yang approach that emphasizes both the up-side and the down-side of every reality.

Each of our many ways of learning, including the dark sides, the "shadow," are part of the whole of the reality; and the parts can be used to contribute to the whole through open-ended collaborative discussion, because the whole of LIFE is a system, a naturally evolved Biosystem that is composed of naturally evolved sub-systems, and that is what the corposystem (also a naturally evolved system) does not understand. That is what is not incorporated into the corposystem world view. The corposystem sees, instead, a very much more simplistic set of mostly either/or facts and imagines that it can be overcome by human technologies.

In the long term, it cannot.

What actually exists, all around us, because that is what we are, is naturally evolved systems, with up-sides and down-sides that operate according to universal facts of LIFE, and not according to corposystem dogma or propaganda (Meadows, 2007).

> ***Reality Number Seven*** *- We, and our parts, and our environments, all ARE naturally evolved systems, as are our social systems and our world views. We are functional, collaborative, naturally evolved LIFE systems (Chapters 04, 06, 07, 09) that can only partly be described by each of the above study methods, or all of them together (Chapter 02).*

It's not a failure of vision that leads us to follow the corposystem down the path toward our own destruction. It is how we – the bad guys and the good guys – are trained by our own social system to use the reality of LIFE systems, and their relationships, *to benefit ourselves rather than to nurture the whole of LIFE.*

It is a failure of our world views. Our paradigms do not parallel the basic reality of the Codes of LIFE.

Codes of LIFE

A code of LIFE is a naturally evolved system that allows individual LIFE systems to communicate with, and respond to, the Facts of LIFE as we experience them. It is also one way that naturally evolved systems communicate with each other. There are many codes of LIFE, and all of them, in one way or another, use natural processes that transmit information. I describe three of them, as examples, in Chapter 09.

It is the human world view code, that I believe is now preventing us from resolving our current human Problem (Appendix A).

So I set out to learn more about world views (paradigms) and how we humans grow and nurture them.

World Views

Learning new things is fun. Ask any happy child. And not only for the "winners" of some artificial competition. At its best, if we nurture our environment on its own terms, rather than try to impose our human preferences on our environment, we could accomplish my goal:

> *To help grow a self-sufficient, reasonably comfortable human culture within a healthy, vibrant and richly productive Biosystem.*

This is a positive result that our modern social paradigm cannot provide: neither the fruitful Biosystem, because that is gone; we have already overgrazed it; nor the sustainable lifestyle, because growth is not sustainable.

More importantly, the human world view is a system over which we have, as adults, a relatively high degree of control, compared with most aspects of our environments. If we want some control over our lives, and especially our contribution to the future of human kind, the best thing we can have is good information that can be used to energize, as nearly as possible, an *accurate* world view.

We need to fact check our information; to learn how things really work, not how the corposystem claims that they work; to know what we can control and what we cannot control. We want our effort, what we care about, to do some good. We do not want to waste all our sacrifices fighting against universal facts. We want to deal with things that we can control, and align those things with the facts that we cannot control in a way that is empowering to the whole of LIFE.

Our human obligation is to avoid behaviors that harm each other and/or our necessary common environments.

> What we can do that is useful is to align our own world views with the Facts of Life. Because the Facts of Life, the facts themselves, do not change. How we use the facts can change, depending upon our world views. So, if we plan our lives to conform to the biological Facts of Life, this will automatically tend to correlate our world views and our common goals with reality and with each other. And it can give rise to some very productive useful and joyful collaborative discussions – as opposed to the corposystem norm, which is to yell at each other in the effort to prove our logic by our dominational expertise (ref. Facebook, nearly anywhere) rather than growing a productive world view that is based in reality.

Systems

(Refs for starters: Margulis, 1998; Meadows, 2007; Capra & Luisi, 2014)

And just about the time I figured out all that above -- another woman, a Californian who obviously holds a similar view, popped into my life. She said, in a (very helpful) Facebook discussion, rather defiantly I thought, as though she were disagreeing:

> "I believe in systems."

Well, duhhhhhhh, so do I. I thought everyone did. I figured that from about 1953 when I took courses in ecosystems and evolutionary systems and genetical systems, back to back, we knew they were systems. To be fair, that is not how those three systems were represented at the time, but it was the first core light-bulb experience (of three) in my life when I knew systems, whether or not I used the term. Of course I believe in systems. I can be (frequently) quoted over the past half-century or so as saying that I've been waiting all these years for someone else besides ecologists, geneticists and evolutionists to recognize systems.

Yes that long ago -- before the mathematicians had adequate computers to study the systems – we knew they were systems.

And how could anyone not believe in systems? They are everywhere. They are us.

And finally, a few decades later, someone did recognize the systems, and nobody told me about it because by that time I was "retired!" And also the modern systems experts tend to speak geek, because they tend to be physicists and mathematicians.

Apparently they believe they invented systems, but the systems have been here all along. Our concept of systems is a metaphor, of course, but it is also a good way to represent the fact of systems, and a fact is a fact. They were here even before I was born, apparently from the beginning of our universe (Appendix E), and very likely the greatest gift of my education was Dr. Salt on that subject when he explained that anything can go out of balance and when it does bad things can happen. Thank you Dr. Salt.

I have labeled my systemic world view, and the subject of this book, as Naturally Evolved Systems of LIFE. My world view has benefited from modern systems theory, but is not about math or physics; it's about LIFE and the Laws of LIFE, the FACTS of LIFE that we cannot change, as best we know them.

So now I have realigned my world view and learned some new words and definitions from mathematicians and physicists and biologists and systems folk, to more accurately reflect the fact that LIFE is an emergent property of a naturally evolved complex adaptive system, the Biosystem, that is composed of naturally evolved subsystems that function collaboratively within their environments, in support of the whole of LIFE as it uses its own complexity and variability to balance itself at the peak of the required efficiency (Heylighen, 2010; Lloyd, 2016; Gell-Mann, 1994).

My new world view is of course logical. Most world views are logical in their context, and it fits together the Facts of LIFE a bit better than the old one did, still without denying any demonstrable realities (that I know about). This book is an effort to bring together all our visions that are not wrong, but not altogether right, and squeeze out a common paradigm that represents the systems of The Creation more accurately than the world view we have been taught.

This book is about sustaining naturally evolved LIFE systems. Saving LIFE, or at least *Homo sapiens*.

And that's the goal, isn't it? To align our own behaviors, and those of our species (*Homo sapiens*) with the Facts of Life so that we can help to grow:

> *A reasonably comfortable, sustainable human presence within a compatible, healthy and abundant Biosystem.*

Rather than destroying what is -- in our vain efforts to make something that we are able to control.

OOOOOOOO

Chapter 02 is dedicated to Dr. Salt, Dr. Womack, Dr. Hearing. Dr. Mizoguchi, and Takahashi Sensei.

Deep gratitude to the Japanese Society for Pigment Cell Biology and the PanAmerican Society for Pigment Cell Biology and the European Society for Pigment Cell Biology. You opened my eyes in two different directions (at least) during the most rewarding and exciting, and yes, fun, period of my life. My greatest sorrow is that I was unable to return to Japan, as hard as I tried, and I did indeed try hard.

Gratitude to The Teaching Company for their DVDs of genuine university-level courses that fill a huge information gap in our educational system for people who cannot live in cities – which is still nearly half of our population.

"The best things can't be said.
That is to say, you can't talk about
that which lies beyond the reach of words.
The second best are misunderstood,
Because they are your statements
about that which cannot be told."
(Joseph Campbell, 1999)

CHAPTER 3

INFORMATION

This book is mostly about the functions of evolution in real life, because I think evolution is the most basic fact of LIFE.

Evolution of LIFE is about the flow of information through all of the Biosystem – all of the systems and sub-systems that must interact if LIFE is to emerge from among the interactions among the systems.

This chapter describes some background that we need, if we are to discuss the basic science (not technology) of LIFE as I proposed in Chapter 02, as we work for our common goal:

helping to generate or regenerate a sustainable human presence as part of a flourishing Biosystem.

We do not usually, maybe we cannot, discuss ideas with each other, even though, (it seems to me) we are essentially all working for a solution to our same common Problem (see Appendix A).

A primary reason we cannot discuss issues among ourselves, in my experience, is because our same words tend to have different meanings for different people, especially if the people have broadly different world views.

Tree is not a tree. It is a code-word, or a metaphor, a word that allows me to tell you what I am thinking about. But even if I showed you a picture of the tree that is outside my window at this time – or the tree that was outside my Japanese teacher's window. To him, the word that images that same tree is ki. Even with a picture, you could not touch, smell, feel or understand my emotions that relate to tree and ki. A tree is a real thing. A word is a real word, but it is not a real tree. It is a tag or a label that helps us to understand each other.

We already knew that.

You and I already knew most of what is in this book. The main differences in our thinking are not about the facts. There are a couple of very nice new facts in here. New to me; in my pride I believe they are also new to science, but of course not to the reality; they were there all along; we just didn't have words for them.

The primary differences among us that we need to discuss openly have to do with how we fit the facts and tales into our world views (see also Chapter 09 regarding world views).

Here is a little example from a couple of weeks ago when the two of us were sitting on her porch in the cool of the day (under a ki), just chatting about our pets, comparing them to ourselves. As often happens in a desert country, the subject of water came up. She was amazed that I did not know we should all be drinking large amounts of water daily, in order to feel healthy. I mean LARGE. Ten or twelve cups for a person who does not do manual labor in the hot sun.

She looks very healthy. She's a sipper. Carries the bottle with her all day, and gives bottles to others.

I was incredulous that she could think that kind of drinking is normal. When I was her age . . . it was not. I do remember there was an advertising campaign quite a few years ago, trying to get people to drink more water. I think it was Coca Cola© promoting water, but I'm sure I said, somewhere in this book that advertising cannot change the reality of how the human physiology functions, and when Coca Cola© speaks I generally ignore them. In my younger days in southern Texas it would take a very hot day for me to normally (in response to the needs of my body) drink 10 or 12 cups a day of water. We all drank when we were thirsty and didn't when we weren't. That's why the body has a thirst mechanism. That's what it is for.

That's what I was thinking

What has changed, then? Why do we now believe it is actually normal to force-feed water to our bodies? In cave-man days, who told everyone to carry around a bottle of water? Who made the bottles? And it might have ended there, except that I have tried drinking more water — and yet more — and it works. If I can manage to glug down twelve cups a day, I do feel better the next day. Or even ten cups.

Then I am hit by another question. What is too much? I do know it is possible to kill one's self from drinking too much water. It occasionally happens during fraternity hazings. So what should we do? What has changed from then to now?

Probably the change relates to world-wide pollution and the increasing normality of pollution diseases ("environmental illness"). Forcing a safe amount of water into our bodies helps the body to get rid of pollution — chemical, electromagnetic — that we pick up from our modern environments.

But it is a temporary "fix," a symptom rather than a cure, and fixing my body does not stop the increase in pollution and pollution-related illness that our children and grandchildren will be required to endure, until eventually the Problem has no solution.

The deepest miracle of LIFE is that it can balance itself, using life and death and extinction and the evolution of information. Right now, the increase in pollution caused by overpopulation of *Homo sapiens,* is unbalancing the Biosystem.

I keep thinking the people who are not yet affected by the unbalance, say, they only need one quart of water a day — that they will want to help those of us who need three quarts a day before all of us are reduced to walking around with a water bottle on our backs, because an out-of-control cycle of pollution is not normal.

To be honest, I was a bit amazed that she was not aware of the incredible increases in pollution. She, on the other hand was no doubt amazed that I was not forcing water into my body.

This conversation was not a win-win interaction. Even though we were both "right," and we used the same words, and we knew essentially the same facts, we were not really talking about the same things, because she was concerned about the welfare of the person who was sitting right in front of her, and I had and have a vision of tomorrow that most people do not want to share. I don't know if she felt "heard" in this conversation. I did not. Hers is the majority corposystem viewpoint. It is not wrong.

However, mine is also accurate, possibly more accurate, and is serious enough that we should all be discussing it.

Why did I not push my viewpoint? Because I have found that the modern corposystem basically can't (or perhaps won't) discuss. Probably because we view a discussion as though it were an argument, and nobody wants to argue, much less lose an argument. We do not understand collaborative inquiry. I did not until I met up with it in my career, but more generally we react as though our words, memes and stories were "put-downs" or dominational weapons.

So —I have written this book, because I also do not like to argue, and what I am trying to say is that there is a different way to use our technologies, including our words, books, memes and stories. Instead of using them to support the growth and profits and dominational behaviors that benefit the corposystem, we could be using them to support the needs of LIFE itself, which after all includes us. And the first necessary step might very well be to form discussion groups for that purpose.

This book is meant to give you a good start. Appendix B defines the most important words. You will see that some of my definitions are a bit different from those of the corposystem. Probably different from yours. That is a good thing. It is why I am defining those words. So we can have a discussion rather than an argument. So that we can relate my words to your words, fact check them all, and discuss the differences as they relate to their biological reality.

Please use my definitions (Appendix B) while reading my words, because I am trying to say exactly what I mean, with no adolescent fluff. Where there are differences between my view and that of the corposytem— that's where fact-based discussion should be most useful.

And for the same reason, please try *not* to use key word shortcuts and *not* skim through the paragraphs, because the function of key words is to jerk you right back into whatever you already know, not to learn or evaluate ideas that differ from the norm, and the result of skimming is to tuck my ideas neatly into your already established world views rather than inform you about mine. Both those actions block the flow of information between us.

Stories, Metaphors and Memes

Metaphorical stories are real. They are real stories and they are often real teaching aids.

Whether or not events in the stories really occurred, they may communicate some of the "best things that can't be said." However, metaphorical stories (by definition) did not really happen, at least not in the way they are told. They are not "facts."

Historical facts are facts because nobody can change them. That is, what really happened — really did happen. Historical facts, and their results, are forever. We cannot change the reality of what happened back then, of course mostly we may not know what happened, but my point is, whatever it was, it was, and we are – must – reap the consequences because we cannot change what happened.

What we can change is ourselves, now. We can change our perception of the reality, or we can ignore it and do what is the right thing to do -- now. The choices that were made historically were in part responsible for our circumstances of today, and the choices we make will be just as permanent and just as important as the historical choices that brought us to this place. Therefore, it is important to the future that we think very seriously about what we choose to do now.

The facts do not change, and the words we use do not usually change. What changes more often is the meanings of our words.

Stories and metaphors and memes are lovely, but they can bring disaster to a human social system unless they are based in real facts or refer to real responsibilities.

The stories we tell are very important, because they grow our world views. Our world views direct our behaviors. Our behaviors are our contribution to our communal future.

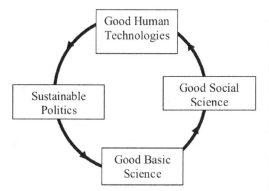

Whether or not we understand the difference between a fact-based reality, such as evolution, and a metaphorical tale such as Harry Potter, the one really happened and is happening all around us in reaction to our behaviors, and the other will not help technologically to resolve our problems.

It is critically important, in this age especially, that our behaviors be as closely aligned as possible to the needs of our biological environment – so that our behaviors will benefit our communal future.

For example, I vividly remember a cautionary tale my father told me when I was about six years old. It had to do with a waterfall, a child who wandered into the water, and several adults who drowned trying to save the child. As he told me the story, I was looking at the waterfall, and to this day I can picture the event that I never saw. For all I know, my father's story was as fanciful as Harry Potter; I know the waterfall was real; and the story was aligned with the reality he wanted to communicate. Water can be dangerous to little children.

Historical choices created our Problem. It is time now that we use that experience to save ourselves, because now we know more than we did then, and our choices now will determine the future of human-kind. It is important that we align those choices with the reality of needs of LIFE as we work to grow a reasonably comfortable human social system that is sustainable. Fairy stories about hope and happiness will not bring this result unless they *also help to align our behaviors with the realities of LIFE*.

An example of disastrous meme, because so many people believe in it, and have used it as though it were true to their interpretation, is "survival of the fittest." I believe in evolution as it correlates with fact-base observation in the course of my life and my career, and this book will tell you why that old meme is not fundamentally true in the way our corposystem has defined fitness — in fact has co-opted the meme to support a dominational ideal and, over the last century and a half, has used the meme to support its naïve, immature and flawed image of evolution; and then has used its image of evolution to support its behavior; with the result is that we are today in the middle of a species-threatening Problem (Chapters 08 and 09, Appendix A).

In fact, the deepest reality of LIFE is its ability to sustain its own viable balance, and the elegance with which it sustains this balance is primarily through collaborative communication that surpasses any simplistic four-word meme.

When we can know them, the real facts of evolution are the most solid guideposts we have, upon which to base a deeply valid world view. We do have enough information to save ourselves if that is what we decide to do.

Words

Words are important. Words represent our world views, and so they do change (McWhorter, 2004). The unconscious changing of words to match our current world view is one example of normal social evolution. Words evolve, so we need to align our words, as much as possible, with reality – for the same reason that we need to take care regarding the real messages we present on TV and the internet using stories and memes.

When I was young, we of the corposystem worked very hard to learn and share our words, as ideas; now it seems the corposystem is working hard, at least in its political wing (Hartmann, 2007); to prevent us from using our words accurately; almost, it seems, as a weapon of war, or at least domination over our thoughts. Changing the meanings of our words – preventing us from using some of them. Preventing us from thinking about our obligation to our own future on Earth.

Have you noticed that debt, starvation, homelessness, smog, are in the process of dropping out of our discourse? And this at the same period of time, less than half of my lifetime, that a LIFE-damaging smog has spread its dirty fingers from the Gulf of Mexico all the way up the valleys nearly to the peaks of the Rocky Mountains, following potentially toxic levels of wifi irradiation (Pall, 2013, 2016).

I drove that road every year from 2008 through 2018, and the pollution lies in layers that every year flatten out in the atmosphere a bit higher up the mountain passes than they were the year before. Have you heard that cities of refugees containing a million or more residents are growing in North Africa and Indonesia (Rawlence, 2016)?

These are real problems: if we really want to grow a reasonably benign, sustainable human culture, we need to talk together collaboratively about our problems, address them not as "ain't-it-awful" memes (Berne, 1964), but accompanied by enough wisdom for fruitful cross-disciplinary discussion toward the goal of resolving their root cause or causes.

Therefore, I believe it is akin to criminal to intentionally change fact-based words and definitions, or to remove important words such as overpopulation, smog, pollution, from our day-to-day conversations in an effort to prevent other people from learning about the reality, or to win elections, or for any other ordinary reason. Our goal is not to "win" something. Our goal is not winning. Our goal is:

to survive by helping to grow a healthy and abundantly fruitful Biosystem.

Birth control, carrying capacity, limiting factors, *suffering* — These words are being removed from our mouths, presumably because, to our political corposystem, they are not problems: because our corposystem finds ways to use those realities in its never-ending pursuit of profits that we do not need. What we need is sustainability.

This method of preventing discussion by changing the meanings of words and other symbols is discussed in Eisler 1989, Chapter 7, and in a quote from Daly (GynEcology, 300-31); Orwell, (1984); all of which complain that discussion is hampered because the necessary words no longer exist. See also Thom Hartmann, 2007; McWhorter, 2004).

Another meme that has been used to sell stuff -- "my glass is half full" -- encourages us to ignore problems as though they were not important; but we ignore our problems at our own peril. Solving problems should be our contribution to the future of human kind, it is in fact our responsibility to ourselves, and we can't solve them if we don't know what they are, or if we just blame someone else or something else that is not the basic cause, or if we actually believe that winning something will solve something.

The corposystem has changed the meanings of the words, terms and memes that my generation of basic scientists MUST use if we are not to be struck dumb. "They" don't listen to us scientists — and then "they" ask why the scientists do not "speak up" and tell us all what is happening. Tell us that we have a really bad Problem and exactly what the Problem is. Meanwhile "we" old-time basic scientists are thinking something like:

> "We tried that, we spent our whole lives trying that. They wouldn't listen.
> We gave up."

And at the same time, the new generations have been educated to the corposystem world view, and cannot understand the Biosystem (see Chapter 09) because the corposystem is based on growth and the Biosystem is based in balance and almost nobody actually will talk about that. But see Heinberg, 2021 (https://www.postcarbon.org/capitalism-the-doomsdaymachine/?mc_cid=5e320d7523&mc_eid=779245bc61&fbclid=IwAR1SVl9CsH2NAvUTblxLIMlzS32pGoyGcTALLhjfpYUjvTLyrLaWgfv3f1l

The net result is that what I say about our common biological Problem no longer makes logical sense to many younger people who were raised within the world view of the modern corposystem; and the corposystem is so stressed by the un-sustainability of its own world view, that it simply tries harder and increasingly harder to resolve our common biological Problem using the same behaviors that caused the Problem in the first place, because those are the behaviors that the corposystem understands.

> *Homocentric growth for gain by competition/domination is not compatible with the balance of LIFE.*

The same words have new meanings, especially new implications and contexts, for the youth and semi-youth of today -- even the scientists -- compared with the meanings of those words when they were coined.

The people believe they have heard and understood; the corposystem perceives that it has heard and understood. But we/they don't understand each other. The discussion (communication) between and among us is not clear and honest, the result is an increasingly chaotic social system.

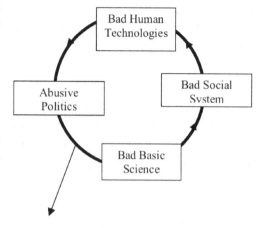

For example, if I say "evolution," you think "survival of the fittest."

You just do, or most people in our culture do; not because you understand evolution; you may or may not; but because the corposystem has scored this channel in your brain (Eagleman, 2015) – and there goes a whole generation of citizens down the wrong road because, at its most basic root, evolution is about efficient collaboration.

For another example, if I say good, or bad, as in the cycles shown in this chapter, you might think about what feels good to you now. The idea of "happiness" may float into your subconscious. I, on the other hand, think about the long-term sustainability of our LIFE systems.

> *To grow a reasonably comfortable future for human kind within a flourishing Biosystem.*

If I say science, it is very likely that the younger generations of moderns think of technology, which has become a *contrasting* endeavor.

Basic science is about inquiry that informs our world views; technology is applied science, seldom basic science, and it is about making tools that we use to reinforce our behaviors.

Or to put it another way, basic science questions how the works of nature, or the works of God, function; technology is the work of man, applied according to his world view. We do not have control over the facts of LIFE, or of God's Creation, which presumably functions as it was created to function. We do have control over how humans apply the technological creations of man. The difference is vast, and we should be using it to guide our survival efforts, if survival is what we genuinely are working for.

The Creation is a real, naturally evolved system. The word that represents the reality of The Creation may (or may not) be evolution, but our human words did not create The Creation or evolution, and also the words do not represent the entire reality of those systems, because humans defined the word evolution and the word Creation, and humans do not know all the real historical facts and events that led to us and our trees and the whole of The Creation of the universe and of the Life of Earth. Humans are not omniscient. Humans do not and can not know everything.

Nobody knows exactly everything about that, and we couldn't change it if we did, because humans are not omnipotent. Humans cannot do everything – especially we cannot change facts. Our understanding of the facts changes as we learn more, but a change in our understanding does not change the facts.

Of course, we do know some things. We know the difference between a word and its reality, between a real tree and the word tree; we know the difference between a fact and an opinion; and we know the difference between real computer games and real life.

However, some very powerful people within the corposystem are trying to change our understanding of reality by changing our words and metaphors, misusing our words to control our world views. And this is important, remember, because our world views direct our behaviors and our behaviors are our unchangeable gift to our own future and the future of human kind.

For example, to quarrel over whether or not there is such a thing as climate change is dominational tripe. There was never any real debate among people who are competent and well trained enough to study the facts as best we can know them, but it has taken nearly two decades and more for us to come to the point where we can talk about it as a reality. How can we deal with what we cannot talk about?

Someone made up that "debate" over climate change, and some people were rather well paid to promote it as a debate rather than a Problem to be dealt with. (Hartmann, 2007). Because the corposystem is in charge of the media, and it does not want us to stop growing because that is how it makes money.

But what is more important? Temporary growth, or sustainable LIFE?

In the current environmental conditions, economic growth can only be predicted to cause more climate change because economic growth conflicts with the requirements necessary to maintain LIFE itself (Brown, 2004, 2008, 2012; Butler, 2015; Catton, 1982; Hartmann, 2017; Hopkins, 2008; Martensen, 2009; McKibben, 2010). That fact is also not a debate; it is quite well understood, so there is no reason for me to make a list and point out which point in the "debate" is real and which is fake and which, most often, is irrelevant. These debates, when we already know the reality, are excuses. Rather cowardly excuses in my opinion, to avoid addressing our real overpopulation Problem.

Nevertheless, some of our corposystem power-seekers are willfully, eagerly, gleefully, joyfully, playfully, compassionately and without much violence simply changing the message of scientific and historical fact so that the people cannot see the reality. And this explains better than I can say why it is NOT ENOUGH to promote the good: wisdom compassion, nonviolence (Antal, 2018; Armstrong, 2009; Berry, 1990, 1992; Bryson, 2002, 2003; Carson, 1963; Dear, 2008, 2013; Easwaren, 1984, 1989; Goodall, 2010; Greer, 2011, 2016; Gore, 2006, 2010; Hartman, 1998; Heinberg, 2007; Heinberg & Lerch, 2010; Hopkins, 2008; Klein, 2014; Rifkin, 2009; Smith, 2001; Loy, 2018; Maathai, several; Makhijani, 2010; McKibben, 2010; Norberg-Hodge, 2000; Orr, 2004; Pall, several; Pineault, 2019; Rawlence, 2916; Ripple, 2017; Salmoney, several; Selak and Overman, 2013; Shiva, all; Steingraber, 2011; Suzuki, 2007; Suzuki & Knudsen, 1993; The Dalai Lama, 2010; The Dalai Lama and Thupten Jinpa, 2009; The Dalai Lama, Desmond Tutu and Douglas Abrams, 2016; Tutu, 2004, 2015; Wolfson, 2007; Wilson, all; Xanthopolous, 2017). In other words, a large number of the references that are listed at the back of the book. It is not enough to promote the good, the truth, the honorable, the wise.

Did I say we should stop promoting the good?

Say it again.

I said it is NOT ENOUGH to promote the good. It is NECESSARY to promote good solutions, that's why I keep doing it; it is essential that we regenerate the positive traits that have led to the survival of *Homo sapiens*, right now our most evil traits are becoming the norm, just as they did in Germany under Hitler, and for similar reasons.

But we can promote good solutions from now until the end of human time and it will only INCREASE climate change, if we ignore the root cause of that Problem. Each and every one of us is under obligation to ALSO promote the COMMON welfare by doing what we can about reducing the overpopulation of humans and the growth of the corposystem as humanely and compassionately as we possibly can.

As I said in Chapter 02 and say again in Appendix A — that is why discussion is essential to our success. No matter what else we do that is fine, heroic and admirable, we need wise compassion and wise heroism and wise solutions to our common Problem. That is not a one-person job. And that will not happen unless we discuss the realities among ourselves, paying careful *attention to both the up-sides and the down-sides of every reality that we discuss.*

> **Reality Number Eleven** - *It is possible to destroy everything that we love WITHOUT violence and, in that way, keep the people "happy" until the very last minute, when the shit hits the fan, and there is no place else to turn. That is not the intention of any publication cited here, nor of most "actions," but I am quite certain there are some very sophisticated organized efforts to "win" the propaganda wars by mis-using the words of our good intentions. Therefore, we should be always aware and make every effort to understand each other before reacting to each other (Chapter 03).*

An internet computer nerd I know, who will remain nameless, told me just the other day that:

> "The web is where the battles for public opinion are taking place. It's where we can introduce new ideas, and build communities to develop them. . . I'm most concerned about concerted attacks (hundreds of abusive emails for certain articles) and paid trolls who attempt to disrupt the conversation and spread fear uncertainty, doubt."

A computer game is a real game, but it is not real Life. The corposystem can try to change the meanings of our words and metaphors, computer games and fairy stories, by a successful effort to gain control over the media and thus silence our discussions of the reality (and they are doing this right now with great gusto and determination), but even if that ploy succeeds temporarily, it will not change any historical or ongoing facts. Rather, it will create an ignorant (that is, uninformed) public, even less well prepared, and unable to deal with the reality of what is happening to us and to the Earth itself, and so shorten the possibility of LIFE of *Homo sapiens* within earth and, more importantly increase the suffering of our generations.

> ***Reality Number Twelve*** - *Trying to change the unchangeable facts is not where our power lies. We have more important things to do (Chapter 03).* Our job, as defined by this book, is to:
>
> *nourish a sustainable, reasonably comfortable future for our descendants.*

We cannot do this by changing facts because we cannot change facts; that's why we call them facts.

> Facts are realities and processes that we cannot change, for example, energy, entropy, information, self-assembly, natural selection, time, gravity.

Our power does not lie in trying to change the unchangeable. Our power lies in *understanding the factual reality as best we can and using the real facts to grow a sustainable human culture within the facts*; to speak for the earth using words based in hard facts; to recognize the dangers of corposystem fairy tales, power ploys and cop-outs. To recognize that some of the things we strongly believe may not be true, and to discuss them with others who are also concerned about our human future.

It seems that many in our corposystem believe that is exactly what we are doing – using our technologies and food fights on the internet. Growing a better future. If it were, then our society would be getting better for us all, not only for the few lucky ones. That is not happening (Rifkin, 2009). I remember.

It is the words that are changing, not the facts.

If we genuinely wanted to behave in ways that could grow a sustainable human culture – then every woman on earth who wants it would have access to free birth control.

The reality is that we do not have a choice. We talk and work together **for the Biosystem** or we will all participate in its slow (or fast, depending on what happens next) change from human-nurturing to something else – to protect its own LIFE.

So, we all need to inform ourselves about the needs of the Biosystem – not the corposystem version, but the Biosystem version.

Whatever method we choose to inform ourselves will require discussion and the discussion will require words and concepts that are OUTSIDE the world view in which most of us were raised,

Discussion

Discussion is not argument, or debate, or winning or any other form of domination. It is collaborative exchange of information around a topic of interest and importance.

> *Information is essential to evolution – evolution, really, is the flow of information through, among and between naturally evolving systems. All kinds of information.*

Without **accurate** shared information, that is, information in the broadest sense, a naturally evolved system cannot sustain itself; it will succumb to inefficiency and entropy and lose its sweet spot; it will fall apart in pieces; in the human case, bits and pieces of broken belief systems, broken lives, social chaos, as climate change matures and our Earth services collapse.

Our discussions will be difficult, first because discussion is always difficult. If collaboration/ discussion were easy, people would stop all the so-called debates, arguments, lies, propaganda, inappropriate innuendo, misused logic and fake photography, and we would do more of good, rewarding discussion that leads to effective win-win-win problem solving (Jandt, 1985).

Domination is easier to understand and to learn, but collaboration is the foundation of LIFE.

Debate, and also much of modern teaching, keep us "inside the box" in a way that can be used to completely control the information and box it into a format that excludes essential elements of the Problem we face. An excellent example of the latter is climate change, now that we are permitted to talk about it, the permitted talk for the most part excludes the actual facts of nature as topics that need to be discussed and understood.

Shared information, not domination, is the key to aligning our world views with biological reality. Shared, accurate information is essential to evolution itself, all kinds of evolution, and it is the key to understanding evolution.

Every link in the naturally evolved systems -- of our world views, of our social systems and of the whole system of LIFE -- consists of shared information of one kind or another. Essential to LIFE is organic (molecular) information. And without the links – the energy – the information -- there can be no system.

Reality Number Thirteen - *Evolution really is about the flow of information through systems (Chapter 03) (see Chapters 07, 08, 09 and 10 regarding evolution).*

So much for that rant.

Proper Definitions

Now that I have convinced you to begin the discussions, I want to change direction and prepare to spend the rest of the book looking at ideas to discuss. Basic biology.

Basic science, as science can be a little confusing. Especially when it is set up in the literary format of the liberal arts, which is not really appropriate to clarify the kinds of relationships that often crop up in science talk. One way to remove the clutter and clarify biological relationships is to arrange our minds in the context of proper definitions.

Definitions are not descriptions, or rather most descriptions, even in many basic science textbooks, where they are most important, are not good definitions.

Proper fact-based definitions are useful in biology far beyond simply describing a thing. When dealing with demonstrable facts, the most useful definition defines the thing *as it relates, by origin or process to* other things. Most of the "things," that we will talk about are naturally evolved systems. Good definitions reflect their evolution and their emergent functions.

Every naturally evolved system, at least every naturally evolved LIFE system, is at least a wee bit (and often very much) functionally different from the others. But they are all related within the emergent properties of LIFE, and proper definitions of these things include an indication of their histories and their origins. Our family tree of LIFE.

For a non-organic example, there is not much point *describing* what is Biology until after we *define* what it is. What is Biology? First and most important, Biology is, or was, a science. Biology is inquiry about LIFE using the scientific method. Without the scientific method, biology is not really biology. It may be better than biology for whatever purpose it is being done, but it cannot be clearly defined as biology.

Biology is the scientific study of LIFE. That definition describes (a) what the thing is (a science, not a technology, or economics, or for example bird-watching or mathematics); science uses the scientific method. (b) which science? (the one that studies the nature of LIFE).

Very likely your idea of that word – science -- does not conform to my definition, because the word has changed, in my lifetime. I watched it evolve to become more and more inclusive. It's a powerful word; everyone wants in on the label. But that is what the word means (or meant); the basic science of LIFE.

Now, in the minds of young people, the label of Biology is attached primarily to the concept of technology, not to a basic science that studies LIFE. Rather technologists made by people. That is a huge difference. Technology is human-made; LIFE is evolved.

LIFE is an emergent property of the evolved Biosystem.

Technology is a human tool, made by humans for their own convenience.

And right there is the beginning of our failure of communication, before we ever get to any difficult ideas and concepts. Proper definitions prevent that misunderstanding by stating the most basic characteristic up front; at least they do if both the speaker and the listener are paying attention to the definitions.

I have provided a proper definition, at least my proper definition, of Biology.

In response to this information, a person who genuinely wants to understand will make sure that she understands the two (or more) parts of the definition: (a) what it is; and (b) which one.

Basic science is: (a) a style of inquiry; (b) that uses the scientific method. We can look that up, part (a) of the definition. We need to find out more about the scientific method. That's easy, you can do that.

Part (b) is not so easy. LIFE. What is LIFE

We have said, in the Preface --

*"**Reality Number Two** – All of LIFE is an emergent property of the Biosystem, which is a naturally evolve system that is composed of other naturally evolved systems (Preface)."*

LIFE is an emergent property of a naturally evolved system. Naturally evolved of course means that nature did it. But what is it? And what is an emergent property?

What is a system?
What is a naturally evolved system?
What is an emergent property?

In this book we will define a system as (a) a group of "things" (nodes, objects, units of matter) (b) that are joined among themselves in specific ways by information-and-energy links of one sort or another. We will us this diagram as our symbol for a naturally evolved system.

A system is a group of things (nodes, represented by the circles), joined together by links consisting of energy/information in some form (processes, behaviors, languages, energy bonds), when the whole group of connected things functions as a unit to perform some specific, usually unique set of emergent functions.

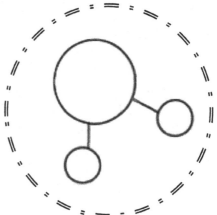

The links (lines) and nodes (circles) in our model represent the "micro-components" (the parts the system is made of). The outer circle represents the emergent properties of that specific system. Each type of LIFE system has unique emergent properties. Emergent properties (S. Johnson, 2003) are specific over-all functions of the whole system that are generated when the parts (the micro-components) work together effectively. Every system has a job to do (a function). I am simplifying the model (that's what models are for) to assume that all the micro-components work together to do the specific over-all function of that kind of system, and that function(s) is its emergent property. The emergent property is different from the micro-components.

Proper definitions clarify and state the relationships between and among the many tightly bonded systems of which the Biosystem is composed.

So let us make some proper definitions and see if they are useful in envisioning the Earth as a system – the Biosystem -- consisting of things (other systems) that are linked together by their history and by inter-connections that consist of information, behaviors, and/or other kinds of energy.

And for the descriptive approach to understanding the system of Earth, which is equally as important as the definitive approach and more common in the humanities, treat yourself to the BBC videos, Planet Earth (2007) and Frozen Planet (2011), narrated by David Attenborough, a respected biologist, educator and communicator, and another version using the similar elegant video and narrated by consumate communicator and activist Robert Redford (2017) so that we do not forget how/why we are here on this gorgeous living planet.

These beautiful DVDs are available in the Chama Library on the shelf below the Over, Over, Over book (Butler, 2015) that was donated by POPULATIONCONNECTION.org, and alongside two fat books of Audubon paintings. Share the humanity of our situation!

Beginning with proper definitions

LIFE is, from our point of view, the most important emergent property of the system of Earth. LIFE is an emergent property of the Biosystem, which is the whole system of our modern living Earth.

The cell is (a) The basic unit (b) of LIFE.

Basic unit in this definition means that the cell itself is alive, but its separate parts are not. As far as we know, the cell is the smallest (least complicated/complex) naturally evolved system that is capable of sustaining its own LIFE.

The emergent properties that define LIFE are variously described, but for here we can say that living things are systems with at least two of the following three emergent characteristics. Units of Life can: (1) maintain themselves by interacting with their environments; (2) reproduce themselves in their environments; (3) evolve over time (generations) compatibly with their environments.

The parts of the cell are molecules and organelles. Separately from the cell, they are not alive. The cell itself, separately from its environment, also cannot maintain LIFE.

The precisely balanced interacting functions of the molecules and organelles (links, processes, information transfer, energy transfer) bring the emergence of LIFE to this complex, intricately organized, collaboratively interacting combination of molecules and organelles.

The cell stays alive because it can use its molecules and organelles – in their environment, which is the cell -- to make more molecules and organelles. The molecules and organelles cannot survive without the whole cell to live in. The cell is their other half — their environment. But that is true of all living things in their environments, so the line between living organisms and molecules is somewhat vague. We don't have to worry about that.

We can also define organelles and molecules, but the purpose of this exercise is not to memorize cellular structures. The purpose is to illustrate an effective way to use definitions so that they specify the interactive and evolutionary nature of naturally evolved systems relative to their environments.

An organelle, in a cell, can be very simply defined as: (a) a naturally evolved system composed of (b) a group of (primarily) organic molecules, (c) that are organized, to perform a specific function(s) within the cell.

For example:

> A lysosome is (a) an organelle (b) that functions in excretion.
>
> A mitochondrion is (a) an organelle (b) that functions in energy metabolism.
>
> A chromosome is (a) an organelle (b) that functions in maintaining and transmitting the "code of LIFE." (actually one of the codes of LIFE, see Chapter 09).
>
> DNA is (a) an organic molecule (b) that functions in maintaining and transmitting the "code of LIFE,"
>
> A chloroplast is (a) an organelle (b) that functions in photosynthesis.
>
> Chlorphyl is (a) an organic molecule (b) that functions in photosynthesis,.

The similarities are as important as the differences.

> Organic molecules are carbon compounds. That is, (a) molecules (b) that contain carbon atoms as basic to their structure.
>
> Molecules are (a) groups of atoms (b) joined together by chemical energy bonds.
>
> Atoms are
>
> Stop, stop.

If biology is the basic science of LIFE, and if the cell is the basic unit of LIFE, then atoms, subatomic particles, quarks and leptons and all that, and the energy of which they all are supposed to be composed – ask a chemist – or a physicist – are not alive.

By definition, subcellular structures are not alive. Because they cannot, on their own, do the activities that LIFE *systems* can do that we described and defined above. Atoms and molecules do not participate in LIFE processes when they are on their own, outside of a living cell.

Let us go back to the basic unit of LIFE and describe the ladder of increasing complexity of living things that make up the body of the LIFE of Earth. If you already know all this, skip to the full-page diagram on the next page, and think of the Biosystem as though it were a giant cell made of all the various combinations of cells.

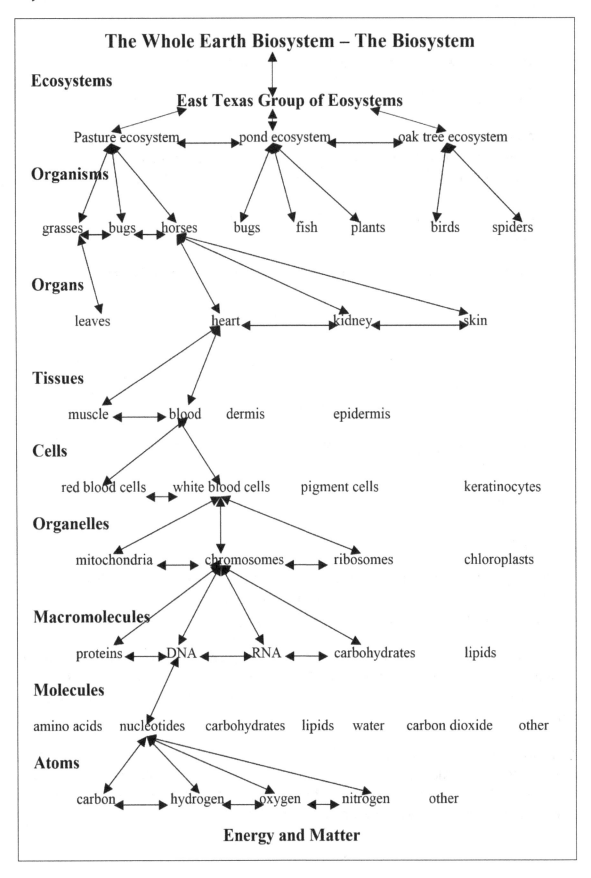

Now we can go up the layers of complexity of LIFE, that make up the body of Earth, from the simplest (the cell) to the most complex.

The cell is: (a) the simplest naturally evolved system (b) that can sustain LIFE. The molecules and organelles are the THINGS of which the cell is made.

Tissues are: (a) naturally evolved subsystems of the LIFE system that are (b) composed of groups of cells that are organized to perform specific functions, either as individual life forms or within multi-cellular living things that are their environment. In other words, tissues are composed of cells that all work together as a system.

Ectoderm is (a) a tissue (b) that covers the outside of early embryos.

Organs are: (a) naturally evolved systems that function within some organisms. (b) They are composed of groups of tissues and cells that are organized into functional units within multi-cellular life forms that are their environment. The environment of your organs is YOU. *The organs are as alive as you are.* Your LIFE is the other half of their LIFE.

A kidney is (a) a naturally evolved organ (b) that functions in excretion.
An eye is (a) a naturally evolved organ that (b) functions in vision.

Now -

What is the difference between a kidney and a lysosome?

What is the similarity between a kidney and a lysosome?

If you got those answers, you are all set to answer nearly any multiple-choice test on this type of subject. All you need is a few more of the proper definitions. You also know a lot about the history of living things and how they are related to each other by descent.

The lungs are (a) naturally evolved organs (if you want to know more, see the above definition of an organ) that (b) function in transport of oxygen and carbon dioxide in and out of the body of some organisms.

That's the definition. Now you know great deal about lungs, without anyone telling you. There is no need to memorize everything separately. If your definition is not set up properly, you can set it up for yourself.

A brain of an organism is (a) a naturally evolved organ (b) that functions in sensory perception, communication within the organism and between the organism and its environment.

And so on through the stomach, liver, eyes, all the organs of a multicellular organism, all of which are composed of tissues and cells and molecules.

> An organ system is (a) a naturally evolved system (b) that is composed of organs that function within their environment to perform specific LIFE functions. The environment of an organ system is its organism.

> For example, the cardiovascular system is (a) a naturally evolved LIFE system (b) that is composed of organs and tissues and cells that function together to circulate blood throughout the body of a multi-cellular organism (c) to carry molecules of food, oxygen, carbon dioxide, waste products, and other necessary molecules to and from all the cells of the body.

> The nervous system etc. etc.

An organism: is an individual living naturally evolved LIFE system. In other words, it has all the functions that are necessary to generate the emergent property of LIFE, including the three that are cited above as definitive.

So, we think that is the king of the hill, right? Organisms rule and we are organisms? And that is as good as it gets? No way.

A biological community: is a naturally evolved system composed of all the organisms, in a local, self-sustaining region such as a lake or a forest or a cliff-side. All the organisms function together with their environments to preserve the LIFE of that biological community within the environmental conditions that exist in that region. Different organisms have different functions in the community, just in the same way that different organs have different functions in your body.

An ecosystem: is a larger LIFE system, or unit of LIFE, or we could say super-organism, that is composed of interacting biological communities, and organisms, and is necessary to the lives of all the organisms that are a part of it, in exactly the same way that those organisms are necessary to the lives of their organs. For example, Wangari Maathai (2006) has referred to the trees of the African forest that was her homeland, collectively, as the "lungs" of the forest community.

A biome: is a very broad naturally evolved system, such as the tropics, the arctic, the deciduous forest, etc.

The biomes function together to maintain the whole climate that is characteristic of the Life form, the naturally evolved complex adaptive system that we know as The Living Earth Biosystem.

All of LIFE is related, both by origin and by its emergent functions. The emergent *function* of the Biosystem, and all the interacting LIFE forms, is to sustain LIFE. LIFE is its emergent property. One of its emergent properties, but for us the most important.

The Earth is the largest unit of LIFE that we know about (Feldman, 2018; Sagan & Feldman, 2018; Lovelock,1988, 2009; Margulis, 1998). The Earth consists of a collaborative hierarchy of interacting biomes, sustained by and sustaining their ecosystems; sustained by and sustaining their communities; sustained by and sustaining their organisms; sustained by and sustaining their organ systems; etc., etc. back down to the basic unit of LIFE; below which the molecules and atoms and etc. may be naturally evolved, they certainly are part of the history of LIFE (Appendix E) but they are not, or don't seem to be, characterized by the emergent quality of LIFE. Their interacting functions are not sufficiently complex to sustain all the requirements that I stated in the above definition of LIFE (and more that I will state in later chapters).

The earth is not a random bunch of separate things that happen to be here together (see National Geographic March 2018). (And BTW Darwin didn't say it was.) The Earth is not a separate playground that was put here primarily to benefit people. If we think of it that way, with the power in our hands today, we will destroy our relationship with the Earth.

The Earth is not a bunch of separate things. All the things, the living things and the nonliving things, are connected in multiple ways by functional links that share information. They are SO intimately connected that they cannot function properly unless their behaviors (links, energy functions) interact properly.

Or they WERE connected by exquisitely balanced functional links. Not as much now as, for example, when I was born. Every extinct species (for example) represents a loss of the *balance of complexity of the nodes and the energy that connects and activates them — and therefore of the emergent properties that sustain the LIFE of Earth. It also represents loss of a big chunk of the genetic code of LIFE that never can be regenerated. Gone forever.*

The Earth is a living system. One, self sustaining, naturally evolved system that functions to maintain the emergent property of LIFE against the power of entropy, using the efficiency and complexity of the interactions among all its organic and inorganic parts (Chapter 06).

Homo sapiens is one part of the miracle of the LIFE of Earth. The living Earth is very much more complex than we are, and that is difficult to imagine. And therefore, to identify the basic properties of ourselves, and ourselves in our relationships with the other systems of LIFE, we use mathematics, reductionist methods of thinking, and metaphorical ways of speaking, such as what I refer to above as proper definitions, and the metaphor of naturally evolved systems, and its symbols, that are central to this book.

The down-side of these holistic efforts to understand LIFE is that we oversimplify the complexity; LIFE of Earth is more complex than we can imagine, and so every time we learn a bit more we imagine that we know more than we do, and naively use the information foolishly, causing problems for ourselves.

The up-side, if we would use these tools to properly represent the (simplified) reality, can be, or could be, to align our thinking more closely with the power of LIFE.

> *To grow a healthy, reasonably comfortable, nurturing interaction with a richly fruitful LIFE of Earth that is our Biosystem environment.*

OOOOOOO

How do we reference a life's work? This chapter I dedicate to Prof Noam Chomsky's two life works to which he made great contributions: linguistics and his activism against the powers that generated first to the social system that arose under Hitler and then to the social system currently arising in the United States, and his many books that give us words to talk about these things. Oh yes, and a third. My activism in retirement, including six years of blogs and this book, arose in response to his words.

"A string of recent breath-taking discoveries
has forced us to acknowledge that
amazingly simple and far-reaching natural laws
govern the structure and evolution
of all the complex networks that surround us."
(Barabasi, 2003)

CHAPTER 4

NATURALLY EVOLVED LIFE SYSTEMS

Barabasi goes on to explain, in his excellent book, "Linked":

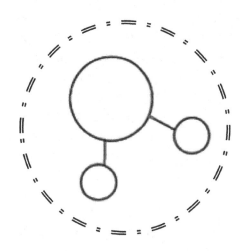

"Reductionism was the driving force behind much of the twentieth century's scientific research. . . The assumption is that once we understand the parts it will be easy to grasp the whole. . . We have been trained to study atoms and superstrings to understand the universe; molecules to comprehend life; individual genes to understand complex human behavior; prophets to see the origins of fads and religions. . . But we are as far as we have ever been from understanding nature as a whole. . . The reason is simple. Riding reductionism, we run into the hard wall of complexity. . . In complex systems the components can fit (together) in so many different ways that it would take billions of years for us to try them all. Yet nature assembles the piece with a grace and precision honed over millions of years" (Barabasi, 2003).

This below chapter describes, in overview, what we naturally evolved LIFE systems are.

A system is a group of "things" that work together to perform a function – to do some specific kind of job that I refer to loosely here as its "emergent property(s)." Using Barabasi's model, we diagram a system using small circles for the "things," the objects that function collaboratively, and straight lines to represent the links (actions) that interconnect the things and define the collaborations. In living systems, the links are complex combinations of energy, entropy, information that connect the "things" by specific functions that happen between and among them (see Chapter 06). Very simply, we can think of them as the energy/entropy that connects matter. Living systems, however, are not simple, so our model is simplistic. The functions (links) connect the things (that we can refer to as nodes), and when energy flows through them the whole link/node system generates an emergent, higher-level (more complex) function that can be referred to as an emergent property, that I have represented by that halo around our model.

This is my model of a LIFE system. For example, the Biosystem. Or a person. Or your pet dog. An emergent property of those systems is LIFE. LIFE is the halo – the emergent property of the system. LIFE is there when all its parts are appropriatedly energized and balanced. It is gone (death) when they are not.

The "things" that make up a living system usually are also systems. As described briefly toward the end of Chapter 03, the basic unit of LIFE (the least complex living thing) is the cell. A tissue is a higher-level living entity. Tissues are composed of cells that have additional links that allow the tissue, composed of multiple cells, to generate its own higher-level emergent property. Organisms are yet more complex systems, as described in Chapter 03. And so on up to the whole living Earth.

For a simpler, non-living system, think of the engine of a car (automobile) that functions to bring together what-all is needed to generate the energy/information that the car requires, if it is to do anything. The engine is a system composed of parts that are also referred to as micro-components. Each part has its own function, enabled by its structure, and activated by energy. All the parts (micro-components) work together, when the car is turned on and connected, that is the micro-components are appropriately connected, to cause the engine to generate usable energy from gasoline. That is the emergent function of the engine; to cause the engine to generate usable energy. The emergent function can be referred to as the macro-property of the engine, an emergent function of the energy system.

Or think of the entire car that has the function to go from here to there. The engine is a system that cannot go from here to there, but the entire car, with the engine, can do so. Each system has its own particular emergent function. The emergent property of the engine is to generate energy under controlled conditions. When it is connected to wheels, etc., the whole car can go from here to there.

The emergent property of the system describes what the whole system can do that none of its parts can do separately.

An emergent function of the Biosystem is to sustain LIFE. We do not know in detail how it does this.

An emergent function of the corposystem is to make a profit using growth.

Both of these systems, both the Biosystem and the corposystem, are naturally evolved, complex, adaptive systems.

A **complex system** – whether or not it is a living system. Mostly it means that the subunits of the systems (the things) are different from each other, not all similar like the kernels on an ear of corn. A zillion pistons could not do the job that an engine does; the engine requires a variety of parts to function properly, some pistons and some other parts. So the engine is a complex system because it has a variety of parts. The Biosystem has an enormous number of parts, like corn and beans and marijuana and dogs and people and cells and tissues; but, of course not a random collection of things. Rather, an elegantly organized set of sets, subsets, parallel sets, most of which are also complex systems that each has its specific emergent properties which contribute to the emergent property of the Biosystem itself, which is, most importantly, LIFE.

An **adaptive system** - is able to respond, to its environmental system. like a thermostat, which is another non-living system. Systems cannot change into *every thing* that is needed. But they can adapt; for example a tree can adapt from summer to winter if that is what it evolved to do. And of course that is one of the defining characteristics of LIFE. LIFE can adapt itself to its environments in order to stay alive. We are already intimately familiar with adaptive systems, because each of us is a naturally evolved complex adaptive system. Your heart adapts its rate of beating to whatever is happening in your life as does the rest of your body. LIFE itself, the LIFE of Earth, is composed of complex adaptive systems such as you and me, each within its environments. Climate change is its adaptation to the conditions in its LIFE.

The Biosystem = the whole giant, complex adaptive system of LIFE.

The corposystem = our modern naturally evolved complex adaptive human corpo-political-economic-military-educational-charitable social system

Energy = the ability to do work.

The entire engine of our car example can make energy available, but one part or another part cannot do that job alone.

The entire Biosystem is also dependent upon its parts for its LIFE.

Another relatively simple, non-living system that is sometimes used as an example is water. H_2O is made of two gases, hydrogen and oxygen, and yet water itself is a liquid. The liquidness of water and the functions of an engine are two different emergent properties that arise in their very different systems because of the ways that their subunits interact.

The Biosystem is an extremely complex, adaptive, naturally evolved system with an emergent property of LIFE.

What is LIFE? (Schrodinger, 1944; Margulis and Sagan, 1995)

> ***Reality Number Fifteen*** - *LIFE is an emergent property of the naturally evolved Biosystem. To maintain this emergent property, the Biosystem requires that the naturally evolved living systems of Earth collectively sustain the balance of their collaborative, efficient interactions that took billions of years to evolve to near perfection. (Chapter 03).*

The Biosystem is composed of energy and matter, of course, and so is everything else. There is a sense in which energy flows through the whole naturally evolved system of LIFE, directed by the information that is stored in the LIFE-giving system (Chapter 05) to sustain the energy links that hold LIFE together.

The primary activities of LIFE are described in most university freshman biology textbooks, and can be summarized as follows:

1. Most systems of LIFE convert electromagnetic energy from the sunlight into *organic energy*, contained in organic molecules. The energy is then used to do the work required to sustain the Biosystem. (Some archaic cells use other kinds of energy sources).

Beginning with the process of photosynthesis, bits of electromagnetic energy are snatched from sunlight and are converted to organic energy by using them to join together carbon, hydrogen, nitrogen and oxygen atoms, and other atoms, to make organic molecules. Primarily proteins, lipids, nucleic acids and carbohydrates.

Then the organic molecules flow the energy around and between and among the bodies of organisms and around the whole Biosystem, energizing the whole enormous system by providing and maintaining the energy and information that causes each of the biochemical reactions to happen at the right time and in the right place (see Chapter 06).

The organic molecules carry with them the energy (in the links of the molecules) and the information (largely in the structures of the molecules) to do the work of sustaining the LIFE of the Biosystem (and all of living things that are part of the Biosystem). The molecules are taken apart and put back together many times during all the processes required for the above, and are recycled, and more energy is added, also many times. The cycle of LIFE maintains itself, and is maintained by the naturally evolved organic molecules.

In this way, biological energy is routed through the whole LIFE system, doing the many kinds of work that are required to sustain the system. The used-up energy is released into the environment as heat, the molecules fall apart, and the atoms of which they are composed are recycled by adding more energy obtained from sunlight.

2. At the same time as (1), and using the same atoms and molecules, the Biosystem adds LIFE *information* to its captured energy as it (the organic energy) is escorted through the Biosystem. The information is stored in the genetic codes of the organic molecules (and other LIFE codes, see Chapters 08 and 09). And also in the structures of other nodes. So the organic molecules carry both the energy and the information required to sustain LIFE.

The information stored in the structures of the organic molecules tells the energy (stored in the energy bonds of the organic molecules) what it should energize, and when, and how, in order to sustain the billions of interacting LIFE functions of the Biosystem.

3. At the same time that the Biosystem is directing the energy of LIFE through the body of LIFE, it must sustain the *viable balance* among all the components of LIFE, that are also naturally evolved systems, and all their individual functions. To do this, the systems use LIFE Codes to drive the processes of evolution (Chapters 08 and 09), including niches, limiting factors, and other relationships that regulate the whole of LIFE that are studied in ecology; form-function relationships that are studied in anatomy and biochemistry and cell biology; life codes that are studied in physiology, genetics and systems. And other regulators of the interacting systems of LIFE.

In this way the organic molecules of LIFE that make up much of the structures (matter) of the Biosystem carry within themselves the energy and the information that is required to make the appropriate activities happen at just the right time and place, each at its appopriate efficiency, where they are needed to sustain myriad systems of LIFE, to recycle all the materials of LIFE, and to sustain the viable balance among all those processes and materials.

We humans, when thinking about this incredible system, tend to forget part three, perhaps because it is even more complicated than parts one and two. But part three, balancing the systems of LIFE is the most important, because when LIFE falls out of balance – when too many important links, processes, checks and balances, are not working, then we know what happens. The failure of energy and the information that integrates and balances LIFE, is what we call death. Or, at a higher level, extinction.

LIFE is unique compared with non-life in the following ways, and in some other ways that I will add later, and surely in other ways that we do not know about. LIFE can:

1. maintain itself by interacting with its environment;
2. reproduce itself by interacting with its environment;
3. adapt itself to its environment;
4. evolve over the generations, compatibly within its environment.

Those are four of the emergent properties of the Biosystem that are required for the emergence of LIFE.

Emergent Properties

Naturally evolved complex adaptive systems have emergent properties. An emergent property is a characteristic of a whole system, that could not happen in the same way without the whole system. Water is not a life system, but it is a simplistic example of a system. Water consists of oxygen and hydrogen that (at moderate temperature) are both gases, not liquids, but the water itself has the emergent property of liquidness that is essential to life processes. The property of liquidness emerges from the combination of oxygen and hydrogen atoms into a collection of H_2O molecules and has to do with the ways in which they are linked together. We use this example because it is simplistic. LIFE systems consist of incredibly complex, largely unknown, interactions among the emergent properties of its component systems.

Emergent properties are also known as macro-properties and, at least in this book, and in naturally evolved systems, they are sometimes known as phenotypes. The subunits of a complex adaptive system are also known as its micro-components. In the water example, the atoms of hydrogen and oxygen are the micro-components and liquidness is the emergent property of water.

All or nearly all naturally evolved LIFE systems are complex adaptive systems and all or nearly all complex adaptive systems have emergent properties.

Four of the emergent properties of LIFE systems are listed above. They (and others) function to sustain LIFE itself. Without them, LIFE cannot sustain itself. (Yes I realize this is a bit of a "circular argument," but indeed we need to stop our linear thinking and develop a more fluid concept of our living reality if we want to save LIFE as we live it and *Homo sapiens* in particular).

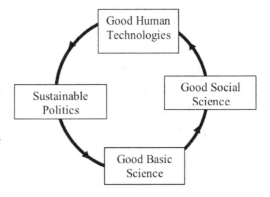

ALL of LIFE is not a circular argument, it is more like a circular discussion, because all of LIFE is made of collaboratively interacting cyclic phenomena.

All the parts of LIFE are also parts of cyclic functions. Problems arise when we interfere with the balance among the cycles of LIFE, because it is the meticulously precise inter-communication among the systems, as I said above, that generates ongoing LIFE.

Systems (Again)

We talk about systems as though we know what they are; and yes, we have recognized some of the functions of LIFE systems from our human prehistory, or we would not have survived. And now, with our invention of writing, and then printing, and then the scientific method, our human system, *Homo sapiens*, is expanding our knowledge at an enormous rate because we humans have developed ways to carry this information forward, first using our language, story-telling, and then writing and printing and now the internet.

Without the ability to store information and pass it forward to following generations. We could not have built so much knowledge on the basis of previous knowledge. We would have been forced to start over with every new observation and conclusion that came into every individual mind.

And now, using the power of computers and modern mathematics, our understanding of the nature of systems is expanding more rapidly than ever. For example, Darwin & Wilson, 2005; Odum, 2004; Lewin, 1992; Martin & Hawks, 2010; Page, 2009; Heylighen, *et al.*, 2010. Now we have more information than we know how to use well. We are not using it well. We are using it for self-agrandizement. That is not how the Biosystem functions.

Before the internet -- that happened in my lifetime -- our linear technologies of reading and writing, and our scientific method, to some extent imposed a reductionist way of thinking upon the information they passed down to us, including our learned logic, our mathematics, and our "social facts," (Chapter 03) (Eagleman, 2015; Gimbel, 2015)

The written word is wonderful! It reaches much further in space and time than the spoken word. Before the internet, it replaced, to a large extent in the dominant Western culture; earlier human forms of education by elders telling stories around the evening fire. It inspired the logic and science of Western philosophers, and organized our thinking into linear and outline format in the pages of written English, French and Germanic and Hispanic languages, in Western texts, spreading out from their origins to eventually guide the powerful homocentric technologies and world view (growth by domination for gain, and in large part that domination is based on information) of our primary naturally evolved social system, the corposystem.

HOWEVER!

The down side to the availability of this modern, homocentric power-of-information is the probability that:

1. we humans, collectively and individually, are naturally evolved systems; and that;
2. clearly, from the above condensed list of LIFE processes we know that linear cannot describe the universal facts that sustain systems; and that;

3. as a result, we don't yet understand everything we need to know if we are to use the power of our information to benefit ourselves in the long run -- rather than merely get rich now and pay later for our mistakes, a reality that is being vividly demonstrated to us by climate change, including its various tipping points, such as fluctuations of the economy, and some embarrassingly uninformed vagaries emerging from the White House when it is confronted with well understood but apparently un-anticipated dilemmas such as the Covid-19 pandemic.

The greatest difficulty in writing this book has been the effort to describe, in linear format, a holistic approach to thinking about LIFE and living systems.

The written word is linear. LIFE itself is not primarily linear. The biological system that gives us LIFE, the Biosystem, is composed primarily of naturally evolved systems.

Naturally evolved systems are not linear.

Functions of Naturally Evolved LIFE Systems

A naturally evolved system must be able:

1. To sustain itself in relationship with its environments;
2. To sustain its emergent characteristics;
3. To adapt and/or evolve;
4. To generate just the right amount of variability so that evolution can function.

1. Survival of the System. Systems must be able to survive, or ultimately they can't be here. They must be able to sustain their *micro-properties* (micro-structure, micro- components).

Naturally evolved systems must behave or function in ways that support their survival within the community of systems; therefore, they must retain their physical construction or micro-structure -- their links and nodes and how the links and nodes interact. Or sometimes change it, to become more compatible with its internal or external environment. The links and nodes limit the amount of variability a system can generate. The system that falls apart does not survive; it must maintain its essential nodes and links (emotional, behavioral, electromagnetic, biochemical, by now you know I am not referring to cement, glass and steel, but to energy interactions).

2. Survival of the (not the most abusive or most powerful, but the most useful) *emergent functions (macro-properties)* of the System.

An emergent property or characteristic (macro-property) is defined as a characteristic of the system that is different from the characteristics of its subunits (micro-properties) and cannot be explained by adding up the individual properties of the subunits of that same system (or other systems). It is more than and different from the sums of the micro-properties. (Page, 2009; Meadows, 2010, Chapter 05).

Each system occupies a unique lifestyle (niche) within its environment; it must sustain, support and enforce its own emergent properties. At the same time, each LIFE system, for its very existence, must contribute to the over-all welfare of the entire system of which it is a part. The resulting yin and yang relationships among the systems, parallel systems and subsystems are accomplished in part by its *niche* and *limiting factors*.

The niche of a naturally evolved system is its life style, which is somewhat flexible within the limiting factors of its environment. The built-in (evolved) limiting factors of living systems are its requirements for LIFE such as water, nesting areas, clean air, food of course, and many less obvious factors that involve relationships with neighboring systems. Whichever factor is in short supply at any given time is its limiting factor, and limits the population growth of the species (Strauss, 2009).

3. Naturally evolved systems must be adaptive so that they can respond to changes in their environments. The environment consists of the other systems with which they interact.

There are constant changes in the systems of LIFE. A constant re-shuffling of relationships. A system that cannot change when conditions change, will ultimately fail. At the same time, there is a limit to the flexibility that is possible without crashing the system. That limit is imposed by numbers 1 and 2 above. This is only one of many examples of the intricate checks and balances that are essential to sustain LIFE. I will not go into detail about checks and balances, feedback loops, except to say they are essential to sustain LIFE, and refer you to (Capra *et al.*, 2014; Meadows, 2002). Or other textbooks about systems. For our holistic view of systems, we already have enough details trying to find their places in our minds, but these limiting factors are of course extremely important because their function is to sustain the balance of LIFE. And then to encode the balance in the genome of the Biosystem (Chapter 09). A beautiful story of complexity.

4. Every naturally evolved system differs in small or large ways from every other naturally evolved system.

This variability is necessary and is promoted naturally by LIFE. There could be no adaptation and no natural selection – no evolution -- if there were no variability. An appropriate level of variability is selected for and enforced by the genetic code and maintained by the energy/entropy/information relationships (that I will call the "sweet spot" in Chapter 06) of the systemic links. We do not need the details of these interactions. We do need to know that low-level variability, such as we can see among all the people around us, is important. Very important. Even more important is the variability among the species. In the media it is often referred to as diversity.

LIFE, we describe as a naturally evolved, complex adaptive system composed of billions of subunits, many or most of which are also naturally evolved systems. In Chapter 03, (under "proper definitions.") we defined some naturally evolved systems as examples of the hierarchy of LIFE systems that have evolved because of the differences among the systems.

Emergent Properties (Again)

We know that the parts of LIFE can and must work together, each part doing its needed function, and we know this capacity is foundational to LIFE. The difference between a dead dog and a living dog demonstrates the reality that its parts, its subsystems and their interactions with other subsystems (some we understand better than others, and some we don't know about) are all, or nearly all, required to sustain LIFE. This fact is most obvious in the study of physiology, but it is true in all of LIFE systems.

LIFE emerges. It is an emergent property resulting from the collaborating functions of the subunits of LIFE, and if the functions get out of balance, or stop doing their jobs, LIFE disappears. If we interrupt the flow of any one of the interactions between systems – their emergent properties -- the flow of energy is changed or interrupted through many or most of its coordinated channels, through the whole system of our example dog – and poof – the balance is gone; LIFE is gone. Only the parts remain.

So we are very interested in HOW the systems of LIFE work together to sustain LIFE.

Using the Barabasi metaphor, we explain that naturally evolved systems are able to work together because the systems talk to each other, or interconnect, using the links that we have been referring to as energy/entropy/ information links, that connect and inter-connect the nodes of LIFE systems.

No.

We said that every system is made of micro-components connected by the links. We said that the connections of all the micro-components of a system, when all the connections are working properly, result in the emergent properties of that system. This is a common characteristic of naturally evolved, complex adaptive systems and you can read more about it in books that describe systems. For us it is important that it happens, because LIFE itself is not a micro-property. It is an emergent property.

Actually, it seems to me a miracle, but LIFE is real and we have it. So we can understand that. What makes it more confusing is the scientific terminology.

So now I want to make a point about terminology.

> *I claim that there is no essential difference, in a living thing, between a phenotype and an emergent property and a macro-property.*

We have already described emergent properties, and we have used the term macro-property, because some systems-people like that term better. Now I claim that these three words, in a general way, refer to the same characteristic of naturally evolved complex adaptive systems.

The word phenotype that are generated in the science of genetics; emergent properties and macro-systems are studied by systems experts; emergent properties were studied by biologists at least for as long as I can remember. So of course there are some different implications for different people using the three terms, but for us here, they all refer to the emergent characteristics of a particular naturally evolved system that is generated by the collaborative functions of its micro-properties.

For example, my life is a macro-property (emergent property, phenotype) that arises because all of my micro-components (cells, tissues, organs, organ systems) are functioning properly – working together as they are meant to do.

> An emergent property or characteristic (macro-property, phenotype) is defined as a characteristic of the system that is different from the characteristics of its subunits (micro-properties) and cannot be explained by adding up the individual properties of the subunits of that same system. It is more than and different from the sums of the micro-properties (Chapter 05; Page, 2009; Johnson S., 2003).

> It is a quality of a system. Often, you can see it or smell it or measure it.
> Or it is a niche of a particular type of bird.
> Or it is a measurable change in the stock market.

That kind of thing, when referring to naturally evolved systems, can be thought of as a phenotype or an emergent property or a macro-system. I tend to prefer emergent property because I think more people have an idea what that means. I also like phenotype, because I am a geneticist.

I think it is likely that the capability of interaction between and among naturally evolved systems — their emergent phenotypic connections — especially those that are preserved in the genetic code of the Biosystem -- that connection is the very source of the flexible complexity that is required to sustain LIFE.

To say that in a different way:

I am suggesting, and will assume, that emergent properties of naturally evolved systems function to communicate with other naturally evolved systems – for example, with their environmental system, or with a partner system such as a mate or a pet, or with a subsystem such as an organ.

Cell surface receptors are a relatively simple example of this kind of interaction among systems. The system communicates with its environment(s), and the environment with the system, using their compatible emergent properties/phenotypes. It is often a two-way exchange of information.

We Tend to Name Systems by Their Emergent Properties

The corposystem and the Biosystem are named for their emergent characteristics. Corpo- refers to the corporate charter, and its primary requirement of profit based on growth. Bio- is a term that refers to life.

The Biosystem is composed of billions of subsystems; we do not need to know names for all of them, especially as their common characteristics are listed above. However, the most important thing about systems of LIFE is how they interact with each other, so we need examples, and I will primarily use the following four systems, named by me, as my examples.

1. Me, the individual naturally evolved system most important to myself. I am a system composed of subsystems (cells, tissues, organs, organ systems) and their emergent properties that function to maintain me. Several of these subsystems were defined in Chapter 03, in the section that defines "things" in terms of their emergent functions (phenotypes). The kidney, for example, is an organ (a system or a subsystem of me) that functions in excretion of urine. I can describe my own emergent properties, I am a subsystem of the Biosystem, by my name, my species, my world view, and most importantly by my behaviors that I use to interact with other systems. I am a human system. An individual system of the species *Homo sapiens*.

2. All humans as a unit, a species, a subsystem of the Biostem, *Homo sapiens*. *Homo sapiens* is defined as: (a) organisms, (b) animals, (c) mammals, (d) primates. We are organisms that specialize in the use of tools and information, and are motivated by a complicated brain that generates our world views, that drive our behaviors that we use to interact with (communicate with) our environments so that we can sustain ourselves.

   In this book, when I say "we are" or "we do," usually I am referring to *Homo sapiens*, or perhaps more often to those of us who were raised in "our" modern social system, the corposystem. So please do not take the reference personally, as "we" are so often inclined to do.

3. The corposystem is a naturally evolved human social system. Because it is a system composed mostly of humans, it has many human characteristics. However, it is not human. It is not alive. It is not an organism; it is a social system -- a naturally evolved complex adaptive system with its own unique emergent characteristics,

including an emergent world view that is based upon perpetuating itself (see the functions of a naturally evolved system, above). It functions to perpetuate itself, not us, and it is caught in an "evolutionary trap" (Robertson & Blumside, 2019). That means its emergent ethic (growth for gain) is fatal to it and to us, in the long term. Interestingly, Robertoson & Blumside recognize evolutionary traps in multiple vertebrate species, but do not associate the problem with humans, which to me seem the most obvious representation of an evolutionary trap. They describe evolution traps as:

". . . when rapid environmental change leads animals to prefer resources that reduce their fitness."

Unfortunately, as explained under the above section "Primary Functions of Naturally Evolved LIFE Systems," the primary function of our modern corposystem, our social environment, is to sustain its emergent ethic, which is growth. That is a "catch 22" – an evolutionary trap – because perpetual growth is not sustainable, and growth is the prime directive of the corposystem.

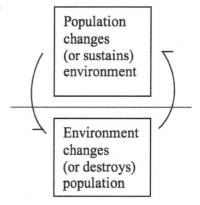

The fortunate possibility is, because we are micro-components of the corposystem, we could change its emergent ethic if we chose to do so.

Of course, the corposystem (relative to us) also has many other properties that we enjoy, and to change it we would also have to change those parts of it that we want to keep. That is the trap. That is why I usually describe the corposystem using its unsustainable emergent qualities, because that is the problem we have to deal with if we, the *Homo sapiens* system, want to sustain our place in the community of LIFE. The most unsustainable, and therefore dangerous to us, emergent properties of the corposystem are *growth by domination for gain*.

4. The Biosystem is a naturally evolved system that is composed of all the living things of earth and the nonliving components of that LIFE which is the Earth itself and its atmosphere that are continually recycled and balanced using the energy of LIFE and the materials of Earth. The primary emergent function of the Biosystem is to sustain LIFE. So far as we know from basic science, LIFE does not sustain human life in particular, nor any human or corposystem world view, but rather the balance among the traits that are required by LIFE to sustain its own self.

    LIFE is defined by its ability to sustain itself.

I am a naturally evolved complex adaptive system. My behaviors cause things to happen in other systems (I am typing right now); my appearance is also an emergent property, blond grey and grey; talking is an emergent behavior; eating, washing, etc. We often evaluate naturally evolved systems using their emergent properties (phenotypes if you wish), so we do understand this concept, though we may not have heard the words: emergent properties/phenotypes/macro-properties.

> ***Reality Number Sixteen*** - *The primary functions of a complex adaptive system can, in a general way, be deduced by the emergent characteristics (that we will from time to time refer to as the phenotypes) of that system (Chapter 04).*

We living things are naturally evolved complex adaptive systems.

Naturally Evolved LIFE Systems are Complex and Adaptive

Complexity

The term complex refers to a system that is composed of many subunits that are mostly not the same as each other, that work together to generate and sustain their own emergent properties. Exactly how they work together probably nobody knows, but I will say just a bit more about that in Chapter 06, Energy/entropy.

My micro-components, kidneys, eyes; all are important to my well being; to my Life; as are my cells and tissues; all my subsystems; but they must collaborate in time and space to accomplish their tasks. It is the collaboration of the subunits of complex adaptive systems that generates the emergent properties of that same system, which in this example is me.

The Biosystem is also composed of subsystems such as trees and animals and water and earth that are not the same as each other. Just as organisms survive using the complexity of our subsystems, so also the subsystems of the Biosystem work together (are connected by energy/information/entropy bonds), to generate and sustain the primary emergent property(s) of the whole Biosystem, which is LIFE.

Another naturally evolved system that is important to us is the corposystem. It is not alive according to our definition, but the corposystem is nevertheless a naturally evolved complex adaptive system. Its primary emergent property is growth.

Adaptive

Adaptation is Not Evolution

The term adaptive, when it is applied to complex adaptive systems, means that the systems are able to change their behaviors in response to their environments (the environments within the Biosystem are also complex adaptive systems). Adaptive systems can change the information content of the energy links, or "turn on or off" links, depending on relationships with other systems. Adaptability is "born into" each LIFE system. It has the ability to adapt to some things but not other things. In this way adaptation is different from evolution, which is a change in the genetic code of a system and cannot be changed back to what it was.

For example an ecosystem, or even my neighbor's pasture, shifts its links (the flow of energy) in a dry year to make sure that LIFE, its most important property, survives. Perhaps different plants are able to grow in some years -- different animals to survive in a dry year, compared with a normal year. The emergent property, LIFE itself, is nurtured and sustained by the entire system's ability to respond to what is happening in its environment: wet; dry; hot; cold; the system as a whole has inborn ways to respond – within its evolved limits -- to its environment by modifying the interactions of its own micro-components.

Adaptation is essential to our survival on Earth; right now especially, with changes happening so quickly all around and in us and other organisms.

How will we adapt? Will we try to do something that cannot be done? Will we reason together (see Appendix A)? Will we continue trying to find ways to kill each other off? Will we learn to listen, to each other and to Mother Earth, and find ways to deal compassionately within the complexities of LIFE?

> **Adaptation** = responding to change without making permanent changes in the genetic code of LIFE.

> **Evolution** = responding to change by changing the genetic code.

What we are now trying to do in response to climate change will not work, is not working.

We are trying to overpower the environment and make it function the way we want it to. In our efforts to make more food for people, we have caused the Biosystem to evolve. The load of our human Biomass is more than the Biosystem can adapt to: therefore, it must evolve – causing the extinction of big chunks of the Biosystem genome.

Genome is defined as the genetic code of the entire system, usually a species. I am unable to find a word that will encompass the entire Biosystem, so I have expanded the meaning of genome to cover all the genes in the Biosystem. Those within the same species interact directly. Outside of the common species they interact in other ways.

The ongoing result of our efforts to overpower this tightly integrated Biosystem genome, is climate change, evolution, that makes our adaptation even more difficult. Living things can bounce back from adaptive changes. We can not bounce back from evolutionary loss, nor can we evolve in partnership with our environments (co-evolve) using adaptation. Certainly not using genetic engineering -- that only adds to the totality of genetic disruption. See Chapters 07 and 09 for a brief overview of evolution. Here I want to talk about adaptation.

Adaptation - Implications

For us, LIFE is the most important emergent characteristic of the naturally evolved Biosystem. Because if there were no LIFE there would be no us. We know – certainly good farmers know – that we must adapt our behaviors to the requirements of the Biosystem if we want to have food to eat. For that reason and for other reasons it is important for us to understand what the Biosystem requires.

As is true of every LIFE system, the Biosystem needs to obtain energy, water, oxygen and smaller amounts of other minerals; it normally obtains these by recycling the parts of its own body; using organic molecules and other methods, it recycles every material thing that it needs to continue surviving, reproducing, evolving, living, basically forever. There is no reason that the Biosystem needs to run out of any material thing, so long as it can continue to use the "things" (materials) that it needs over and over again, to recycle its own parts.

It normally does this, by balancing the birth, growth and death of the various parts of itself, and eating other organisms or/and raw materials -- using energy from outside of itself, from the sun, to drive the necessary process and maintain the necessary balance among the micro-properties of all the systems.

If we want to help the Biosystem maintain its balance, we must do as much of our own rebalancing as we possibly can to replace our growth ethic with one of sustainability.

But that will not be enough.

Sustainability means we must fit our species (*Homo sapiens*) and ourselves into our own niche within the Biosystem and stay there. Defining our niche will be part of the discussion we must have if we choose survival over growth.

That is what the Biosystem is telling us, using its own emergent behaviors to communicate with us -- climate change, the pandemic, starvation, etc.

Meantime the corposystem is also a part of our environment, and it tells us (by its behaviors and also by its propaganda in its media) that we must grow, grow, grow, because that is what the corposystem needs for its survival (and for our jobs, money, and of course the internet, and lots of fun toys like highways and automobiles that we get from the corposystem).

The corposystem is not the Biosystem. They overlap, of course. Like a Venn diagram, broad areas of both systems are the same or similar, but the emergent properties of the two systems are irreconcilable and continue to diverge. The Biosystem has been doing what is necessary to the sustenance of LIFE for more or less five billion years. Our human social system has deviated from the goal of LIFE, and specialized in the goal of growth for more or less 10,000 years, and it ran out of surplus materials, that it was giving to us, some time around the beginning of this century, depending upon how one measures it. What we are still doing is arguing over the measurements of the fact -- while ignoring the fact itself, as though our measurements of reality were more real than the reality.

The corposystem is a real, naturally evolved human social system that functions to do all the things that human social systems do. Education, politics, all those human social tasks that are important to us as humans, but not as important as LIFE itself. One of the defining emergent characteristics (phenotypes) of the corposystem is growth.

The corposystem can't think. It is not a person. But if it could think, I expect it would be in a panic right now because it would believe that there is no other way to survive except for more growth, and there is nothing left to grow with. Fortunately, if we think about something other than growth, if we listen to other alternatives, that concern is not actually true, because sustainability does not require profits, but only maintenance. But growth is obviously what the corposystem is programmed to do, and so the corposystem continues to try harder and harder to survive by growth, and without considering the other aspects of its reality.

The reality is that growth of the population or of the corposystem, at this time, is the surest way to make the Biosystem even more unbalanced, even to the point of crashing both systems.

And the catch 22 is -- the corposystem needs the Biosystem as much as we do, or more. It always did. And to save itself and us, it and we must align (adapt) OUR BEHAVIORS to the needs of the Biosystem. We must stop the growth.

The Biosystem requires balance. Right now, that means less growth: otherwise the climate change is sure to get worse, and other worse things will continue to happen, such as pandemics, wars, droughts, starving babies, pollution diseases, inadequate medical services -- because when we force other systems to change it upsets the balance of all the systems: politics, economics, religion even (Witt, 2017).

We can blame the President; there are good ones and bad ones, but no president can stand at a crossroads holding a stop sign and change how the Laws of Nature and God function to sustain LIFE. Some people actually believe they can; we need to talk about that, so we can adapt ourselves – DO the things that could help, ignore the things we cannot change, or work them into the program.

The corposystem itself never stops proselytizing and propagandizing, in large ways and incredibly subtle ways, for more and more growth. Now it is using its own human anti-corposystem activists, the charitable sector, to cause growth. The corposystem doesn't care who grows or what grows, so long as it can make profits using growth. It will use anything we humans put out there, so long as it can grow.

Unfortunately, the growth of the corposystem breaks links in the Biosystem, causing genetic evolution rather than adaptation, that cannot be reversed, destroys resources, and disrupts the necessary recycling of the components of LIFE. It sucks the LIFE out of the Biosystem. It programs our children to believe that growth is the source of LIFE, rather than its greatest danger. It tries to train our children that humans have dominion even over God and The Creation, and even the laws of physics that sustain The Creation.

We do NOT want to EVOLVE the Biosystem away from what it is good at, but that is what we are doing with every species that we bring to extinction, and if we don't stop, the end-point is our own extinction, because without the myriad of biological connections that have created the Biosystem, It cannot sustain itself. And whether we know it or not, we do NOT know how all those connections fit together.,

Humans do not have these powers

Solution

I know that many economists understand these facts and are working to change the behaviors of the corposystem – to conform to the needs of the Biosystem. This effort is necessary, unless we just let it crash on its own, but it is also putting the blame and the responsibility on something other than ourselves; blaming not the President, perhaps, but oh, say capitalism, or some other –ism. No –ism will save us unless we ALSO conform our behaviors and especially our belief systems (world views) to the reality of how the Biosystem generates its emergent property of LIFE (Witt, 2017).

That is why discussion among the people -- of how the Biosystem functions and how it got out of balance (Appendix A), must accompany any other efforts we make to save ourselves. Otherwise we are doomed to continue flailing about in all directions, using our various belief systems and their charitable organizations, trying to adapt to changes after they get here rather than to be ready for them, without understanding what it is we are doing – we who are causing the Climate Change problems to which we are trying to adapt – forcing the Biosystem to change – and that we are generating toxic – potentially terminal -- evolution rather than reversible adaptation.

And the only positive way that we can behave now is to stop the growth.

What do you mean by forcing the Biosystem to change? And why on earth would we do that?

You tell me! Why do we keep on trying to force God and His Laws of Nature to our will?

"Science is the controlled observation of nature; technology is its controlled exploitation." (Huston Smith, 1985)

We could stop exploiting nature for our own "happiness," and start using our technologies to help nature to sustain Herself. Not as we think nature should maintain herself. We do not know exactly everything that nature needs, because we have no idea what all that information is in all those systemic information links, but so far we have been using what we do know to grow the corposystem in our dedication to profits – not to just back off and permit nature to heal herself in our dedication to LIFE.

The systems are "talking" among themselves; we are not listening. They are talking about balance. We must stop messing up their communications with our behaviors.

To make any serious choice that affects other people, we need to understand not only what *is* happening but also what *will* happen, or is most likely to happen, depending on the choices that we make. We humans have been gifted with a cause and effect thought system, but cause-and-effect only works **for** us when we understand the causes and their probable effects.

What we could do, that is not impossible, is to evolve our social world view to conform to the reality of LIFE itself, and then adapt to that reality.

OOOOOOOO

This chapter is dedicated to Yoko Kawa, and to Ivy Williams

"In the beginning, God created the Heavens and the Earth.
The Earth was without form, and void;
And darkness was on the face of the deep.
And the spirit of God moved over the face of the waters."
(Genesis 1:1-2)

CHAPTER 5

I AM A NATURALLY EVOLVED SYSTEM

Homo sapiens is the naturally evolved species of humans.

I am an individual *Homo sapiens*; I am an individual naturally evolved living system. I am part of the naturally evolved human species. This means that all the previous generations of my ancestors DID fulfill their responsibility to me for about the last 4.5 billion years, generation after generation, without a break, passing forward the information that gives me LIFE.

Isn't THAT a miracle!

I believe this means that I, too, have an obligation to the future of my environment, as it is now, at this time in history (Horan, 2019, links below)

https://www.ncronline.org/news/opinion/faith-seeking-understanding/christmas-all-gods-creatures

https://www.ncronline.org/news/earthbeat/faith-seeking-understanding/climate-change-most-important-life-issue-today

All humans have a radically new obligation to the survival of our species and our environment and to our own sense of compassionate responsibility -- to make sure those who survive have a place to survive in.

Severn Cullis-Suzuki, 1992. https://www.youtube.com/watch?v=oJJGuIZVfLM
Greta Thunberg, 2019. https://www.youtube/watch?v=KAJsdgTPJpu&t=144s

A Biosystem that still has viable links with us.

> *My goal is to help grow a reasonably comfortable human presence in a richly bountiful Creation.*

I am a naturally evolved system, and so is my physical environment, the Biosystem, and so is my species, *Homo sapiens,* and my most powerful social system, the corposystem. And it is important to understand that my world view is also a naturally evolved system (Chapter 08; Eagleman, 2015). We all are naturally evolved, complex adaptive systems, each a little or a lot different from the others, but all with the same basic characteristics of naturally evolved systems (listed in Chapter 04). Our world is full of naturally evolved systems because it is composed of naturally evolved systems.

Reality Number Two – All of LIFE consists of naturally evolved systems. We humans cannot change how they evolved or how they function to sustain LIFE. Just as the growth of the human embryo requires the womb, and the mother cow feeds the calf, so do all the mothers and all the species require the appropriate environment for their survival (Preface).

I am a system. A system is a group of objects or structures or things (nodes, such as organs and organ systems and cells) that are linked together – the nodes communicate using their links; their tightly interacting processes and behaviors and communication and energy. Together, all the links and nodes that are part of me generate my body and mind — my own particular emergent characteristics (phenotypes). Some of my emergent characteristics are (using proper definition style, Chapter 03): I am an organism, a mammal, a human; I am a fair-skinned blonde, I am getting older; I love to think and learn, and usually I am a pretty nice person, but that depends upon a great many things including interactions with my environmental systems.

The nodes that work together to make me what I am – my subsystems -- they are also naturally evolved systems. They are essential parts of me, but they are not me; they are other naturally evolved systems: digestive system, respiratory system; cardiovascular system, each with its own emergent characteristics, its links, its emergent properties, all collaborating to make me.

Also part of me and of my systems is/are a variety of tissues and their individual special functions, plus billions of cells, plus whatever parasites, commensal bacteria (and other symbiotic organisms) are associated with me. They are all naturally evolved systems (watch chapter 06 of Feldman, 2018).

I am the emergent result of their ongoing interactions. Of our mutual links.

As a naturally evolved living system, my primary function is to do the work required to perpetuate myself using resources that are provided by my environment.

At the same time that I am an individual system and an environmental system for my parts, I am also a subsystem of my environments. The whole of LIFE – the LIFE of Earth, is the sum of its links. The Biosystem, or the whole of what we often call nature -- is my primary environment, but I interact with many other environmental systems.

I am a thing: a node – a subsystem in the multidimensional web (mesh) of LIFE; I am a node within the body of the Biosystem, which is also a naturally evolved system. I am linked to other nodes by the work I do and the information that I exchange using my emergent functions, behaviors, and communications, processes, and any form of energy and information that is involved in making changes happen, at the right time and place, according to the codes of LIFE (Chapter 09), to sustain my own welfare while at the same time contributing to the welfare of the whole of LIFE.

The primary function of every naturally evolved system, is to sustain itself. It does this by its interactions with its sub-systems and with its environmental systems.

I am a naturally evolved complex adaptive system. I do all those things, and I don't even have to think about it. The Laws of LIFE made me alive.

Who made the laws of LIFE? I do not know, but if you ask me straight out my answer will be that my Creator must have made all the laws that govern the operation of our entire Universe, including the Laws of LIFE that generated me.

I Am a Naturally Evolved System

I am alive. I am a living system. I do not argue about decisions that were made by my Creator some billions of years ago, that have guided evolution all the way to me. Whatever is The Creation – I have no reason to assume my omniscient knowledge of it, and therefore even less reason to believe in my omnipotence over it. Such beliefs in our own powers are great fun, but they are suicidal for today and irresponsible for tomorrow.

I sustain my life by all the energy links as we have defined them – functions, actions, behaviors, information, processes -- in myself and between myself and the many systems with which I must interact in order to sustain my life: those of which I am composed, and those that are composed of me (plus). That would be everything, wouldn't it? Nearly (Martin & Hawks, 2010; Sutherland, 2013).

On this day in 2018, just to make a small example, I tried to list some of the links (relationships/behavioral interactions/energy exchanges) that I noticed, between myself and some other systems: environmental systems; internal subsystems; partnership systems.

This account just touches the surface. It is very, very far from a complete list of all the naturally evolved systems (and some human-made systems such as my pickup) with which I had information exchanges on this day.

The purpose of the exercise was:

1. Just for fun, as it was my birthday.
2. To expand my awareness into the more important non-linear dimensions of reality, and to develop a feeling for how very firmly and inextricably every one of us is embedded within the matrix of LIFE.

HAPPY BIRTHDAY LYNN!

First thing in the morning, of course, there is all the usual morning stuff that a biological animal system must do, whether it wakes to the clanging of prison bells, the singing of a rooster, or the sun rising from behind the cliff outside the window. Communing with our subsystems, organs and organ systems.

The particular living system that I wake up in is a deep mountain canyon – a biological community (https://factfictionfancy.wordpress.com/2012/10/24/bare-bones-biology-129-community-iii/) which consists of many organisms that collaborate to sustain the canyon community as a whole system.

I wake in the frosty part of the morning (it's June we are talking about and yet there is a frosty part of this morning).

Bladder subsystem wants to be emptied; stomach subsystem wants to be filled; deep breath of clean air.

Feeling good, I jump into the flannel-lined jeans from Vermont Country Store, the sweater JoAnn gave me, under the down jacket Sheila gave me, and cover with the fuzzy hat I got at the village store. Bitsy snuggles under our pile of comforters to wait for the sunlight to reach our yard and turn up the heat.

Next, I plug my human-made not naturally evolved system – the coffee maker, into the inverter of my own personal technological solar system (actually, Mick made that) for the morning cup of coffee – anything hot is welcome on this crispy day, and my naturally evolved environment does not offer hot drinks.

The canyon community begins to take its slow, deep morning breath. Its golden energy, flowing down the Western slope, washes across our yard as the sun rises over the cliff behind us, pushing last night's cold air in front of it, until there is no place left for cold. Bitsy somehow knows that it's time to crawl out from under the bedcovers and move to that warm spot out on the porch, where the sun first shines on our solar panels, and then on our yard.

She trots to the door with her eager little-bark, we both go outside, leaving the door open, and she stretches out on the porch, in the sun. I sit opposite, my back to the sun, watching a snake warm itself under the overhanging floor of Bitsy's porch.

A young Kaibab squirrel, one of my favorite creatures, and endangered, forages in the creek bed, and a scrub jay comes down to see if there is any food to be shared.

Bitsy and I and the snake, squirrel, and jay, all and each are animal systems that are components of the LIFE of the canyon community. We move organic energy around and through the canyon system.

An animal, by definition, is a multi-cellular organism that can wander about to obtain food from its biological environment and leave behind bits of partially digested effluent. An organism is a naturally evolved, individual subunit of LIFE. Subunits of LIFE, as LIFE functions on Earth today, from the individual cell to the most advanced animal, which many would claim is us, or even the Biosystem itself, all require the same basic resources for maintaining our lives. All except a few ancient bacteria.

We need:

1. oxygen in, carbon dioxide out;
2. water and food in, wastes out;
3. a sensory system to "feel" (hear, see, or sense) what is going on in the environment and send that;
4. information to the genetics system (and the other codes of LIFE) that organize survival behaviors;
5. An energy system so the behaviors can happen and the cell can respond to its environment. (Energy is the ability to do work, by definition, so, if work happens, by our definition, energy has been used even if we don't precisely understand how);
6. A way(s) to obtain the materials (carbon, oxygen, nitrogen, hydrogen, water) of which the organism is composed.

The grasses and trees ever-so-gently wave their leaves at Bitsy and me, as the canyon inhales the energies it needs. For just a few seconds, between frozen and evaporated, a drop of water forms at the very tip of every tiny end of all the branchlets of all the green cedar trees and, in every drop of water, if you look at it just right and use your imagination, you can see a tiny rainbow glowing — until the sunlight flows on down the hill and all the little droplets evaporate into a rising mist, forming a cloud that hovers under the shadowy overhang of the cliff for a few moments and then becomes part of the clean, sunlit air.

The cedar trees, the grasses, the ponderosa pine and scrub oak, aspen and spruce, and a variety of unlabelled bushes are plant systems.

Plants are also organisms, with the same basic LIFE requirements. Plants generally are not capable of moving about to get food, but they, unlike animals, can make food, by converting light energy to organic energy, by using it to link together atoms of carbon, hydrogen, oxygen, nitrogen (and others) in various ways to make the organic molecules needed to build a cell. Organic molecules are mostly carbohydrates, lipids, proteins and nucleic acids that make up the bodies of organisms, along with water.

There are other categories of organisms here in the canyon, beginning with the basic unit of LIFE, the cell, and at higher levels, biological communities, ecosystems, the also fit the definition of living entities. They all have different ways to fulfill the needs of all LIFE systems, but the needs are essentially the same:

1. They use organic energy as their food;
2. They contain the genetic instructions (and other LIFE codes) for their own functioning;
3. They can reproduce themselves, including their LIFE codes, in collaboration with their environmental systems.
4. They can evolve, within their environmental systems.

Bitsy and I love to sit in the drenching warmth of the early sun on a crispy morning mountaintop before it gets hot-hot and think – or perhaps not-think – perhaps meditate.

We thought about that on my birthday morning. Well, to be honest, I thought about it. Probably Bitsy was just enjoying the sun. Bitsy probably doesn't think very much, analytically; her mental system is different from mine.

Maybe she thinks in memory pictures.

Unlike Bitsy (maybe) I do think about God as playing a role in all this confusion of systems that includes both of us as organisms. I'm not sure at what level God might be or emerge. Certainly, far above our level of complexity, so not an organism; perhaps not a living thing; perhaps incomprehensible.

I do not believe that God would literally "mold" a human person out of clay, but that and many other origin stories (Campbell, 2011; Campbell & Moyers, 1999) describe The Creation metaphorically in ways some people have not considered.

I think God created the whole shebang, and made it to function the way it does function. And so, I honor the whole shebang, the universe, and I love learning of Its functions as a way to know more about God. Like a physical Bible that communicates using energy without the words. Words are human; communication is, perhaps, universal. And, knowing

God, or even a small bit of the reality of LIFE, one does not blaspheme The Miracle by messing It up, either in little ways such as littering, or in big ways, by playing King of a Hill that we have not even climbed — that we are just beginning to understand.

So that's what I was meditating about. I could be wrong, but the concept doesn't disagree with any of God's universal facts that I know about.

Sometimes I meditate about nothing; sometimes I don't formally meditate, but I do think of meditation as an energy connection/link.

On this anniversary of my birth, the perfect morning temperature faded very quickly into hot, and the snuggly hat was replaced by a blaze orange baseball cap with a dark brim to save my eyes, then the down jacket went back to its place where it can always be found in case of drastic change in weather. And I picked up my tools and began to spiffy up our local environment. I carefully cleaned the kitchen space of the cabin after our breakfast, so as not to invite the *Peromyscus* mice or the pack rats or a passing bear, for lunch. I added the wash water to the slop bucket, and was about to dump it on the compost heap when Bitsy called – her very serious come-here-right-now-there-is-a-real-problem bark that I have heard only six or eight times and every time it was a rattlesnake.

Splash! I dropped everything and came, and sure enough Bitsy was staring at the corner of the house, near the front steps.

So, I stared too. Those things are SO HARD TO SEE, unless they move. I saw nothing – just grass. I stared closer, looking, listening (I'm a wee bit deaf). Closer yet - then:

> "What are you doing?" I asked myself. "Bitsy has told you what you need to know! It is not necessary to be bitten in the face to fact-check her information!"

The rattlesnake moved; I got the snake tools and killed it.

Well, I really, really, really hate killing rattlesnakes, especially this one who I saw a few days earlier when she was in basking mode, and she was beautiful. But, reality is what it is. They are hard to see, and harder for my half-deaf ears to hear and their bite is, after all, poisonous, and we are a long way from neighbors, and this time it was threatening Bitsy.

I couldn't bring myself to eat it, though it surely must be the most organically grown protein available, and the primary function of us animal systems, relative to the whole of LIFE (in addition to helping to sustain the balance of oxygen and carbon dioxide in the atmosphere when we are alive), is to help recycle the organic energy when we are no longer alive.

It got recycled. The skunk came around a couple of nights later and dug it back out of the compost heap and carried it away, and then Bitsy found the decomposed skeletal remains up by the barn and she ate part of that.

But, back to this birthday morning, Bitsy and I headed for our dominant naturally evolved complex adaptive social system -- the corposystem -- to photograph the Citizens' group demonstrate against one of our President's more than usually inane, biologically insane behaviors.

After that, Bitsy and I went to our house in the village to water the baby apple tree, deal with laundry, buy groceries, fill up the car with gas, fill up the water bottles, and process the photographs, and then a good hot bath for me.

Unfortunately, I am sensitive and becoming more sensitive both to human pollution and to the abnormal, polarized electromagnetic irradiation with which the corposystem has blanketed our formerly lovely land.

Or more likely, there is more pollution and EMR to be sensitive to.

> www.eiwellspring.org

> http://annmccampbell.com/sample-page/story/

> Steffan et al., 2018. Trajectories of the Earth System in the Anthropocene. PNAS www.pnas.org/cgi/doi/10.1073/pnas.1810141115

> https://nca2018.globalchange.gov/downloads/?fbclid=IwAR2hHW1mxmK
> Z x2Uw2NLT3SkcID4xpqdySmjKc4xi6SfT2mLQyglLkrZPdE
> https://www.ipcc.ch/sr15/

So I try to not spend a lot of time in places that are dominated by the corposystem, especially in the tourist-time of summer and autumn. I try to NOT fall asleep in town.

I fell asleep.

About 1:30 AM, I woke up with the onset of what I think of as "whole-body nausea," that is caused by overexposure to human-made chemicals such as perfume, laundry detergent, combustion products, and various other pollutants of our village and yours.

GET ME OUT OF HERE!

Out of the toxic corposystem. I don't know of any chemicals that can cure an overexposure to chemicals, nor any EMR that can prevent EMR sickness.

We took off, jumped into the pickup in the dark of night, and headed out.

On the way out of town, we missed a collision with an even darker bear-shaped shadow in the headlights, fortunately a fast-moving shadow. There are no street lights out here; it takes getting used to.

That slowed us down a bit, for the last twenty miles to the canyon -- where the Biosystem is still in control, mostly free of toxic chemicals, and radiation pollution, and so much less scary than the corposystem.

About 2:30 of the black-dark morning, we slowed for the turnoff into the canyon, and I kid you not, out the right side of the pickup, there on the mesa-top behind the next town were the moving lights of an unidentified flying object. Moving lights hovering over the mesa.

In spite of my nausea, I burst out laughing, stepped out of the pickup, and took a good long look.

And then I remembered that the annual UFO conference, hosted by the Jicarilla Apache Nation (a different naturally evolved complex adaptive social and physical system), was held that weekend at the reservation.

If you find all this hard to believe, maybe it is part of that King of the Hill thing. It does get in the way of healthy listening. But it is all true.

I got back in the pickup and drove the three miles into the canyon and slept until nearly noon the next day.

That's enough of that story. You do not need a minute-by-minute exposition of every linking interaction that involved me on that day. It would take forever. The point is that we can equally imagine all of each of our lives -- our behaviors, phenotypes, interactions – as links (pleasant links and unpleasant links and links we don't even know about) within, between and among ourselves and other quite well defined systems. We never thought about them as systems, but in fact they are, and the more we can learn about how naturally evolved systems function, and the more we respond to them accordingly, the better off we can be.

And we already knew that, we just didn't think of it that way, and it is very important to be aware of it, because that metaphor explains our interactions, and it is fact-based, and very much more closely aligned with the reality of LIFE than the metaphor that is preferred by the corposystem-- to serve its own ends of growth by domination for gain -- survival of the fittest and a vague sort of idea that things don't change. They do, especially when we mess with the other systems.

The interdependence of our systems is one of the universal facts of LIFE. And our behavior is *now* – not tomorrow. In small ways and big, whether or not we think about what we are doing, we each have a forever effect on the future of The Creation.

I Am a LIFE System

"I think of LIFE as a poem, consisting of actions."
(Joseph Campbell with Bill Moyers, 1988)

We can be aware of the nature of these links, our links with other naturally evolved systems that sustain us, and we can consider every one of them as an interaction with LIFE, and we can try to make that interaction a win-win-win, or at least a win-win (Jandt, 1985) exchange with the energy of life expressed by other systems.

And what is the reality of LIFE, really?

LIFE is (1) the emergent property of the naturally evolved complex adaptive system of Earth, the Biosystem; (2) that evolved within a complex (nonliving) environment and is capable of sustaining itself in collaboration with its environment(s).

We already knew that too.

Our Problem is not the academic effort of understanding what LIFE is. Our Problem, partly because of our linear and outline-format conditioning, partly because of our reductionist approach to science, is that we tend to think of everything separately. It's not separate. When it begins to be physically separate, that means systems are coming apart. The links are breaking. Things are dying that should be reproducing.

Healthy systems are very much together with and between and among themselves and our common, intersecting environments.

"Every single part of the Earth reacts with every other part.
It's one thing. . .
If I could get every Earthling to do one circle of the Earth,
I think things would run a little differently."
(Astronaut Karen Nyberg, IN: Beyond the Blue Marble, by Nadia Drake, beautiful photographs by Martin Schoeloler, National Geographic, March, 2018.)

We are all interconnected, interacting naturally evolved complex adaptive systems, and it is important that we humans make the effort to see ourselves as we are, if we want to develop a rational and positive relationship with the Mother Earth, because we have become a very powerful part of her existence, and she is, without a doubt, the most magnificent, most complex system ever evolved (that we know about), short of the whole universe.

We are doing better as a society than we were when I began this project about 18 years ago. At that time, the corposystem was trying to teach the people that climate change is a figment of our imagination; today, most of us are sensibly and logically concerned about our human future within the reality of climate change. The problem now is that we are trying to use the same corposystem world view, that caused our Problem, to solve the problems that it created. That kind of behavior only makes the problems bigger.

To truly re-integrate ourselves into the LIFE of which we are a part, we must learn to think of the Biosystem, not the corposystem, as the source of LIFE for *Homo sapiens* and for our social systems and partner systems and subsystems and all of our environmental systems.

For all of the LIFE of Earth.

OOOOOOO

Chapter 05 is dedicated to my parents, who taught me to think about such things.
And to Mr. Lagoria, who sent me back to graduate school.

"Energy is the ability to do work."
(many dictionaries)

"Energy makes physical systems do things;
Information tells them what to do."
(Lloyd, 2006)

CHAPTER 6

ENERGY, ENTROPY AND COMPLEXITY

In our model of naturally evolved systems, it is the links that represent "what happens" between and among the nodes.

The nodes are the things of the system, the physical parts. The links are the energy that makes something happen within the system. Actually, the links are the information - that  is, the energy AND the entropy that tells them what to do.

Each specific kind of system – an oil well, a person, an ecosystem -- has a unique function that contributes to the welfare of its environment (or not) and is expressed through its emergent properties. That is why I feel free to name each kind of naturally evolved system according to its primary emergent function. What is the emergent function of the fracking system shown above? Perhaps to contribute to the welfare of the corposystem in a specific way? What is the emergent function of an ecosystem? Clearly to contribute to the welfare of the whole Biosystem, its environment.

Green plants are systems that have the specialized function of photosynthesis. The green plants convert sun energy to organic energy, by generating organic molecules out of atoms linked together with energy bonds. Organic molecules are mostly carbohydrates, lipids, proteins and nucleic acids. This is the "food" for the entire Biosystem. Or nearly.

A primary emergent function of animals is our ability to move around in a purposeful fashion so that the food is distributed to nearly all the parts of the Biosystem.

All the activities of LIFE require energy, primarily organic energy that is generated by plant systems and circulated by animal systems.

Again, we refer to the Barabassi model of a system, composed of physical things that are linked together by energy in some form, reminding us that this universe and its parts are not a mish-mash of chaotic stuff that just swirls around in a cosmic blender. Rather, it is an intricately organized complexity of specifically related naturally evolved systems that communicate (share information) with each other using organic energy.

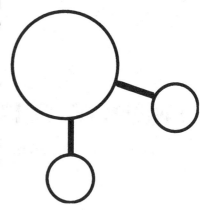

Within the model, the links represent the energy exchanges and the nodes represent the structures that are required to support the energy exchanges. In fact, the two functions are not separate, and that is one reason for the elegant efficiency of the naturally evolved system. Every part contributes to the welfare of every other part through the emergent properties of the whole.

But our minds cannot visualize the whole. It is too complicated. So we can use our model of systems to visualize any system at any level of LIFE to roughly outline these relationships. Every organic molecule can be thought of as a naturally evolved system; a whole person is a more complicated naturally evolved system; the entire Biosystem is the most complex naturally evolved system that we know about except for the entire universe.

The links and nodes of each system interact to support the emergent functions of that system. The emergent functions of each system communicate with precisely interacting emergent properties of other systems to integrate the whole.

The structures of the nodes contribute to the functions of the links, and to the exquisite precision of efficiency that is required at each link/node interface to permit organic energy to flow naturally "downhill," as it does its work in orderly sequence, through the link/node combinations that make up the cycles of LIFE. In each interaction, energy "flows" through the system, associated with entropy, in accordance with the laws of thermodynamics.

Thermodynamics is a field of physics that studies the behaviors (dynamics) of energy. (See also Grossman, 2014).

The First and Second Laws of Thermodynamics (Grossman, 2014):

> I – Energy cannot be created or destroyed, but it can change from one form to another. Light energy has more free energy (that can be used to do work) than organic (chemical) energy than heat energy.
>
> II – When "something happens," if energy changes naturally, it will change from light to organic to heat, and that is what we mean by energy "flowing downhill." Energy never spontaneously changes from less free energy to more free energy (some people refer to that kind of change as "uphill;" that is, up the gradient from a state of low free energy to one of high free energy). If it changes spontaneously, the relative amount of free energy is reduced. High amounts of free energy can change spontaneously to low amounts of free energy. And to a higher level of entropy. And do some bit of work in the process.

FYI, Dr. Seth Lloyd's book, Programming the Universe (2016), does a good job of debunking the simplistic idea that the complex reality of LIFE conflicts with the Laws of Thermodynamics, specifically the second law. Dr. Lloyd's enjoyable lectures can be found on UTube or the Santa Fe Institute website https://www.youtube.com/watch?v=5He7bYM7beM&list=PLZlVBTf7N6Gp 1GlndwLnyS44OqJoRphOK&index=1 (See also Lewin, 1992; Gell-Mann, 1994; Heylingen *et al.*, 2010).

It is best to consult physicists on this subject. But for a hint, the reason that entropy does not conflict with the second law has to do with the evolution of complexity. The complex interactions among the links and nodes of the systems of LIFE, that I described above, each is exquisitely related to its specific function, and its necessary efficiency. They all together provide what Dr. Lloyd refers to as the "cutting edge" of LIFE between the simplicity of high-energy and the chaos of high-entropy.

Energy and Entropy

Each link in our model represents a naturally evolved link/node interaction that is exquisitely balanced so that the energy can do some bit of the work of LIFE on its way from high energy organic molecules to low energy inorganic molecules, before it is released as heat energy that helps to balance the climate system.

For a life-size example, to visualize such a link/node interaction, we can use our elbow, or our knee. The energy flows through the nerves and muscles (structures) that are attached to bones (also structures). The energy of muscle contraction causes the muscles and bones to move. The structure of the elbow or knee is designed so that it cannot flop around randomly when the energy tells it to do something. When the energy says: "do something," the structures of the elbow or knee, the arrangement of the muscles and bones and nerves, tells it what to do. The resulting movement of the joint is smooth, efficient, purposeful. It is also perfectly designed for the needs of that particular system.

For example, the "elbow" joints of a rabbit are designed for the needs of a rabbit and therefore differ from those of a human arm in just the way that provides for a high efficiency of the needs of a rabbit.

That relationship is referred to by biologists as "form contributing to function," or a "structure/function" or "form/function" relationship (also briefly described in Chapter 07). Biologists would not use the word entropy for the structural contribution. Entropy is a word of physics. But it seems to me the basic observation, or the basic principle, is not different. Some combinations of structures (things) contribute to or help to direct what happens (energy). And this basic fact is a focus of evolution.

Evolution tends to preseve the combination of things/energy (form/function) that are the most appropriate for each and every interaction (link) in LIFE. That is why it took billions of years of evolutionary "experiments" to perfect the relationships/interactions that make LIFE what it is.

This means that every energy/entropy interaction at all the different levels of LIFE is somewhat different from every other, primarily because the structure (entropy) part of the energy/entropy "link" is different and exquisitely designed to implement its necessary task.

So now we switch to another sort of example and show that the same basic principles (big ideas) also operate at the molecular level of LIFE to help regulate the precision and efficiency of each chemical process, and generate the *complexity* that is a necessary property of LIFE and that "balances LIFE on the edge of chaos."

Organic molecules use the form/function principle. (Check your biology textbook under the topic of the structures of proteins. For the elbow, look in the physiology section of the text to see how anatomy relates to physiology in the bodies of organisms).

Likewise, every link and node combination of an organic molecule is precisely designed (selected by evolution and reproduced by genetics) to do what is needed when energy tells it to do something. If a larger organic molecule is based on sixteen carbon atoms that are linked together with each other and with some hydrogen atoms, then you can imagine our model as sixteen nodes (circles) that are held together by links (energy). The energy of the links holds the molecule together. The structures of the atoms direct the functions (energy) of the links. They "tell it what to do."

Every node/link relationship in LIFE, that is every structure and its relationship to its functional links, has been selected because they just naturally fit together (the structure and the function fit together so they tend to come together by self-assembly) and then they have been used by nature to do a job that needs doing, and then they have been perfected over millions of years of natural selection (Chapter 09).

So that combination of events and structures is rare, perhaps uniquely useful. So then the *information* that describes each form/function combination is saved by the genetic code of LIFE and passed on to every new generation in the form of a system of links and nodes that is recreated in every generation at the right time and place where it is needed to do its special emergent function.

That is evolution, not adaptation (but see Chapters 04 and 09 for a more precise definition of evolution and adaptation).

Every link in our model of naturally evolved systems represents energy, collaborating with entropy to do the work of sustaining life while at the same time directing (informing) what work may be done by this particular node-link combination.

That is one reason why LIFE is more efficient than non-LIFE.

It is also a primary reason that LIFE is so incredibly complex -- at all levels – that we cannot substitute our beautiful tools (technologies) for the very much more elegant link/node interactions of LIFE -- and the more we interfere with these interactions the more we REDUCE the essential efficiency of the over-all system of LIFE.

But to return to the basics:

> Energy is the ability to do work.
> Something happens. Something changes.
> Whenever something happens, energy is involved.
> And entropy is also involved.

Entropy can be defined as the degree of dis-order, chaos or randomness, looseness, compared with tight degree of order of the structure(s) that are interacting. The exact amount of "looseness" or in my above, more intricate examples, the shapes/structures that are required so the interaction (exchange of information) can happen. Bones and muscles in the elbow example, molecules in the biochemical example. I think of it as the "sweet spot" of the collaborative interaction; information is a description of the relationships that are required – the requirements for the interaction. If it is sometimes measurable, the information exchange (the complexity of energy and entropy), can be defined in bits – like a computer.

Balance
  Matter – Recycling
  Energy – Efficiency

Naturally Evolved Systems (chapter 04)
  Emergence
  Phenotype

Self Assembly (Chapter 05)
  Energy
  Entropy
  Information
  Adaptation

Evolution (Life Codes - Chapter 07)
  Genetics
  Variability
  Natural Selection

If energy makes the physical system do something, then entropy describes the way in which the structures of the physical system contribute to what it does. *Complexity* is the sum of the interactions, and information describes the whole.

Information, encoded in the genetic system and sustained (or improved/modified by the evolution system), perpetuates and perfects the emergent LIFE of the Earth.

And so here we begin the discussion of the fourteen big ideas that are the basis of my new view of LIFE.

Background – Fourteen Big Ideas

The first four big ideas we have already introduced. The most important is *balance* of the whole system of LIFE within the universe of non-LIFE, and then the idea that the balance consists of interacting *naturally evolved systems*, that have special functions that are characterized by highly specific nonrandom *emergent phenotypes*.

And we have introduced the idea of *recycling* all the matter of LIFE (Chapter 04) so the system does not run out of the materials of which it is composed.

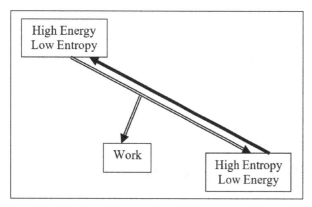

In this chapter we cover the next four big ideas. The energy that "makes something happen" and the entropy and the resulting information (interaction between energy and entropy) that determines what will happen. The complexity of the interaction and the information that makes its evolution possible.

We will start there, with physics, but LIFE is more about how the systems direct the purposeful flow (inform the flow) of energy and entropy to generate the *complexity* of each action, as in the elbow joint – and then store the information so that it can be passed from generation to generation, and modified in response to its environment by its genetics and evolution. The biggest idea that includes all the others, is *evolution*, and we will talk more about it as we go along.

Energy, Entropy, Complexity

Energy is the ability to do work, and is represented in our model by the links

Entropy is associated with energy and represents ways in which structure of the physical systems contribute to its function. If it is an organic molecule, for example, the molecule itself contains both energy and structure, and they both influence how the molecule interacts with other molecules (or not).

Together, energy and entropy, function and structure, are represented in our systems model by the links and nodes that work together to enable the interaction.

Complexity is the result when the structure and function work together as a living unit.

The first law of thermodynamics is usually reported as: "Energy cannot be created or destroyed, but it can change from one form to another." This explanation gives the impression that entropy is one of the other forms of energy. Probably it is not. Not as I have broadly described it above.

Right now I am thinking about organic molecules, using the diagram above. An organic carbohydrate molecule, in this example, is made of carbon, hydrogen, and oxygen atoms that are linked together with energy bonds. The diagram shows a sugar molecule that breaks apart so the biochemical energy that was linking them can be used to do some other kind of work, somewhere else. We do not care about what work it is doing. We just want to talk about how the removal of the energy (the links, or some of them) affects the sugar molecule. The sugar breaks apart into smaller molecules, the energy that was holding the sugar together goes away (to another process) and the entropy of the parts increases because they are not so tightly held together. Their entropy (looseness) is increased.

This part of the reaction goes from high free energy to lower free energy. It also goes from low entropy (the structure of the molecule tightly held together by the energy) to high entropy as the energy is taken to do other work in a different reaction.

The energy is doing the work of holding that sugar molecule together – linking all those carbons and oxygens and hydrogens together, and when the energy is taken away to some other work, then the "links" (of our model) go somewhere else, because energy cannot be created or destroyed, and of course whatever the links were keeping together, in this example some of the atoms of the sugar, separate from each other. There is less free energy associated with the sugar, and the sugar molecule falls apart because the links are gone, and the result is we no longer have a sugar molecule, but more molecules that are smaller. Water and carbon dioxide. Small molecules with few links, therefore low energy and high entropy.

Entropy is the degree of moving-around-ness. As the energy links are taken away, the atoms have more freedom to move around.

Somewhere between high and low energy (low and high entropy), for some combinations of atoms or molecules (or people, or whatever is interacting) there is what I call a sweet spot, with just the right amount of energy to make this particular reaction happen and just the right entropy, where the relationships are just right – or perhaps more right than in other spots, so that the reaction is free to happen.

When all the energy is used to link the atoms together, they cannot come apart or move around, their moving-aroundness is severely restricted. But somewhere in the spectrum of freedom-to-move relationship with energy -- there is a "sweet spot," with just the right amount of energy and the right freedom-of-motion that permits this particular reaction to happen without forcing it to happen.

The sweet spot also depends upon the particular environment and may be different in other environments.

The sweet spot is a condition where all the participants in the process fit together most comfortably. All the participants – the energy the entropy and the environment are necessary for the best, most useful sweet spot.

Sweet Spot

Energy
Entropy
Environment

If the interaction has a sweet spot. Many do not. Every combination of energy, entropy and environment is different. If there is a sweet spot, then it is the most comfortable association of those three characteristics. A change in any of these conditions can cause the sweet spot to shift, and that is how a lot of work is done inside cells – simply by arranging the interaction so that the sweet spot changes.

For a very elegant example of a molecule that has two different sweet spots and uses them both to do its function, hemoglobin is the molecule that carries oxygen in our blood, all around the body so that every cell has the oxygen it needs. Oxygen, of course, comes into our bodies when we breath it in. The hemoglobin molecule is floating around in the blood stream. When it gets to the lungs, where the level of oxygen in the environment is high, the sweet spot of the molecule causes the shape of the molecule to change in such a way that it attracts oxygen and clings to it. And later, when the hemoglobin, let's say gets to the leg or anywhere that cells are low in oxygen, the hemoglobin changes its shape again, to the other sweet spot required by the different environment, and the oxygen falls off the hemoglobin and is available to nearby cells that need it.

The body of LIFE uses such structure/function; energy/entropy relations to regulate many of the functions of LIFE, at all the levels of LIFE.

Interactions among organic molecules are rather well studied. If you want to read more about how they fit themselves together, using energy and entropy, an excellent example, in your basic biology text you can read about the primary, secondary, tertiary and quaternary structures of enzymes.

People interact. They interact with other people and with their own cells and enzymes, and with the ecosystems and social systems. I believe these interactions proceed, in general, using this same *pattern* of functioning (not the same processes) using the structure/function relationships that are available at the different levels of LIFE from cells to the entire Biosystem. The same basic fourteen principles (and no doubt more that we do not know about) apply to all the levels of organization, from the molecular level to the whole big Biosystem.

The energy flows through the system because the system is designed to flow the energy through it using the basic principles that we associate with the first and second laws of thermodynamics. Evolution has learned to use the form/function relationships of each interaction to increase the complexity of the LIFE system just enough to temporarily reduce the effects of entropy until in the end, after many exchanges through many sweet spots, the energy is changed from organic energy into heat energy that has less free energy. The energy has been used to sustain the complexity of LIFE and the complexity of LIFE is just sufficient to sustain LIFE against the force of entropy.

Ultimately, the LIFE is in the complexity that is maintained and applied and perfected by evolution, using the systems of genetics, and natural selection, and in the information that applies, sustains, and replicates the complexity of biological interactions..

Complexity

The above description of energy/entropy and form/function is quite amazing. It starts with two big ideas that describe two basic characteristics of LIFE systems – energy and entropy – within their environments -- and ends up with the complexity of the whole of LIFE. That would seem to be impossible, wouldn't it? Getting LIFE from the interactions between two basic functions? Not forgetting their environments, and that adds up to three big ideas.

Perhaps.

However, one purpose of this book is to make it clear to every citizen, biologist or not, the incredibly dangerous homocentric hubris of the way we are using our technological power. Perhaps it is impossible to generate LIFE from a base of two fundamental natural laws such as energy and entropy. Perhaps there are five or six fundamental natural laws contributing to the mix that we do not know about, on top of the ones we do know. How would we know what we don't know? The point is that we do NOT know, and we are staking the life of our species on our ignorance without ever questioning it, because it is profitable and because it works – at least temporarily.

Another point is the wisdom passed down to us by our ancestors, that we seem to have forgotten altogether: "First, do no harm."

We do not know what harm we are doing to ourselves, because we are using our own ideas without testing them against reality. And indeed the vast majority of new ideas do NOT fit into the scheme of LIFE as it has evolved. Evolution takes millions of years to find just the right sweet spots among all the energy/entropy combinations.

Perhaps it is time to pay attention to the folly of politicians and activists who are trying to make our decisions for us, based on homocentric issues that are set for us by the corposystem and do not relate to the needs of the Biosystem. Or vote the real issues, rather than the fun money parties. The real issues are more than LIFE size, and bigger than anyone. And so far I have not received any "election-year survey," that even bothers to mention them. I do not watch debates, first because they are manipulative and dominational, and second because they do not debate the LIFE issues, but only homocentric winning-and-losing crap.

You already know that.

So to get back to the question; can the complexity of LIFE be generated from only one or two initial variables? Consider the following example as evidence that we can indeed evolve an enormous amount of complexity, using only two sorts of variability. And then remember that life is more complicated by far than light switches. And light switches are not and cannot be alive.

An ordinary light switch uses electrical energy to give us two choices. Yes the energy is flowing through the wires, or no it is not.

Two choices; yes or no; no emergent properties.

Make that a dimmer light, switch that you turn a knob and the intensity of the light increases gradually from none to full, and this switch can already produce a vast number of different, measurable, outputs.

Now we add a second dimmer switch that controls a different property of light – let's say color, the full spectrum. Again, this is a property that can be measured. It has information content that can be replicated, saved, manipulated. It has replicable information.

Now tell me how many combinations of light can be produced using these two switches. Quantity combined with quality, how many different color and intensity combinations can be produced?

How many emergent characteristics?

I cannot answer those questions. What I do know is that energy quantity is more complex than a simple electrical light switch and so is color of light, and the reason we can regenerate and manipulate and preserve any particular combination of the two (including emergent combinations) is because of their measurable information.

Information

The complexity of energy/entropy; function/form; link/node interactions exists as information that can be preserved, manipulated, reproduced, and improved – not by us – no way – we do not know enough about the Biosystem– but by the Biosystem itself, using evolution of the information. Life Codes (Chapter 09).

When information can be recorded, replicated and reproduced, it can be used to define the characterstics of an energy/entropy link. When this can be described mathematically, the information is stated in bits, as in a computer. We rely on mathematics to give us this information, but numbers may not define or describe the structure/function relationships of the nodes. Biological information is not so simplistic. For example, the entropy of any interaction depends upon the environment, and we cannot define the environments in LIFE, because they change over time. Therefore, while we know that the information of all LIFE processes exists to be used by LIFE, we also know that we cannot measure most of it. Even if we could measure every biological interaction that drives and corrects the essential balance of LIFE, it would take so long to do all the measurements that there would be no point to it.

The Biosystem, on the other hand, manages all this information at the same time, biologically, and it also adapts itself to change as it happens. The ability to adapt is built right into the information of the link/node/environment combination – just as it is built into the hemoglobin molecule, that we talked about above, to change its sweet spot when its environment changes. To adapt. It has evolved the ability to adapt.

Similarly, summer and winter generate a host of interacting changes that are built into the biological interactions of the ecosystem. Stress and relaxation are built into the human physiology. Those changes are examples of adaptation, not evolution.

Using our sugar example again, sugar can dissolve in water -- it can change back into crystals, if the environment changes again, and the water goes away. That is not evolution. It is an innate characteristic of sugar. Evolution uses these innate characteristics of the sweet spots to increase the useful complexity of information that is available to LIFE. That is, evolution uses the adaptability that is available, but evolution itself cannot normally change back and forth. Evolution is forever or, if it is a harmful evolutionary change, it is for nevermore.

If the information to make an arm, or a salmon, or a carbohydrate molecule or a flower is lost -- then that particular complexity of information is gone forever.

Evolved information that took perhaps millions or billions of years to evolve just right – just so -- interacting almost perfectly with the other systems of LIFE, is the very source of LIFE.

Gone.

That's one reason that the Biosystem must start over at the beginning after each great extinction event. When enough of its interacting parts no longer have other parts to interact with – sweet spots, compatable emergent properties, adaptations -- the links fall apart and the system is reduced once more to its basic unit (cells) and must begin again. No dinosaurs this time. No humans next time.

Adaptation is NOT Evolution.

We seem to believe that extinction of other species is not important, or even a good idea. More room for us. Chapter 07 answers this misconception. So we thoughtlessly divert, destroy, add links of energy and information to the metaphorical book of LIFE, and LIFE adapts to these links as any living system adapts, but in so doing, we are tweaking both adaptation and evolution, because we are "stirring the pot" of information that the Biosystem requires for its LIFE. And the result is among many other effects, climate change.

When we moved from adaptation to evolution and extinction is (was) when the whole of LIFE began to evolve in response to our overpopulation – extinction of other species removed their information, their links and nodes, from the information of LIFE interactions -- that is when humans started to break apart our own links with LIFE as it was. The LIFE that we evolved within.

Evolution is beyond adaptation; adaptation changes back and forth between the seasons and the natural disasters, within limits of tolerance of the Biosystem environment.

Evolution is the cause of climate change. It is the beginning of our end if we do not change our ways, because we were born into a code of LIFE that connected everything up to give it all LIFE, and without the connections – the whole genome of the Biosystem, we do not have a LIFE to live in.

When we are willing to actually change the information of LIFE, either by inadvertent extinctions or by adding or changing the genetics of anything, we are mucking around in the playground of the Gods and we do not understand the game. We do not understand the Biology, so we just do whatever the corposystem tells us is good. Whatever the corposystem will pay us for.

Reality Number Nine – *As citizen activists, we should learn the rules before we try to fix the game (Chapter 02).*

We should NOT be, but we are, using nearly the full power of our technological sciences and mathematics trying to "fix" that which had already evolved to a near perfection over the past 5 billion years or so, even though we have no real understanding of the information links we have destroyed and continue to destroy in the process of trying to fix something that doesn't need fixing.

What we need to fix is ourselves.

We should absolutely avoid trying to change, or inadvertently changing the information content of the Biosystem, for any reason, either by causing the extinction of other species about which we know very little, or by using our technologies to modify the information content of LIFE. Or by changing the environment that was meant to nurture *Homo sapiens*. The information content that is passed on to the future – and expressed within LIFE at the right time and the right place, largely by the energy/entropy/information links of the systems of LIFE.

Balance

And so you rightly may say:

> "I am not trying to change anything. I have struggled through your description of molecules and entropy and elbows and knees, but what is the point? And also – who cares? What has that to do with anything I care about? We normal people are trying to sort out a pandemic, a Presidential election, no job, and a sick child and we are sad, and worried, and all at the same time. What does that have to do with anything that matters?"

Yes. That is the point. You do understand. *It is all connected.*

Especially it is connected with the welfare of your sick child.

You are a biological system. Imagine the balance of your entire body, mind and soul, on that gradient between too much energy and not enough energy. Between too much entropy (chaos, social or biological disturbance) and not enough.

Right – you do not need to imagine it, you are living it.

You know that a sweet spot exists in your relationship with your environment and you automatically try to stay there in that sweet spot. Or if you cannot stay, then you try to come home again, even though home might not be there any more because the environment has changed. Adapted or evolved. Your whole body system automatically tries to recreate that home – or if you had a very bad home, to create a better one, to find the sweet spot you know must be out there somewhere.

The Biosystem is going out of balance. Because WE HUMANS ARE OUT OF BALANCE with the Biosystem. And the processes of evolution are "stirring the pot" in response to the imbalance. That is what evolution does, and it does it automatically.

We have changed the Biosystem so much that it can no longer adapt to the changes, but must actually evolve itself in order to save itself. That is climate change. We have failed our pact with God.

"So what should we do about that?"

We cannot "fix" the Biosystem, it was already fixed before we messed it up, and the harder we try to fix it using technologies, the more we throw it out of balance. We cannot force the Biosystem to do anything. It will do what the universal laws of LIFE ordain that it must do, and if there were no universal laws of LIFE then there would be no LIFE, so there is no point trying to come at it from that point of view. Our technologies are not more powerful than the universal laws of LIFE.

We must fix ourselves; we must turn to our Creator and return our species to its sweet spot within its appropriate environment. Individually, we must not bring any more babies into life unless there is a sustainable LIFE to bring them into, and when they are here we must do everything in our power to stop the suffering that we are bringing down upon their heads.

OOOOOOOO

Thanks to physicist mathematician Dr. Tanmoy Battacharya, who answered the most basic reality questions when others would or could not. A solid base for a new perspective on LIFE.

Reality Number Seventeen – *The primary function of naturally evolved complex adaptive systems is to perpetuate themselves. They have evolved and survived because they CAN perpetuate themselves, and they do it primarily by their uniquely efficient ability to balance energy, entropy and information in their relationships with their environmental systems. Not by dominating, changing or destroying their environmental system from which they emerged*
(Chapters 05 and 06)

CHAPTER 7

THE SPIDER QUESTION

"Did you know how much of our food all the spiders on Earth eat?"

It's a Corposystem Ploy kind of question that confuses the uninformed citizens of our country, and in that way sets up debates and arguments, and generally "stirs the pot," and prevents us from using our combined human power to solve our common human Problem.

Why does the corposystem resist solving the Problem?

Because the corposystem is not an individual, rational, caring person. It is a naturally evolved social system, and the primary function of naturally evolved systems is to perpetuate their own emergent characteristics (see Chapter 04). Not ours.

> The primary emergent characteristic of the corposystem, its requirement for growth, would be reduced or eliminated if we were to give our support to the primary need of the Biosystem, which is sustaining LIFE.
>
> *LIFE is an emergent property of the naturally evolved Biosystem (Chapter 04).*
>
> *To maintain this LIFE, the Biosystem requires that the naturally evolved living systems of Earth collectively sustain the balance of their collaborative, efficient interactions that took billions of years to evolve to near perfection (Chapter 04).*

I would like to say that "God took billions of years to evolve," but would that eliminate half my audience? Do we pretend that we know exactly what was happening and how during all those billions of years? What difference does it make how it was done –the question is of no use to argue over – our goal is the future. A future. The useful question is how do we nurture our "Garden of Eden" so that we may survive in IT. With reverence for what IT is (Chapter 01; Woodruff, 2001).

Both the corposystem and the Biosystem are naturally evolved systems. Each evolved to sustain its different primary emergent function. They are on a collision course because of the power-based dominational methods of the corposystem that conflict with the collaborative requirements of the Biosystem.

The Biosystem is a biological system composed largely of living subunits that are also naturally evolved systems. It maintains its emergent property of LIFE by sustaining the collaborative balance among its subsystems, primarily using the process of evolution (see Chapters 08, 09 and 10)

The corposystem is a human social system that is composed of people, corporations, etc. It sustains its emergent property of growth by manipulating the people, using primarily information -- our beliefs and behaviors. For example, by taking control over our educational system, our medical system, and the internet and other media, using advertising and psychological games such as asking bad questions and stimulating debate over topics that are not relevant to solving our primary Problem.

> *If we ask the wrong question,*
> *We will get the wrong answer.*
> *(Or: "garbage in/garbage out.")*
> *All computer nerds know this.*
> *Or did in the good old days.*
> *The corposystem also "knows" this.*

Both systems use various kinds of information to direct the flow of their existence. The Biosystem is much the more honest of the two. When you begin to notice the bad questions, the irrelevant debates, the bait and switch tactics that abound on the internet, you will identify many of the "games" the corposystem cons us into playing with each other (Berne, 1964) that do not address the Problem we face because they are human games that are not intended to consider the needs of the Biosystem. Rather, they are designed to stimulate growth of the corposystem.

Asking bad questions is better, perhaps, than the old-fashioned method of domination (cracking heads), but psychological games are equally harmful to human welfare. Because they are emotionally dishonest, they destroy our trust in our own faux-compassion system, generate fear of the LIFE that gives us our lives, hatred of those we believe responsible, and conflict as our long-term outlook.

The Answer

There is a big difference between our technology-based corposystem world view and a LIFE-based world view, but it usually doesn't seem like it, because the difference is mostly not about the facts. It is about how we use the same words (representing the same facts, see Chapter 03) to describe a view of a world that can sustain LIFE or one that cannot. Given that it is one of our special gifts, we often try to find the answers to the questions in our lives using our innate human logic applied to our evolved world views. Our innate human logic is logical in its context – but it is not always right relative to the Facts of LIFE. Everyone's logic needs to be fact-checked at every possible step. That is why the scientific method, applied to good information, is so useful.

There are many logical ways to make sense of information. I know my world view is logical because I have spent years, decades, fact-checking my world view against the biological reality. Also and at the same time, I know my world view is somewhat different from yours, because our available information is somewhat different, and some of yours is wrong and some of mine is wrong, depending on our environments and the needs of our social systems. Even though we may be using the same universal facts, our backgrounds and training are different. We have evolved different world views.

There is only one over-all holistic biological reality of the Living Earth, at any given time, so we do need logic -- both logic and a good understanding of how naturally evolved systems interact among themselves to generate what is. And even then, we humans have at least two perspectives on most subjects, the homocentric, "we will fix the works of God" corposystem view, and the LIFE-centric view that the Biosystem will fix itself if only we stop throwing it farther out of balance (Smith, 1976; Wilson, 2002, 2016).

The more accurately we are able to describe the Bio-friendly realities (Carroll, 2015) -- the more closely we can align our human world views with the universal facts and processes that created LIFE in the first place – so the more likely it is that *Homo sapiens* might survive the next few decades, which I think is more important than word games.

As Steven Johnson points out, in his 2003 book EMERGENCE:

> "Emergent behaviors, like games, are all about living within the boundaries defined by the rules . . ."

"Do you know how much food all the spiders of the earth eat every day?

"That we could have available for people if we would kill all the spiders?"

The answer to that is no – to both bad questions. No I don't know and no the amount that they eat would not be available to us, because we do not eat flies. The much better question is:

"How does LIFE maintain (sustain) itself?"

The rules that maintain the primary emergent property of the Biosystem (LIFE) are the same rules that sustain the Biosystem. And they are very strict, because the Biosystem, and each of its interacting parts, must balance every part of itself on the "cutting edge" of its required efficient function – on the sweet spot that was described in Chapter 06, where the influences of energy, entropy and information most naturally connect to generate self-assembly (Seth Lloyd Lectures, 2016; West, 2017) .

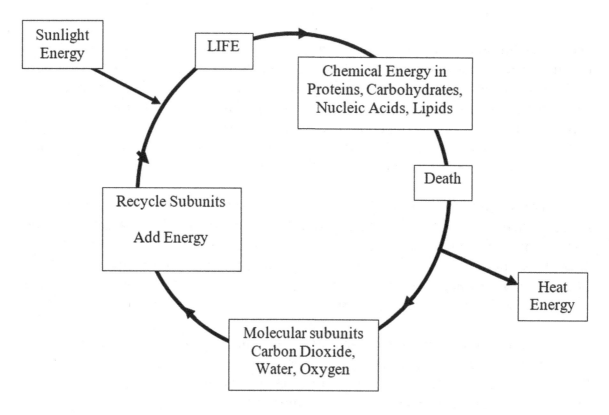

As illustrated in Chapter 05, and re-emphasized below, the over-all requirements for LIFE are almost identical at all of the many levels of LIFE, beginning at the level of the individual living cell, all the way up to people and beyond to the whole LIFE of Earth. The processes and Laws of Life that flow energy through the systems, that are discussed in Chapters 05 and 06 – and the resources that are recycled that are discussed in Chapter 04, are very nearly the same, except for their increasing complexity, at all the levels of LIFE.

LIFE, we said before and will expand later, is:

1. the emergent property of the naturally evolved complex adaptive system of Earth, the Biosystem, and of its living parts;
2. that evolved within a complex environment,
3. and is capable of sustaining itself by reproducing, adapting and evolving in collaboration with its environment(s).(Chapter 04)

The cell is the basic unit of LIFE.

The spider is a life form; it is mostly composed of cells; it can reproduce itself; it can evolve.

Living cells are made of water, organelles and organic molecules. Every living cell, in collaboration with its environment, creates most of its own organic molecules and organelles, using information from the genetic code of LIFE (and other codes of LIFE) plus biochemical and electromagnetic energy, and the organic molecules of which LIFE is primarily composed: carbohydrates, lipids, amino acids, proteins. For the most part, living systems get the materials (small molecules and atoms) that they use to make their own organic molecules by eating or otherwise recycling other organisms.

Using the materials and energy contained in the organic molecules, the cell makes complicated structures, called organelles, that are responsible for the same basic functions that we talked about in Chapter 04 that are listed below. The cellular organelles are responsible for all the same necessary functions (or nearly) that our organs perform to keep us alive.

A – At the cellular level, in order to survive - to be alive - a unitary cell uses its parts (molecules and organelles in water, informed by the information of LIFE – Chapter 03, 05, 09) to constantly provide:

1. *oxygen* imported into the cell, carbon dioxide exported;
2. *water and food* imported or allowed to pass into the cell, wastes out;
3. a *sensory system* to "feel" (hear, see, or sense in some other way) and to know what is going on within and around it in the environment and send that
4. *information* to the system that organizes survival behaviors and stores the information.
5. An electromagnetic *energy* system so the behaviors can happen and the cell can respond to its environment.
6. A way to obtain the *materials* (carbon, oxygen, nitrogen, hydrogen, water) of which the cell (the molecules and organelles) are composed, so that the cell can construct its own body, using the information and *organic energy* and the materials to sustain itself and make more cells.

Every kind of organelle and molecule has a specific function relative to the above requirements, and all must work together in an integrated way to maintain all the functions of the cell, or of any higher-level organism such as a spider, that is composed of cells.

Every kind of living system makes a unique contribution to the whole of LIFE and thus to all other kinds of living systems in the over-all system of LIFE.

B – A spider is a naturally evolved unit of LIFE at the organismal level of complexity. Spiders are made of organs and the organs are made of tissues that are made of cells. The spider has separate, naturally evolved systems, organs (kidneys, spiracles, brain, etc.) to do the functions that must be done if the spider is to survive, the same functions that are done by organelles in living cells.

1. oxygen imported, carbon dioxide exported
2. water and food in, wastes out
3. a sensory system that uses electromagnetic energy and other kinds of environmental energy to "feel" (hear, see, or sense in some other way according to what the creature eats and how it gets what it eats) and to know what is going on in the environment and send that
4. information to the system that organizes survival behaviors and stores the information
5. An organic energy system so the behaviors can happen and the spider can respond to its environment
6. A way to get the materials (carbon, oxygen, nitrogen, hydrogen, water) of which the spider is composed and cycle them into its own cells, to sustain itself and make more spiders.

To survive, the spider must have food of the right kind available at the right time in the right place in its environment.

C – You are also a naturally evolved unit of LIFE at the organismal level. You, like the spider, are an organism composed of organs (made of living cells) that must work together efficiently to accomplish the same tasks, and to do this you must get the materials and energy and interactive information from your environment, including from the food you eat and drink. That is what the process of eating and drinking is about.

1. oxygen in/carbon dioxide out — your lungs and circulatory system
2. water and food in, wastes out — your digestive system and circulatory system
3. a sensory system using electromagnetic and organic energy to "feel" what is going on in your environment and send that
4. information to the system that organizes survival behaviors and stores the information in your sensory system;

5. A "nervous system" that uses both electromagnetic and organic energy to respond to your environment
6. A way to get the materials (carbon, oxygen, nitrogen, hydrogen, water) of which you are composed and cycle them into your own cells to sustain yourself.

To survive, you must have food of the right kind, available at the right time in the right place, in your environment. That is managed by the codes of LIFE (Chapter 09) that tell all of LIFE what to do and when and where.

All of your organ systems, and organs and tissues and cells must work together in an integrated way, coordinated by the information of LIFE that is an integral part of every organic molecule, in collaboration with your environment and at a biologically appropriate level of efficiency, to maintain your Life.

Food is materials that are being recycled – organic molecules, minerals, water that are ingested -- plus the energy/information that drive the processes at each step within and among the systems. This cycle of food also and at the same time sustains the environment -- all at the same time in the same bite. Otherwise LIFE cannot be maintained.

Animals cannot eat sunlight; they eat food (organic molecules). The energy that LIFE requires is biochemical (organic) energy gathered by plants and used to link together the atoms of organic molecules that are made by the plants. We cannot eat solar energy or light energy or heat energy. We cannot make food without further unbalancing both the recycling of the materials of LIFE AND the energy balance of LIFE. Therefore it is not correct to say that "plenty of energy is available." Only organic energy found in organic molecules contains both the materials and the information that are necessary to sustain the over-all system of LIFE.

D – The Biosystem is a naturally evolved unit of LIFE. Like the spider and the cells and the organs and the people, and plants and all other sentient beings, today's Biosystem requires the same set of over-all processes to maintain its LIFE:

1. oxygen in/carbon dioxide out
2. water and food in, wastes out
3. a sensory system to "feel" (hear, see, or sense) what is going on in the environment and send that,
4. information to the system that organizes survival behaviors.
5. An energy system so the behaviors can happen and the Biosystem can respond to its environment.
6. A way to get and cycle and recycle the materials (carbon, oxygen, nitrogen, hydrogen, water) of which the Biosystem and every sentient being are composed.

Instead of (actually, in addition to) organelles, or organs, the Biosystem uses organisms to do the necessary tasks of keeping itself alive — you and me and the spiders and every other species on earth— each has its individual task to do to sustain itself AND OUR COMMON ENVIRONMENT -- all coordinated in the living, multitasking unit that is the Biosystem. We humans do not know what information the spider brings to the cycles of LIFE.

Every unit of LIFE is a naturally evolved system that recycles the organic energy and the materials as food for the others. Without them – the cycles of LIFE would slow to a halt.

Every naturally evolved living thing, all the time, in its breathing out and its breathing in; in its drinking and urinating; in its eating and defecating; recycles the climate required by every other naturally evolved living thing. At the right time, in the right amounts, at precisely the right places in the Biosystem. In its living it grows the organic molecules that find the sweet spots of their complex interactions, in every cell and every behavior, and every interacting phenotype, to link together the flows of energy and entropy; and to reproduce the information that operates the whole big system of LIFE. In their living are the cycles that sustain the emergence of LIFE every minute of every day and night.

And in their dying, they pass on and recycle the materials, the matter, that is required to grow new bodies for the next generations of energy and information to fulfill their obligations to the LIFE of Earth.

And the whole big system is coordinated by the integrated genetic code (and other codes of LIFE) – the information inherent in the whole big one-system. Every time we make a species extinct, we are destroying a part of the genetic code that coordinates all of LIFE as it is on Earth today. Every time we break a link, we divert the energy of the Biosystem into a different path than that which evolved specifically to the peak of the efficiency necessary to support that link and its interactions with the other links of LIFE.

Without the energy carried by organic molecules, nothing would happen; there could be no LIFE as we know it.

Human solar technologies cannot replace organic energy because we cannot at the same time tell every molecule and cell and body how to use the energy inside our bodies, and because, without recycling the materials that make up the structures of the molecules, there would be no solid parts, the solid parts of the spider as we see it; the earth would pile up with dead bodies until nothing could change, or it would run out of materials.

> ***Reality Number Eighteen*** *- Technology can move food around to serve people. Technology cannot, at the same time do this in a way that incorporates the cycles of energy, information and materials that sustain all the cells and all the organs and all the species that maintain the next higher level of LIFE on Earth, the ecosystems and the Biosystem and their emergent properties (Chapter 07).*

That is why the meme: "Survival of the Fittest" is wrong in our corposystem interpretation of it. That is also why the meme: "There is plenty of energy," that I have been hearing for fifty years expounded as though the speaker actually cared about the outcome -- should be corrected every time we hear it -- so that the people can know the truth rather than kill the Biosystem in their ignorance. What kind of energy? What is it good for? What will it do to unbalance the codes of LIFE? How many MILLIONS of MORE people are eating up the energy of LIFE today than the first time that meme was spoken at least fifty years ago?

There is plenty of energy falling upon the earth, but there is not an overabundance of *information* to tell the energy what to do. And with every species that goes extinct, some of that information is lost forever.

There may be plenty of sunlight, but there is not plenty of biochemical energy/information in the earth system to feed the LIFE of earth and all of us humans, all at the right time and the right place required by all the cells and organelles and organs and organ systems and organisms and higher levels and kinds of living entities, including ecosystems and the whole LIFE of Earth itself. And the more trees and other natural energy-providers that we rip out, the less irreplaceable biological energy is available that is integrated into the cycles of LIFE.

There is, or was, just the right amount of information and complexity to direct the flow of energy as we need it for our lives. Not so anymore.

If we killed off all the spiders in an effort to use their food to feed ourselves, we would find that the system as a whole has LESS food remaining for us, not more. Less energy, especially less information, fewer sweet spots, because we would have broken one of the important sources of LIFE. In fact, we are already learning this lesson; it is the cause of climate change. It enables pandemics. Broken links; lost information, evolution.

And we probably could not survive by eating flies.

And the flies are also important to the whole of the Biosystem.

LIFE is the emergent property of the naturally evolved Biosystem that functions as the laws of God and nature created it to function -- every link in the system in balance with every other link, and the balance sustained by the information carried inside every living cell.

Our job is to nurture this system, not to destroy it. Not to use it to crown ourselves Gods of the universe, but to make it available unto the seventh or the 700th generation or beyond (Lyons, The Dalai Lama). Every link in the system is an interaction that has been honed over several thousands or millions of years to SUPPORT the gift of LIFE itself – so that LIFE can then support humans. Not the other way around.

When we kill off any one species, we not only lose some of the biochemical energy that functions to support the emergence of LIFE in the Biosystem. We also lose oganic materials that are made unavailable because they are not recycled (because only spiders eat spider food) and above all, we irreplaceably lose a big chunk of the genetic information and other codes that tell the Biosystem how to function – how to do what and when and where. See examples in Chapter 09

If we want to save people, then our very first and most important priority must be to

SAVE THE SPIDERS!

> When I moved to south Texas in the 80's, the best part of every day was the early morning display of dew-sparkled spider webs, hanging from trees, filling the 2 x 4 squares of dog fence, spanning the horse trail, way up at my head level.
>
> Thousands of them. Everywhere.
>
> It's all gone. Mornings now are drab and relatively lifeless.
>
> When was the last time you had to wash the bugs off your windshield?

Save the whole big one-system of LIFE: its complexity; its efficiency; and above all its balance. If it's not too late.

The Complexity of the Biosystem

LIFE systems that are descended from one-celled organisms have added, within the overall emergent property of LIFE, additional characteristics, so that now the number of systems that are capable of LIFE -- based on the same requirements as the spiders, but each with its specific life-style and dietary preferences – is truly immense; and their diversity, and the complexity of their interactions is awe-inspiring. And the more diversity and complexity is intricately intertwined, the more firmly LIFE is able to balance on the edge of entropy (Chapter 06).

For example animals are alive. Animals are loosely defined (see Chapter 03 on the subject of good definitions) as: a) organisms, that is living things; b) that can move around.

Organisms are living things. Animals are organisms. Animals usually have legs (or some kind of moving-around gear that may be modified as legs, or wings, or fins, etc.)

> A horse is: a) a multicellular organism b) an animal c) with four legs d) one-toed hoofs e) and other unique horse characteristics.

A cow is a) a multicellular organism b) an animal c) with four legs d) two-toed hoofs etc

A bird is a) a multicellular organism b) an animal c) with wings –

Animals can move from place to place. They function to distribute and recycle the materials and energy and information of the LIFE of Earth. Because there are many different kinds of animals, the materials/energy/information are recycled in many different ways.

But animals cannot do photosynthesis.

Trees are plants. They are also organisms; we are all related in our histories. Trees cannot run, but they can do photosynthesis to get their food energy.

Animals eat to get their food energy.

The result of the specialization of LIFE into many different species is that every living thing has its own *niche*, and is specialized for the energy/information and materials within that niche. Spiders have their webs. Birds have the sky; horses do not. Every kind of bird has its own space in the sky and trees. There are even whole ecosystems of living things deep under the ground that we know almost nothing about, but that we are nevertheless destroying with our fracking activities (Choi, 2013; Scudelluri, 2011).

> LIFE systems as we understand them have most often tended toward becoming more intricately complex (specialized), collaboratively interacting with each other as they co-evolve their specializations into an emergent whole that is greater than the sum of its parts. That is one way that emergent properties can balance complexity on the "cutting edge of entropy." Another way is the intricate specialization of the efficiency of the links of LIFE that are discussed in Chapter 06. Organic energy is being recycled nearly everywhere on and in the outer crust of the living Earth and that is what makes it alive – the living Earth Biosystem.

There is a reason for this specialization in the uses of both matter and energy, and for the complex niches and other checks and balances that evolve by specialization. It is a way that LIFE:

1. can generate more food (by making different kinds of food) using the same amount of space and resources. More different kinds of organisms can more efficiently use the food potential of our planet because each is somewhat different from the others and generates and/or distributes the food somewhat differently; the whole adding up to emergent LIFE, more than the sum of its parts.
2. can sustain the balance among its parts, with feedback loops and other biological versions of the checks and balances that you can learn more about in your study

of complex adaptive systems (Capra *et al.*, 2014; Meadows, 2007; Page, 2009). A good practical explanation of feedback loops is shown in several videos at https://feedbackloopsclimate.com/ narrated by Richard Gere.

LIFE can sustain itself when the raw materials of LIFE – the things it needs to stay alive -- are available and accessible. When we re-distribute them, divert them to other functions, we unbalance the Biosystem, reduce its efficiency, and endanger our selves. Right now our climate change is the Biosystem trying to rebalance its own LIFE; there will be more and bigger changes to come.

The Efficiency of the Biosystem
Is Higher Than – and More Complex Than -- our Technologies

The most obvious methods that evolution uses to regulate efficiency of living systems, are:

> Form/function collaborations
> Multitasking
> Recycling

Efficiency – Form/Function

When early biologists asked this question about animals
and plants and cells.:

> "What does LIFE need to stay alive?"

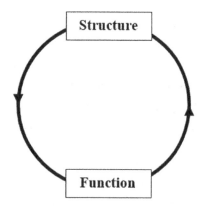

They found that the physiological functions of organisms,
and parts of organisms, are intricately related to their structures. Most Freshman Biology texts give examples of this.

Two examples of structure/function relationships were also given in Chapter 06 in the discription of the information component of energy.

1. The structure of the arm enables its functions, and both relate to the way the muscles and bones work together as a lever (and of course energy to make the work happen, and entropy to help find the sweet spot). If the arm/muscle/nerves did not have that structure, you could apply all the available energy (to contract your beautiful biceps) and the arm/muscle combination would not be able to do what you need it to do. Its structure (solid parts) and its functions (energy parts) are inseparable. The whole does not work properly without both the structure and its functions that collaborate with the energy/entropy and the information to make the right thing happen at the right time and place. This is an example of how complexity can influence efficiency.

2. Organic molecules also, and even more elegantly, combine structure and function in the same system. You can read about this in your Freshman biology textbook, in the section on protein structure.

Efficiency - Multitasking

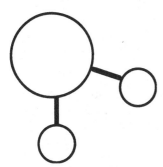

Imagine again our very simple model of a naturally evolved system. The straight lines are metaphors for the energy/entropy/information that holds together the "things," or nodes, represented by the circles. I just said the functions of the "things" of the Biosystem (their physiology) are inseparable from their structures (their anatomy). I say again that the structure/function of the things are not separable from the energy/entropy/information that we discussed in Chapter 06.

The energy causes the system to "Do Something." The flow of energy through the system links the structures in ways that tell the things what to do. The way the energy flows through the system enables the behaviors of the things. The structure, for example your arm or your knee, tells it what to do by making various options available – by the way the nerves, muscles and bones are fastened together. Or not.

As a generalization, the links and nodes of naturally evolved living systems use their complex collaborations to "multitask" or collaborate, at all levels from the organic molecules to the entire Biosystem, to do at least three tasks:

To cause the work to happen;

To inform the work - tell it what to do, make the options available;

To determine the relationships of the work with other systems – communicate with other systems, coordinate the responses. Because communication can only happen when there is BOTH a well-designed sender AND an appropriate receiver that can respond relevantly.

Efficiency – Recycling

Did you think that the breeze "cleans the air?" No. The breeze mostly just pushes the air around from one place to another. In the natural Biosystem there is almost nothing to clean from the air. The matter is all passed from one system to another, with the flow of energy through the organic molecules of the Biosystem, and used again.

LIFE recycles all its materials. There are no waste products (Lovelock, 1988; Margulis, 1998; Margulis & Sagan, 1995; Macey & Brown, 2014) and there are no extra shipping charges and there are no unnatural and/or toxic products messing up the natural chemistry of the cells -- getting in the way of the smooth flow of energy directed by the information of LIFE that mostly knows how to construct and manage and use its own organic molecules and does not know what to do with the artificial pollution that humans are generating in massive quantities – medicines, hormones, poisons, -cides, etc. – the greatest part of them just because we can – and to make the corposystem grow.

This is perhaps the primary reason that human technologies cannot save our species unless we reduce our populations and their effluents to a level that the earth can recycle biologically, and do so without causing harm to its own living body.

Implications – Recycling – waste not/want not

The meme 'Waste not; want not' is a bit of wisdom that, according to Susan Goldberg, editor of National Geographic, in the issue of March, 2020, can be traced to the 1500's. She went on to say:

> "But we *do* waste, in ways big and small. The result is this shocking fact: of the minerals, fossil fuels, foodstuffs, and other raw materials that we take from the Earth and turn into products, about two-thirds ends up as waste."

And the remainder of that issue is largely devoted to the concept that we humans can recycle our own waste products better than the Biosystem can do it. You already know what I think about our modern dedication to re-making the cycles of LIFE using our technologies. I think it is very important, and now at this very late stage in our response to the Problem it is necessary, artificial recycling is necessary.

But I also think it is a CAUSE of climate change, not a solution to climate change. We are caught in an evolutionary trap (Robertson & Blumstein, 2019) that we created, and it is essential that we talk about *our behaviors, that are our links with our environment,* rather than continuing to just do whatever seems logical and makes us feel important -- at our time and place in history.

Why do I so firmly believe this to be a fact of LIFE?

1. Because we are intentionally and routinely destroying the naturally evolved links that sustain LIFE and replacing them with technologies. Many or most technologies not only destroy the links of LIFE; they also destroy the species upon which LIFE balances itself. Our technologies cannot recycle either the matter or the information in ways that support Biosystem health. To the contrary, our technologies change the balance of the information of LIFE and so change the climate.

   Our technologies, for example, change the balance of the DNA, including the balance of the species that have evolved to sustain LIFE. The climate will not stop changing. It cannot, so long as we continue to change the information that keeps it in balance, the DNA and other codes of LIFE that direct its behaviors. Our technologies cannot replace the information of LIFE and hold it in balance. What they can do is cause massive shifts in the evolution of human kind; they can break our links with LIFE itself.

2. Because humans, or the corposystem, are trying, in essence, to grow a separate system, that we can control – outside the cycles of LIFE but dependant upon those life cycles for materials, energy and food; and as a result we have the misfortune to be the generation that is on the earth at the time when we have finally overgrazed its resources.

We can put the resources back into the ground, or the air, or use them to make more stuff for the trash heap, but we do not know how to put them back into the balanced, organic cycles of the Biosystem, and the harder we try to change the nearly perfect cycles of LIFE, the more we will destroy them.

3. Because cycles that are outside the naturally evolved cycles of LIFE are not appropriately efficient to sustain LIFE. This is for at least two reasons.

   a – because they ignore the biochemical and behavioral sweet spots that are necessary for the balanced flow of energy through LIFE (the energy/information components of each biological interaction. They take materials out of the cycle of LIFE and dump them in our back yards, in our air, in our soil, in our water. All of our human methods of recycling materials, perhaps with the exception of "organic compost," are OUTSIDE the cycles of LIFE (those same cycles that are informed by and energized by organic molecules) and therefore do not effectively address the Problem of sustaining LIFE.
   b – or, given the example of some chemicals, perhaps asphalt would be a good example, they may actually become entangled with the organic molecules of LIFE in such a way that they directly cause physical illness or mutation of the codes of LIFE by changing the organic molecules of LIFE: DNA, RNA, protein and other natural molecules.

Our waste products are largely toxic to LIFE. Recycling them technologically cannot be done within the efficiency limits to LIFE. Toxic is toxic, whether or not we recycle it back into the Biosystem.

We do not and never did need most of the products that are on the shelves of Wal-Mart© and its kin. Even the food products. We would be better off growing our own food, but of course most of us cannot do that either, because there are too many of us.

The answer to our Problem, the answer that might work, is not to get together and jump uncritically onto every "one-term" technological solution to the problems that were created by the previous technological solutions that didn't work. That is what I mean by our evolutionary trap. We have been doing that for 10,000 years or so, and that is what we know how to do, but the result will be quite simply that it will not work again unless we turn our attention to removing the cause.

Our mistakes were not because of bad science, but they are primarily the result of bad over-all understanding of the relationships of technology to LIFE. They were largely because we did not understand, until quite recently, how systems function; and because we continue to misuse our technologies to satisfy our greed, and now our fear of the symptoms, rather than to secure our future.

In other words, the ancient wisdoms of humans were mostly more accurate than our modern desperation. Even without our technological know-how, ancient humans understood how our mis-behaviors negatively impact our lives. That information is in all the wisdom traditions. But we have turned away from the God of LIFE and created our own human idol of our technologies, and our religions are suffering for it.

We cannot save ourselves by doing more of what is crucifying the earth. Now, the Earth is overgrazed in its every corner (Martensen, 2009, the free DVD). Substances that were removed from the cycle of life have been thrown out in our back yards with no way to return them to the cycle of Life. These waste products make us sick. They cause chronic "environmental (pollution) illness", and then we try to treat the illness with medical technologies (Selak & Overman, 2013) that may or may not make the problem worse, individually, but for the biosystem they simply add to the pollution, and so the pollution illnesses among the people.

The resulting pollution diseases of humans ensure that our next major "unexpected" crisis – or maybe the one after next – is more than likely to be pollution diseases that cannot be cured or relieved by adding more pollutants into our environments.

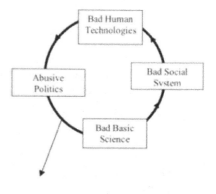

Pollution diseases activate your body's general alarm system, but they usually do not point to specific symptoms, because humans have not evolved specific neurological responses to these novel threats, and the result to the individual is fear. Fear of an unknown or un-targetable threat, and that fear activates nonspecific symptoms. The result is you cannot explain to your doctor or anyone else what is wrong, but your body is telling you to get away from the harm and it is not able to tell you where to go or how (Selak & Overman, 2013). Because medics are not taught the relationships among these symptoms, they generally assume it is "all in your head." The only difference from yesterday is that they don't use those words anymore.

Like a war veteran, you are living in a world that ignores or denies your reality, criminalizes the only pills that actually help, and then blames you for the whole scenario by claiming that you have an "addictive personality" (try Alkaseltzer Plus© or some brands of CBD) and then tries to grow its own self by selling you more expensive, man-made, toxic chemical "cures." That add to the pollution problem.

The result is that we become less and less able to tell what is real and what is not physically real. We grow more and more disconnected from our primary source of LIFE.

The links are breaking; the systems are falling apart.

And the more trash we throw into our environments, the sicker we will be, as individuals and as LIFE, because we are disturbing the natural ability of the emergent properties (macro-properties, phenotypes) to "talk to" each other – to communicate between the systems – between our organs and our bodies and between our bodies and our Biosystem.

As a result, we are running out of limiting factors to our overgrowth, short of extinction or a sudden attack of responsibility to the future of human-kind.

Implications - Pollution Sickness (aka "Environmental Illness")

The two basic sorts of pollution disease are becoming rapidly more prevalent. Of course, because LIFE is composed of matter and energy, these are illness caused by materials pollution (aka chemical sensitivity) and/or illness caused by energy pollution (aka EMR pollution, electromagnetic pollution).

1. Chemical pollution is caused by man-made chemicals that are being recycled through our bodies from the air we breath, the water we drink, and the food we eat. (I have given several examples above. The "things" or nodes of our model. Air, 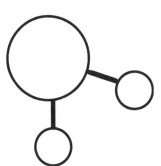 water, organic molecules, recycling the toxic chemicals with which we have saturated our environment and our bodies. Childhood asthma and the modern illnesses of aging, such as Alzheimer's disease, are examples of the body's response to chemical pollution).

   https://soundasacrystal.com/2014/12/07/canaries-in-the-coal-mine-multiple-chemical-sensitivities-myth-vs-reality/

2. Just as the links differ from the nodes of our systems model, EM (electromagnetic) energy pollution differs from substance pollution. Electromagnetic energy is not the same as organic energy, but it is equally as essential to LIFE of Earth. Organic energy, as we have said, forms the links of organic molecules, and so it cycles both matter and energy through the Biosystem with the organic molecules.

Although energy can change from one form to another, EM energy does not come to us originally from our organic molecules, but from our sun, and is described by its many wavelengths. Energy pollution is caused by our bodies' reactions to the various wavelengths of electromagnetic radiation. Sunburn is a natural example; X-rays, light, sound; more problematic is the artificial energy that is produced by our technologies. That includes electrical and electronic appliances, and also the polarized EM of wifi, G5, and other communication devices that carry information unknown to us or to the cells of which we are made (See Chapter 09) (Sivan, S. and D. Sudarsanam, 2012).

Materials pollution illness (MCS or multiple chemical sensitivity) is caused by imbalance of the realities represented by the nodes of our system model. Energy pollution is caused by imbalance in the energy/information links of our model, or by imbalance between us and our natural and artificial environments (Martin Pall, all; Hertzgaard & Dowie, 2018.)

In a normal environment, within which humans evolved, many dangerous and harmful things in the environment can be recognized by our sensory systems – they taste bad or smell bad or we can see them coming. In our modern polluted world, our sensory systems are not able to recognize and respond to all the harmful sources of chemical pollution or especially of electromagnetic radiation.

We often can smell or taste chemical pollution, but we can be standing right in the middle of harmful energy pollution and not feel it. X-rays are a good example. Even sunshine can cause a delayed reaction burn that can be harmful, but we cannot see, hear, feel or taste X-irradiation, and we know that is harmful; and that is true to various degrees of a broad spectrum of natural and technological irradiation. Overexposure can be harmful in small and large ways.

There is no way that man-made chemicals or modified EMR can help LIFE to balance itself on the peak of its own complexity because man does not understand the details of the complexity of LIFE and has not appropriately tested, most of the pollutants.

The solution is to stop unbalancing LIFE in the first place.

Evolution Sustains the Balanced Efficiency of the Biosystem Or at least it tries.

It required billions of years for the Biosystem to evolve. Even with computers, it would probably take us billions of years to test all the different link/node combinations of LIFE that evolution has already tested for us (Lloyd, 2016).

Our technologies cannot contribute to the over-all efficiency of our life systems unless they are as efficient as the life systems (Goldsmith, 1981; Gorschkov, 2002). As far as I know, they are not and can not be as efficient as LIFE systems, because we humans do not know about all or even most of the structure/function relationships, the links and multitasking agreements, the layers of regulatory controls, between and among the systems of LIFE.

Energy/information cannot flow through the system of LIFE unless the system is designed in such a way that it 1) is an organic part of the LIFE system (this means that it uses and recycles organic energy); and 2) is organized in sequence "downhill," relative to the energy/entropy/information (again, organic energy) exchanges of each or most of the interactions of the system.

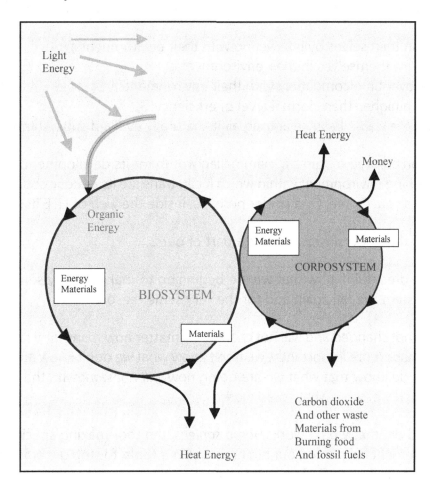

Otherwise, our technologies direct both the energy and the materials of LIFE into the trash. Or into the corposystem, as in the above diagram.

We will run out of materials; we do not know what will happen as a result of EMR pollution, but we seem determined to find out.

Balanced Efficiency of the Biosystem

As a scientist, if I try to look at the details of LIFE, I get confused. Too many words that describe billions of interactions that involve other interactions.

When I mentally look down at LIFE from above, the astronaut view, holistically taking in the whole thing, I see just a few primary processes going on, over and over -- at every level the same basic principles that are used in a myriad of different ways by our fourteen big ideas, but often described with different words – at all the different levels of the complexity of the Biosystem from cells to the one LIVING Earth -- to generate the LIFE of Earth and all its parts.

The emergent properties of living systems are variously described, but for here we can say that living things are complex adaptive, naturally evolved systems that can:

1. maintain themselves by interacting with their environments;
2. reproduce themselves in their environments;
3. evolve over time compatibly with their environments;
4. sustain a higher-than-normal level of efficiency;
5. sustain the viable balance among all its naturally evolved subsystems.

Just as a human embryo requires a mammalian womb for its development, so LIFE itself needs a nourishing environment within which it can translate its genetic code into a living system. Such as you. Or me. Or a spider perhaps, inside the web of LIFE itself.

We are part of the spiders' web and it is a part of ours.

Wouldn't it be dreadful if, now that we are beginning to make a really serious effort to save our Biosystem, we fail again and for the very same reason?

The facts have not changed and will not change, no matter how many fairy tales we prefer to believe. Perhaps more importantly, we don't know what we don't know about the Facts of LIFE, but we do know that what we are doing now *will not work* with the facts that we know about. And we know what could work.

What we could do, that would work. *Homo sapiens*, the tool-making species, could use our special emergent properties, our big brain and our tools, to stop generating suffering and learn how to reduce suffering by figuring out a way to compassionately reduce the overpopulation that rewards untested "solutions" to our Problem.

Not to dominate evolution, but to save The Creation.

We could do that; it is not biologically impossible; but first we would have to stop believing in survival of the fittest and learn more about how evolution really does function.

OOOOOOOO

Special thanks in Chapter 07, to Paul for the spider question and Consuelo for the best answer. And to one of my special heroes, Martha Crouch (1990) who saw this crisis coming and chose to not contribute her technological skills to our destruction of our Biosystem.

"Like any human technology,
there's a plus side and a minus side,
and a stupid side you didn't anticipate.
Pick out any technology; it's true of them all."
(Atwood, 2019)

CHAPTER 8

WHAT IS EVOLUTION?

The Biosystem uses the laws of nature (including evolution) to sustain its emergent property of LIFE.

Evolution is about change and choice; the flow of information (energy/ entropy) through the Biosystem.

As described in Chapter 04, the basic function of each naturally evolved system is to sustain its own emergent properties. To do this, biological systems use the natural law of evolution, that includes variability and change, natural selection, and genetics.

In the case of the Earth, these processes (of course working with many other processes; probably most we do not know about) has been used to create LIFE.

Atoms – molecules – cells – people -- the more complex the things become, the more different ways they can interact – the more complexity arises using re-combination, complexity, variability and natural selection.

The extraordinary quality of the system of LIFE is that it has evolved ways to keep itself alive with checks and balances and feedback loops that prevent any of its combinations from becoming too complicated or not enough complicated to stay in its own sweet spot and let the other systems stay in their sweet spots.

Perhaps an example would help to illustrate how a system interacts over a period of change.

This Chapter 08 is a made-up story about how the interactions (communication) between a social system (not a living system) and its environment leads to evolution of the social system and of the environment.

The Trash Company

Our fictitious example is a trash company. Not in my town. I lived in a city far away and not so long ago, while this organization grew up almost by chance in a small fictional community called Winter Wonderland that sat on a mountainside in far rural America, sometime in the 19th or 20th century, when it had few connections to the outside world, and where very few of the people had any idea of the elegantly intertwined natural systems they were trashing every time they broke open the ground, or perhaps "knowing" the elegance of how the living earth can grow itself back together again if it is not too badly unbalanced. Or, more likely, not thinking about that at all.

But that is the old story of the sustenance of LIFE.

This is a nearly up-to-date make-believe story of a modern human evolutionary "success."

Winter Wonderland

In that older time, transportation down the trail from Winter Wonderland was by horse or foot; neighbors knew each other, really to talk to; the road was several miles down the rocky hillside path and only accommodated horse-and-wagon traffic; and the radio, if there was one, only worked in the summertime, when everyone was working.

It was a rough life, but the residents pitched in and helped each other. They liked each other, and got together about once a month for their town meeting and casserole dinner at the local church.

One year, toward the end of harvest season, discussion at the community center focused on trash pick-up. With everyone working to bring in firewood, to pile the hay in the barn and the potatoes in the cold-shed, and maybe to throw up a shack or two to shelter the sheep and cattle over winter – well the fact is the whole town was beginning to look a bit trashy, and the community agreed to get together after harvest and clean it up. And so they did.

It turned out to be quite a pile, so at the next town meeting they appointed a few of the older folk to keep the town clean and carry off the trash to another town down-country that had a designated dump. They agreed upon a small donation from each household to cover time, labor and other expenses. It was a win-win-win accomplishment (Jandt, 1985) that emerged from interactions within the community. The older folk and their horses had jobs and a tiny income, the trash was recycled, and the environment looked better and was safer for children and livestock. Triple win.

This group of friends might evolve into a system, or maybe someone will become angry and it will fall apart. Most embryonic naturally evolving systems do not develop full term. Remembering that the primary function of a system is to perpetuate itself, if this group of friends is to become a self-perpetuating social system, it needs to gradually evolve ways to do that. To perpetuate itself, even in the hard times. Paperwork; interactions with the town down the hill; perhaps a better defined identity and a logo. For sure money will change hands. And eventually a corporate charter in writing. All this is exchange of information. Whatever is needed.

Or the community may hire outside professionals to do the job. And with that expense it starts looking for ways to make a profit. In the first generation after that, it raises the prices. By the second generation, both the company and its human political environment have changed. The original goal was: "see the need and fix it." I remember that mantra. But it was long ago, and the society has changed. Now its trash company needs to perpetuate itself in the new societal environment that has become -- in the meantime -- more and more like today's corposystem, which could be described as: "make a profit or else." Not much about need.

Give it one more generation, and it will begin to look like the corposystem, its new environment, the social system of which it has become a part. Nothing about individual need remains, but only the primary requirement to make a profit off the rich people, and the secondary requirement to avoid problems that might get printed in the newspaper that has sprung up in the next town down the hill.

Meantime the town of Winter Wonderland has chosen to move away from its origin within the Biosystem toward a much greater dependence upon the corposystem that is growing up around it. The trash is carried down the hill to disappear someplace, certainly not to be recycled. More and more the town of Winter Wonderland finds ways to depend, not on its natural environment, but on the money it can make to buy what it needs and carry food, entertainment, medical care up the hill, and also to educate its children in the ways of the corposystem.

Mostly the trash generated by poor people gets thrown in the river, which is nobody's property, or burned by the side of the road, which is everyone's property. This is not an improvement over throwing it in the back yard. It cannot be recycled through the Biosystem because it is toxic; more and more it does not come from the earth and cannot be returned to it; it pollutes the earth, air, water. People get sick. The environment is damaged in many ways.

Meantime, the trash company becomes a corporation, a self-perpetuating system that is responsible to nobody. Its new primary goal is growth for gain (as required by the corporate charter). It makes or invents a law that everyone living in a "residence" is required to pay for trash pickup, "whether or not they need it."

This new law is not a tax. The new corporation does not want a tax, because the people would be required to vote on that, and would become aware that the trash company has become more for-profit than for-service. If someone asks, the trash corporation does explain to people that it is "like a tax, to protect the forests." While the forests are burning up, along with the roadside trash.

The trash company, given that it no longer provides a service to the local area, and now is required by its corposystem environment to make a profit, rather than just break even, begins to have trouble collecting this non-tax, and starts placing liens on the properties of people who do not pay. This step creates some angry customers and some bad publicity, and so the next step, of course, is to not send bills and instead simply to wait. Old people and dead people rarely cause trouble.

This fictitious human social system evolved naturally from a communal service to a money-making system. The next obvious step might be taken by the property assessors, who might find it advantageous to label every conceivable abode as a residence, from regular homes to tents to those old sheep and cow-sheds that were thrown up the year the trash company originated (whether or not it is a residence, whether or not it has electricity or running water or sewage disposal or an outhouse) – to label it as a residence that must pay for trash pickup according to the law that is not a tax.

This community service has become a scam that you must pay for "whether or not you need it." (Perhaps they mean: "whether or not you know about it.") The trash corporation then arranges the system so that hardly anyone really needs it or knows about it, and as many people as possible end up paying for nothing.

As populations increase, of course the poverty increases, as more and more people try to survive on less and less land per person, likewise the profits increase to the corporation as these multiplying small properties are labeled residences.

A service that benefits the environment has evolved into a scam that benefits the corposystem. Notice the back-and-forth communications between the system of Winter Wonderland and its environments. It began as a system within the Biosystem and ended as a system within the corposystem, with its ethic all along the way reflecting and benefiting its environment.

Which is not a person, does not behave like a person, and has no human instincts.

What Has Changed?

Did all the people become crooks? Probably not, although we do tend behave in ways that we learn from our environments. Probably what changed was the system itself, that began as a service and changed to accommodate the needs of its changing environment, which has evolved into a new kind of system based on money rather than biological energy.

The primary function of a system is to sustain itself *within its environment*. What changed in this example was its environment. Evolution is the process that causes systems to conform to their environments.

This scam. unfortunately for both the company and its environment, is not sustainable because it causes enormous harm to the town of Winter Wonderland. The emergent property of the trash business has veered away from STRENGTHENING the community ties to weakening them. Some people get rich and move away, the community system of the village itself begins to break down into a set of competitions, rather than collaborations, and church membership drops and there are no longer any monthly casserole dinners and most people do not know their neighbors.

The imaginary system described above is only one possible outcome for this trash company. If the members had defined it differently it might have survived as a service, even within the corposystem environment. There are many examples of successful service organizations. Consider the Mayo clinic for a more positive example in approximately the same historic time.

The point is that naturally evolved systems emerge from a successful combination (recombination, self-assembly) of factors within their environments, and co-evolve with their environments. And then they succeed or fail depending on their relationships with their environments.

This fictional trash company is an evil system (Peck, 1983), partly because it ends up as a Ponzi scheme, but mostly because it causes harm to its own environmental system.

What is an Evil System?

Natural law is not about evil or wonderful or good or bad. It is about cause and effect – and about balance (Chapter 07), and about survival of the whole naturally evolved system. That is why the scientific method is so powerful; when properly used, it cuts through the human emotions, the individual good or bad, to aim at the universal realities that are not good or bad – they just are what they are (Chapter 01).

But for people, good and bad are real. For me, good means sustainable, relative to the Biosystem, which is the source of human life. Not according to the corposystem which, if it continues will very likely be the end of the Biosystem in the form that we humans require it for our lives.

One definition of evil (Peck, 1987) is causing intentional harm to the system of which one is a part, especially to the future of that system. Or causing intentional harm to one's own environmental system as, in our example, the trash system evolved from a win-win-win to a win-lose system. The environment was progressively and permanently damaged by the trash company, as were some but not all members of the community.

Because we humans are a social species; because we can do cause-and-effect thinking; we know that the harm we do to our environments will have an effect on other people. To knowingly cause harm to the environment of all the people -- for the benefit of a few of the people -- is evil. The trash company became an evil system because it caused harm to the environment and defrauded some individuals, for its individual, temporary enrichment. But even more because when today's children become of age, that is what they will know how to do. They will know that it is OK to cause harm to our environmental Biosystem in order to get what they want.

> **Reality Number Nineteen** - *The function of community is to create safe places for people and their environments. Instead of growing safe communities, evil systems are evil precisely because they destroy safe places (Chapter 08).*

Does this mean the humans who grew and operate the system are evil? Should we blame them? Again, the answer is no, mostly not as individuals, although we must hold individuals responsible for their individual behaviors, we are also responsible to design our human rule of law (currently the corposystem) so that it parallels the reality needs of LIFE. And we must enforce that rule of law.

The charter of nearly every corporate organization, and the modern corposystem, is defined here as growth by domination for gain. We do not need to argue over this reality, because we only need to listen to the corposystem propaganda. Make a list of the words used in its advertising. They will not actually say domination, but the dominate ethic is very clear both in it's advertising -- especially advertising aimed at children and young people on both sides of the goodguy/badguy divide -- using soft domination based around sex and more lately "happiness," and the progressively more violent aspirations that range from winning games to debating irrelevant questions, to war stories on the web, to war for real.

The primary unique function of the corposystem is growth by domination, usually for financial gain. The evolution of the corposystem will therefore follow the path toward doing the best and most efficient job of growing, as it has already done with making millionaires. Unless we take charge and intervene.

The primary unique function of the Biosystem is to sustain LIFE, which is essentially a collaborative affair, because LIFE would be impossible without a very high level of interactive complexity.

Wise compassion is the effort to understand the difference.

In the town council today we see two votes for money today; two votes for LIFE tomorrow.

What will we see tomorrow?

Our generation is faced with that choice because our parents chose to pretend that the reality is something else.

Nobody has a right to do (or to ignore) things that are harmful to the whole community.

> **Reality Number Fourteen** – *The environment of every naturally evolved system (including us) is essential to the LIFE of that system -- is literally the other half of the LIFE of that system. The function of every naturally evolved subsystem is not "survival of the fittest." It is co-evoluton. The function of a naturally evolved system is to collaboratively enable the welfare of its environmental system(s) and to change their social system if it does not align with the Laws of LIFE – for example if it is causing climate change. If it does not do this, the environmental system will eventually weed out the unhelpful subsystems or destroy itself. This is how evolution functions (Chapter 03).*

We have the power to influence our human social systems, but the baby bird solution – screaming for the corposystem to help us is PART OF THE PROBLEM – IT WILL NOT SOLVE THE PROBLEM. THE CORPOSYSTEM WILL NOT HELP US; IT WILL HELP ITSELF.

If we behave as the corposystem requires, we just give the corposystem more power and more money.

We do not need an evil corposystem; if we are forced to choose, we need a healthy Biosystem.

We could try education. I mean education to the realities. We were given the gift of a human brain to think with, not to think how to cut the neighbors' fences in order to overgraze today and who cares about the health of the forest – it takes a long time for a forest to die from overgrazing. We won't know what happens, and our children will never know who killed the forest, but they will have to live with it.

Why do we destroy our own water-table by overgrazing our forests, and then rage at the man who lights the match?

> Two votes for money today and two votes for a healthy future? Who wins?
> Why are we voting from such deep ignorance? And proud of it!

> We could try actually talking about our religious ideals.
> What is unwise love? What is unkind compassion? Who cares?

We could try controlling the corporations that are controlling us – make them function for the benefit of human kind. How about requiring a clause in every corporate charter, of both for profit and not-for-profit organizations, that requires each dot-com AND dot-org system to "do no harm" to the community of LIFE systems? And spend some time thinking about what means "harm?"

They would have to stop the growth.

We would have to stop arguing and actually discuss some relevant questions.

OOOOOOO

This chapter is dedicated to Ivy Williams and Donna Hanna-Calvert and Janis Atkins.

". . . the structure of a natural system
is not random but highly directive or
purposive; i.e. it must be that which
best favors the survival
of the whole."
(Goldsmith, 1981)

CHAPTER 9

CODES OF LIFE

In this book, naturally evolved systems are defined by their emergent properties, not by their boundaries. They may or may not have "boundaries." First, of course, because we are using a metaphor when we talk about systems. A simplistic links-and-nodes metaphor for interactions that, in reality, are very complex. Even more complex than the human mind.

Those simple, flat shapes in the diagrammatic metaphor represent a real phenomenon that is too sinuous, translucent and intertwined with other systems to actually pin a label on it and see where it starts and where it stops. It doesn't "stop." It is all connected, at least via the emergent properties. Our diagram is based on a simple water molecule, but if we actually knew how the Biosystem is linked together within itself we could, in principle, diagram the whole, humongous, multidimensional, naturally evolved system. We do not know very much about how it is linked together, we will not know, and if we did know, it would probably take a computer as long to make the diagram of all the connections as it took the living Earth to grow itself. (Carroll, 2015; Gates, 2006; Gimbel, 2015; Schumacher, 2009, 2015; Tyson, 2012) . Probably much longer for an ordinary today computer.

In fact, there are additional sorts of links associated with a molecule even so simple as water, both within itself and between itself and other water molecules. So please do not take too literally the metaphor of links and nodes. It's true in principle; but usually it is not discrete and specific, because it is very simplistic. And because LIFE is adaptive, naturally evolved systems change (adapt), in response to their environments.

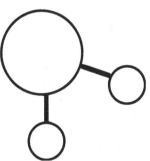

As simplistic as our metaphor may be, it is helpful, so let's pretend that this diagram is a water molecule consisting of one big node and two little ones (atoms in this case), linked together with energy bonds. At least three kinds of energy bonds according to my Freshman Biology textbook, but all represented by the one straight line between the hydrogen atom and the oxygen atom and the other straight line between the other hydrogen atom and the same oxygen atom.

Naturally Evolving Systems May be Discrete and Enclosed Or Not

From that simplistic perspective, I will say there are two major sorts of naturally evolved living systems. One, like a human body, or a cell, has boundaries. The other, the climate

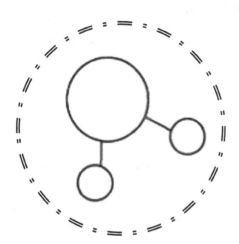

of Earth for example (Wolfson, 2007), is a system without obvious boundaries. The halo in the diagram above does NOT represent a boundary, but rather the emergent properties of that system. I do not consider boundaries in my metaphor, because they are fluid and because they are not as important as the emergent properties of the system.

Therefore in my model, the systems are defined by their emergent functions, not by their boundaries. And the functions of each individual system are its emergent properties (phenotypes, macro-properties) with which it interacts with other systems.

I don't intend to talk about this point – just to make it, because you probably by this time have wondered about it yourself.

The Biosystem uses whatever works. It uses variations on this theme of systems that are enclosed, interacting with systems that are not enclosed – or any combination of the two -- as one part of Its control over the flow of materials and energy through Its whole self. It is not necessary to discuss these differences; just to not let them confuse us. The reality is very complex; the model is necessary; the model is necessarily simplistic. That is one of the functions of models.

Both kinds of naturally evolved systems communicate with each kind of other system(s). For our climate example, the atmosphere can be thought of as a system (Johnson, 2003; Wolfson, 2007) without boundaries. And the air. Natural earth air is a system composed of carbon dioxide, oxygen, nitrogen, water, and other natural compounds that are put there in normal proportions by the living and nonliving components of a successful system of LIFE.

It is very unlikely that humans can improve on natural earth air for our long-term welfare, because we evolved in natural air. Natural air, as I am describing it for this example, is not composed of pesticides, asphalt, propane, diesel, and so on. However, our air, in our Earth atmosphere at this time in history, does have all those things in it. Enough to cause pollution diseases in many or most of our children and our elderly, and increasingly also in young, vigorous adults -- and dangerous levels of carbon dioxide -- because there are no boundaries to keep the unnatural and toxic compounds out of the air, and because we are using the air as a waste dump.

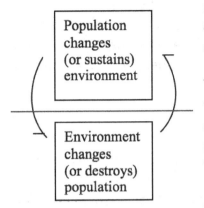

The cells of our bodies work hard to remove the pollutants from the air we breath, and then from our bodies, but they are overwhelmed by the enormity of the task – 7 billion people is NOT what the Earth evolved to support, nor does the human body have systems designed to eliminate every man-made artificial chemical or electromagnetic toxin. We evolved in natural air, and we cannot adapt to manmade chemicals (because we are animals that do not have the necessary systems to adapt with) and also we cannot evolve the necessary systems, because evolution uses the genetic code, and the genetic code requires many generations of reproduction to generate new systems.

Biochemically and biologically, our cells know how to "talk to" (how to deal with) other chemicals that were in the air when the cells were evolving. They do not know how to deal with chemicals they have never before encountered.

Inventing more new kinds of chemicals and electronics in hopes they can cure the symptoms caused by the last batch will not save us from our own overpopulation; it takes too many generations. Genetic engineering does not work that way either (check your up-to-date Freshman biology text). Artificial chemicals do more harm than good to human welfare. They mostly make money for the never-ending growth of the corposystem.

The air system of earth is a subsystem of the climate (system) and influences the functions of the climate system. The natural air of earth is a subsystem of the LIFE of earth.

Cells are systems with boundaries -- membranes that actively work to keep the inside things in and many of the outside things out. Your skin also works to keep the bad things out – if it can recognize the bad things. You are a system with boundaries.

The air system is without boundaries, but it is even more important to you than your skin.

Well, no, let us say they are both essential, and neither knows how to cope with toxic chemicals.

The nodes of this air system can also be thought of as systems. Non-living systems. Atoms or molecules consisting of different combinations of electrons, protons and neutrons. And even those elementary particles apparently are systems composed of more elementary particles classified as quarks and leptons and -------- .

But we set out to talk about basic biology -- not physics.

In one way or another, all the naturally evolved systems of LIFE are connected by their emergent properties, and need each other – therefore they need their emergent properties, their connections -- for their natural functions. The energy and information of LIFE "flow through" those connections (links). These are places where energy and matter join together to generate information (Chapters 06 and 05).

Information

By now it is clear that naturally evolved biological systems must be able to communicate with each other, or they could not keep track of all the things that must happen, at the right times and places, to sustain the whole LIFE of Earth. Or any subsystem of it. Obviously the systems of LIFE do communicate. The ways in which the systems of LIFE share information are referred to here as LIFE codes. They range from simple diffusion, to human courtship behaviors, to the birth of lambs in my neighbor's pasture.

Many LIFE codes, working together, flow the energy/information of LIFE through the Biosystem, so that the right processes happen at the right times and places on Earth.

Information (source)	→	Transmitter	→	Message (signal)	→	Receiver	→	Information (Destination)

The communication links between and among naturally evolved LIFE systems are emergent properties of the relevant systems. The emergent property of one system (transmitter) connects with a receptor (receiver) of an appropriate other system. A process happens. That process or sequence of processes (the message) is a LIFE code.

The messages are communicated by the emergent properties. Emergent properties arise from interactions among the micro-properties of the same system. Apparently that is what systems are for – to communicate messages -- energy/information (see Chapters 04, 06). To provide a framework that enables the flow of information.

Emergent Properties

We can study the micro-properties forever (using our reductionist science), but in most cases we do not and cannot know how they actually give rise to their emergent macro-properties (phenotypes, emergent properties) that are essential to the flow of energy/information among the systems of LIFE. Even if we did know, the links differ from each other. Probably every link is different from the others, or nearly, and it would take forever, from our perspective, to reconstruct them. And then, of course, we would end up with what we already have. An emergent LIFE system that works.

Reality Number Twenty-One - *We can not add up all the reductionist functions of every subsystem to understand the whole of a naturally evolved system, because at every step we encounter emergent properties (macro-properties/phenotypes, Chapters 04 and 05) that we do not understand how they emerged (Chapter 09).*

We would make mistakes. Better to keep what we have and cherish it with our every thought and care, because evolution does not work backwards. By the time we got half finished trying to copy it – it would be something different and *Homo sapiens* would not be here.

We know that the parts of the Biosystem must be working properly and in balance with each other or the Biosystem will have no LIFE. Without LIFE, it would be like Mars, or the moon. If the important parts of the Biosystem die, it can – in fact it must -- evolve into a different sort of Biosystem, and ALL of it changes because all of it works together to generate the emergent property of LIFE.

Better to change our world view to something that is sustainable.

As it is, we are ignoring the micro- and macro-property complexity and the codes of LIFE that it controls, rather than recognizing our ignorance of how these higher-level emergent properties function to generate and regenerate LIFE. We do not understand it, and it may be too complex for humans ever to understand. So we ignore it.

Ignoring the reality will not help us, and what we DO understand that is the other half of the problem, that we could control, is how to stop human overgrowth. Nevertheless, if you turn on the TV right now, you will see the corposystem working full time to promote the growth of human systems. Count how many times you hear the word growth spoken or implied, as though it were the goal of all LIFE.

That is just plain foolishness based in ignorance.

Nobody is forcing us to remain ignorant.

We humans are micro-properties of the Biosystem. Or of an ecosystem that is a micro-property of the Biosystem. We do not know how the higher parts of these systems are integrated using transfer of information. We already showed in Chapters 06 and 07 why we cannot "fix" or improve LIFE by substituting technologies for natural processes. Because we do not know how to integrate the technologies into the flow of biological information, especially the flow of organic energy/information (proteins, lipids, nucleic acids and carbohydrates) that is required to sustain the whole of LIFE. Because we don't know how to make the "right" properties emerge at the right times and places in LIFE. Because do not know all of the codes and messages required to accomplish those goals.

We do know that the whole of LIFE is necessary to sustain human life, and the whole of LIFE requires the naturally evolved balance among its emergent parts to sustain itself.

When we believe wholeheartedly in the parts, separately, or the simplistic metaphors that are debated on the web and discussed in the laboratory, and when we build our technologies and therefore our world views around reductionist facts, we are very likely to lose sight of, or take for granted, the emergent property that is the most important of all to us — LIFE, and its requirements.

When reduced to its parts, LIFE has no life. LIFE is an emergent property of a functional whole Biosystem.

LIFE is an evanescence that depends upon the balance between its environment and its internal makeup for its existence.

And when (if) we DO get a mathematics of emergence (Johnson, 2003) – what do you bet? – there will be no LIFE in it. Mathematics (including big math) squeezes the LIFE out of LIFE in its effort to understand LIFE. So do physics and chemistry.

Because LIFE requires the *complexity of emergence* to generate the enormous numbers of messages that are necessary for LIFE to exist. Or, to say it again.

Everything in the whole of LIFE must happen at the right time in the right place on Earth for the whole of LIFE or any of its parts to exist in their present form. This requires communication (exchange of energy and information, Chapter 06) among all the systems. Using LIFE codes.

Breaking the links of a LIFE system changes the LIFE system into something else. LIFE requires that all or most of the systems of LIFE must be linked together in specific ways, using the many Codes of LIFE, in essentially the same way that they evolved.

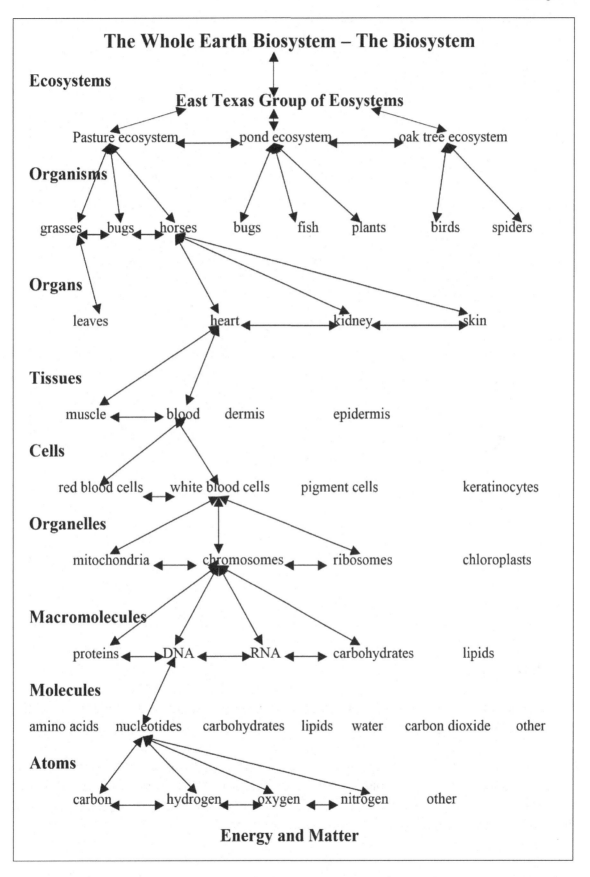

137

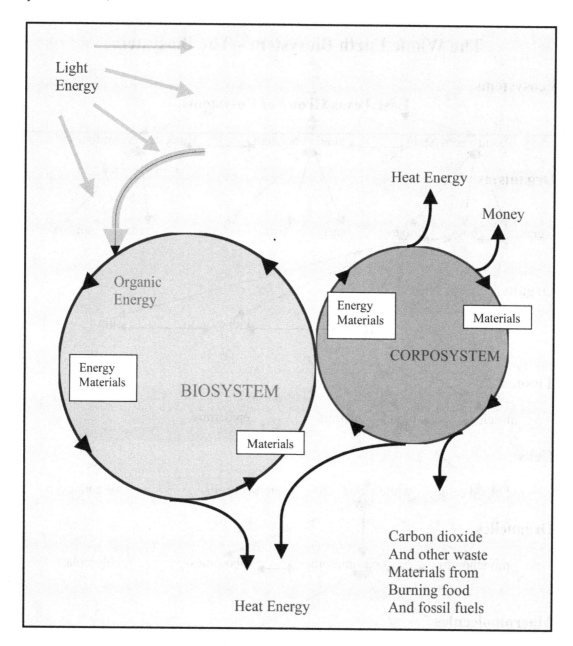

CODES OF LIFE

The Codes of LIFE function to communicate the information that LIFE uses to make the right things happen at the right times in the right places to sustain LIFE.

All of the levels of organization of systems shown in the diagrams above, and many, many more, can and do interact within the whole Biosystem in exquisitely specific ways that are organized, and replicated, using the information transmitted by the (many) codes of LIFE that we humans have barely begun to understand.

The right kinds of trees, for example, grow in the right places and shelter hundreds, thousands, of organisms that all know how to reproduce within its branches -- where the food is -- and not somewhere else that is not right for their babies; and this is true of other biological systems from the great, global whole of the Biosystem, down to the tiniest detail of every inch of soil.

How can that "big blue marble," all those multiple billions of subsystems, hold itself/ themselves together without the parts communicating?

Answer: It couldn't. It doesn't. The parts do communicate, of course mostly not in English or Hebrew or Sanskrit, but using many kinds of information generated by energy/entropy/ environment combinations, the energy/information links that make up the codes of LIFE. And that is the subject of this chapter.

What a mess (perhaps the proper word is chaos) that bunch of probably more than billions of systems would be, if every action were performed separately. Or continually. Neither condition would be organic; or efficient; it certainly could not be alive.

It would be what we see in inorganic (nonliving) situations, such as mountains, or waterfalls (excluding the lives therein). Primarily entropic -- everything tumbling down, sooner or later, toward a level plane, not precisely organized to accomplish the functions of LIFE, not organically connected with the Biosystem, and not nearly as efficient as LIFE must be to sustain its necessary multitasking complexity, community and integrity (West, 2017).

LIFE is based upon the ability of naturally evolved systems to:

1. maintain themselves by interacting with their environments;
2. reproduce themselves in their environments;
3. evolve over time compatibly with their environments;
4. sustain a higher-than-normal level of efficiency;
5. sustain the viable balance among all its naturally evolved subsystems
6. and communicate among themselves, using many different types of LIFE codes (Chapter 09 below).

LIFE is not so simple as a human technology or even a human world view; it is not so simple as a function separated from a structure or a function/structure relationship that is separate from its environment or the codes of LIFE that inform and activate the whole.

LIFE requires that the right functions should happen at the right times. The matter and energy and information inform the functions of the systems. The CODES of LIFE communicate among the systems to determine how, when and where their functions will happen.

What is a Code?

Codes are methods of retaining, storing, communicating and using information, across time and/or space and sometimes other boundaries.

All LIFE codes, working together, function to sustain the balance of LIFE.

Each code, in its most basic function, can be diagrammed as follows.

Information (source)	→	Transmitter	→	Message (signal)	→	Receiver	→	Information (Destination)

The information may be transmitted using any method or medium that is effective in accomplishing the appropriate response from the intended recipient. All those energy/information links in our model.

The most obvious methods of communication use emergent properties/phenotypes such as cell surface receptors; sensory receptors on organisms; behaviors, visual cues and displays, sound, words, thoughts, and of course their receptors. In Chapters 04 and 05, I began describing the emergent properties of naturally evolved systems as phenotypes, and the links as "holding hands" between the information source and its destination/response. This relationship between systems I refer to as a code. The code transfers the information (message) from its source, across the hand-holding, to its destination, its receptor (receiver).

A code is a system that functions to preserve, transmit and translate information (see Chapters 03 and 04). To function as a specific code, in living systems, it is necessary that there be a sender, a transmitter mechanism, a specific message, and a receiver that can interact and respond appropriately to the message. For example, sound is a form of electromagnetic energy. For a sound to have meaning (to transmit information), it must be heard. And the hearer must "know" how to respond appropriately.

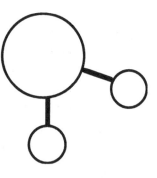

What is meant by appropriate response?

That depends upon the system. A biological code is appropriate if it provides information that helps the receiver to do its "job" using a message (emergent property/phenotype) that the receiver can understand and to which it can respond. The "job" of the receiver is to do some large or small task that helps (or at least does not harm) its environment and itself. The "job" of a system is usually described by its primary emergent property(s). The "job" of the Biosystem is to sustain LIFE, its primary emergent property.

The "job" of your heart is to push blood throughout the body. Messages come to the heart from various sources and behaviors, from epinephrine to exhaustion, and the heart knows how to respond to the specific messages in specific ways.

An appropriate response for the genetic system, when it receives a signal, might be to determine when and where to make an organic molecule that codes for a protein. Maybe a digestive enzyme is needed in the gut, just after you ate a meal that is heavy on the carbohydrates. That would be a molecular message that stimulates an appropriate molecular response.

At the organism level, a message might be the call of the baby bird in its nest, calling for its food. The energy/information link is the call, the sound. Sound is a form of energy and if it is used in that way it can provide information at the same time. The receiver is the mother or father; actually a sensory receptor in the mother or father bird, processed in the brain into behaviors; the result is food in baby belly.

That response is instinctive, inherited, evolved, and appropriate, and of course there are quite a few more steps (links) in the chain of information/energy between baby and parent. We are highlighting the primary holistic cause and effect of Biological codes. Not the details of how they happen. Just the concept of our encoded living biosystem.

System Codes

The first priority of every naturally evolved system is to perpetuate itself (Chapters 04 and 05). Naturally evolved LIFE systems generally consist of micro-components that work together to support the emergent properties (phenotypes) of that system.

Examples

>**The primary function of an individual green plant system (say, a tree)** might be to sustain its individual life using earth, air and water provided by the Biosystem in order to accomplish its unique capacity for photosynthesis (in its own unique niche) to convert electromagnetic energy (EMR) to organic energy- with-information that it stores in organic molecules, with which it grows its body. Energy and information. This is very useful to its own LIFE and also to the LIFE of the Biosystem.

>**The systemic function of an individual human system,** is to sustain its individual life, its physiology, in balance with earth, air, and water that are provided by the Biosystem; using biochemical energy and information provided by green plants and/or other animals; and also using its unique world view and skills to sustain its own life within the Biosystem. Energy and information.

And every naturally evolved system has its own set of requirements that support its particular systemic function within the limits of the Facts of LIFE.

And the codes of LIFE hold it all together, in balance, by telling each system what to do and when and where. Providing the necessary information for these necessary tasks, using the information codes of LIFE to maintain the cycles of which the systems are composed and in which they participate.

> **How the Biosystem sustains itself, for example** -The over-all function of the Biosystem is to sustain its emergent phenotype (LIFE) by maintaining the balance among its subsystems (micro-systems). It does this by exchange of information – that is, using the codes of LIFE.

> **How the Corposystem sustains itself** - The over-all systemic function of the corposystem is to sustain its own emergent phenotype (profit or gain), to do this in our age, it uses growth (evaluated in terms of money) and domination, advertising for example. Propaganda. Often false or misleading propaganda that upsets the natural balance of the systems. For example, its intent is to lead you and me to buy something that is harmful to the Biosystem (or even harmful to us) that we would not otherwise have bought, rather than all of us pulling together to solve our Problem (that was caused by the above system). I think of that kind of control as "soft domination," because its result is that the people end up not understanding our factual Problem that we should otherwise be taking steps to deal with.

The problem is that growth system is not cyclic, therefore not sustainable. The result, instead of maintaining a viable space within LIFE, is that that the corposystem uses its energy to grow itself at its own extremes. Measured as money, this is extreme wealth and extreme poverty, with less and less in the middle. This is a mathematical reality, as well as a fairly obvious outcome that should be available for study in our age.

Our corposystem has learned to use "soft" domination, mostly by formal and informal "them-or-us" education. Men versus women, black versus white, teacher versus student, rich versus poor, who is better than whom. Who is the in group: for example, using communication, information, advertisement, various kinds of social games such as special offers, competitions, withholding information) -- for example, influencing what we are allowed to talk about or believe. Censorship.

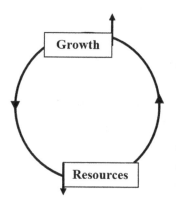

For the most part, we cannot even think about ideas we have never heard, and if our minds are all filled up with irrelevant soft domination, we are not out there communicating, communing, collaborating with each other toward a goal of sustainability. Especially if we think that having fun is the goal of LIFE.

As the corposystem becomes again more desperate for growth it will probably again crank up the hard domination (discrimination, war) in its effort to sustain its own growth.. We ignore the real solution, which is to reduce our own populations to a point where there is enough "stuff" for everyone -- mostly because we have never thought about the systems that created the Problem.

Even many or most systems people continue to use their understanding of systems to promote growth, rather than LIFE.

The solution to war is to voluntarily reduce the overpopulation – not to grow our culture of haves and have-nots. The solution to war is not to increase the growth/competition for scarce resources, but to compassionately reduce the numbers of people who need the resources.

This is particularly obvious right now, before the election, when all the politicians now actually understand the Problem but won't talk about it, even in the debates, because they can't win unless they lie, either overtly or by keeping silence. The political issues have nothing to do with birth control, or even biological survival. Yet biological survival for humans at this time requires birth control and is more important to our welfare than anything that is being widely discussed.

And since when is it OK to raise up babies and then send them off to war just because the corposystem says we should. Because it is profitable. Selling. All those diapers, uniforms, guns, funerals.

And more recently, the corposystem has invented a new quirk in the game – a quite novel approach to increasing its own growth. Charitable and educational resources. Right now (this changes, depending on the political climate) many of the so-called charitable organizations, rather than discuss possible solutions to our problems, are horriblizing discrimination (who is better than whom, domination) in their competition to generate income (growth).

Making money by horribilizing (whatever flies), or at least not talking about saving LIFE, which would require a reduction in our corposystem plans for growth.

The charitable organizations are now fully integrated into the corposystem. They say "give me money." I expect they will not use that money to effectively accomplish very much, except to further grow the corposystem. Which is why the corposystem gives them money in the first place. It is a broken link in the corposystem world view,

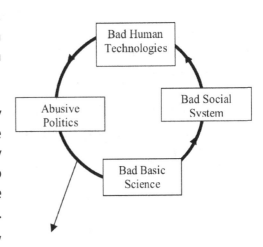

based on a belief that the emergent property of money can accomplish what we need better than the emergent property of LIFE can do. And of course it works for the few with the money.

In reality (see Appendix A), growth of the corposystem at this time, when the Earth is full, will maybe fix a thing or two somewhere, AND it will cause MORE discrimination, because both the corposystem and the Biosystem are now out of resources; thus competition and costs are rising, making it ever more difficult for many "minority" populations ("them") to access the necessities of life, or to raise their babies in a collaborative environment that includes all peoples.

Up side, this campaign reminds us of our ideals and our goals, that is, to not discriminate. Down side, the campaign grows the corposystem and the growth increases the discrimination. Because it becomes ever more difficult for "them," individually, to feed their babies and fulfill other basic needs.

The best solution is not to kill each other off, or ask our politicians to give us things that can't be got because we are running out of resources, or improve the efficiency of getting things and in that way kill off other species that balance the Biosystem.

The best solution is to discuss these issues, get together, and reduce our populations AS COMPASSIONATELY AS POSSIBLE so that however many people who are already alive and beathing have access to reasonable amounts of whatever resources really are available while we are using our fact-based information to align our behaviors with the reality of LIFE and what IT needs to maintain ITSELF.

Because the corposystem has already not enough resources to survive as it evolved; and because the resources are taken from the Biosystem, which is already overgrazed; therefore, there are not enough resources for all the people. Therefore, increasing the growth of the corposystem most likely will NOT reduce the discrimination. It will increase the need of individuals (individual systems) to fight over the remaining resources.

And now, as I review the above a few weeks after I wrote it, the anti-discrimination campaign is essentially over with, and the flow of our most available information has gone on to horribilize something else –another good cause, but it will further delay the discussion of reality.

Pretending that the growth of the corposystem will "fix" something horrible that is actually caused by the growth of the corposystem. Finding someone to blame. Pouring money into false goals. Did I say false Gods?

THREE CODES OF LIFE

The miracle of interdependence of all of LIFE is inseparable from its many codes that together contain all the information necessary to sustain LIFE, to wrap a cell membrane around the information that is imprinted in its DNA, and then to copy the DNA and pass it on, generation by generation for four or five billion years (Appendix E), molding it into one form and another that fit together like a self-sustaining, multidimensional jigsaw puzzle to the end of the LIFE of Earth, perhaps a few more billion years from now if we decide to do our job.

What is the greatest miracle of LIFE?

Sustainability, as described in Chapters 04, 05, 06, 07. As long as electromagnetic energy from the sun can be captured, changed into a usable form (biochemical energy) and all the matter can be recycled using the same energy/information biochemical molecules – as long as that can continue, then the activities of LIFE can sustain themselves.

Living Things

1. maintain themselves by interacting with their environments;
2. reproduce themselves in their environments;
3. evolve over time compatibly with their environments;
4. sustain a higher-than-normal level of efficiency that is appropriate to each link;
5. sustain the viable balance among all their naturally evolved subsystems
6. and communicate the information that is required for all these activities, among themselves, using many different types of LIFE codes (Chapter 09).

This is what the Biosystem has evolved to do; this is what the codes pass from generation to the next generation, so long as their support system can continue to provide the energy/information in the form of biochemical molecules. In the form of organisms that are able to do the right processes at the right times in the right places. That is, maintain the balance of LIFE through ontogeny and phylogeny, directed by the Codes of LIFE.

> *Ontogeny* is the development of the individual organism, including the production of sperms and eggs; fertilization of the egg; development of the tissue layers of the embryo, if it is multicellular; then development of the organs and organ systems; birth if it is a mammal; and further development, especially of the brain during maturation (see world view below); and then death. Or the equivalent developmental process in the other species.

The instructions for these complex processes of LIFE have been carried by the genetic code from generation to generation of ontogeny throughout our phylogenetic history.

Phylogeny is the process of the entire development of LIFE of Earth over the past 4.5 to 5 billion years more or less (Appendices B and E); from the first LIFE, a cell that was capable of reproducing itself in the environment of that time; to the first organisms that were composed of tissues; to complicated organisms containing organs and organ systems; to social organisms (that is, organisms such as humans who develop family groups and other social systems); biological communities (BareBonesBiology; https://factfictionfancy.wordpress.com/2012/10/24/bare-bones-biology-129-community-iii), and ecosystems (Gimbel, 2015); all within the development of the body of the LIFE of Earth.

There are many codes of LIFE. Not only the genetic code. Probably hundreds or thousands, depending upon how we recognize them. LIFE codes, because they direct "what happens," are associated with energy. Just to give a glimpse of the sorts of control they have over the processes of the Biosystem, we will talk briefly about three higher-level examples that are important to us.

The genetic code of the whole LIFE system
The world-view code of *Homo sapiens*
The universal electromagnetic code.

The marvelous **genetic DNA/RNA/Protein code** records and reproduces the "blueprint" of the entire Biosystem (as it is continually improved by evolution), and is used by evolution to balance the ongoing phylogenetic Biosystem "physiology," based on the interactions among Its living subsystems (including us) that control the flow of biochemical energy/information through BOTH ontogeny and phylogeny -- and the recycling of matter -- through the whole Biosystem in such a way that every process balances with every other process while flowing energy "downhill" (Chapter 06).

Our elegant human **world view code** functions, in part, to balance the interactions among humans, our social systems, and neighboring, parallel systems such as pets, children, trees, the air we breath, and our environmental ecosystems and the whole of the Biosystem. Our human world view code, for example, is indirectly responsible for climate change, by its understanding (or failure to appreciate) the cause-and-effect relationships between human behaviors and their impacts on the Biosystem.

The biological use of the **universal electromagnetic energy code** connects our living Earth with the cosmos; protecting and informing us. Within our bodies, through our nervous systems, and in every cell, electromagnetic energy helps us to sense the ordinary dangers of our daily lives at every systemic level, and connects the biochemical interactions at every level with the electromagnetic phenomena of Earth all the way to outer space, and in many ways that we do not yet understand. All species use natural electromagnetic energy as part of their relationship with their environments.

Beyond the individual Codes of LIFE, the whole Biosystem is balanced by adaptation and evolution that we have mentioned from time to time already, and will come back to at the end of this chapter and summarize in Chapter 11.

First – The Three Example Codes.

A - The Genetic Code of LIFE

The genetic code controls the key functions of the cell or organism by making proteins that either are structures in the ongoing LIFE of each new system (cell or organism, node) or are enzymes that cause biochemical interactions to happen (links), or other molecules that turn genes on or off at the right time in the right place where specific proteins or nucleic acids are needed. In this way the genetic code regulates both the links (energy/information) and the nodes (things) of individual and collective LIFE. It sustains what is alive today (ontogeny) -- It also preserves the code through the generations (phylogeny).

> Hoffmeyer (2019, referenced by Tonnessen, referencing Gregory Bateson --see Nora Bateson in the references), referred to this aspect of evolution as "code duality." The genetic code participates in evolution both of the present time and of its own future, by its interactions with its environment. It participates in the betterment of nodes and links today, and passes the information on for tomorrow.

The genetic code is reasonably well understood; you can find a useful description in your good college Freshman biology book (preferably an up-to-date text intended for Biology majors. Look for biology texts at Half-Price-Books).

The DNA/RNA/protein (genetic) code may be the LIFE code that we know most about. It is very important because it is physical. Hand in hand with evolution/natural selection it maintains the code – my code, your code, more or less since the beginning of modern (eukaryotic) cells of which we and the trees and birds and fish and other species are composed.

Like writing on a stone tablet, the message written in the DNA does not go away when the writer dies, because it consists of molecules that are copied and re-copied, potentially to the end of LIFE. The genetic code even has feedback methods to make sure there are not too many mistakes in the code, and that there are enough mistakes to generate the variability that evolution requires.

The genetic code is ubiquitous, though not universal, within the LIFE of Earth; we humans and most other creatures have the same genetic language. In the same way that our English language puts together letters to make words, and then puts together words to make sentences, the sequences of nucleotide molecules in the whole gene and the whole chromosome – the sequences contain the information:

"Do this! Now!"

"Do that!"

Mostly, the DNA code is the same code as the RNA code. Normally the code is either copied for the future or used to make proteins to sustain LIFE now.

Each protein, like every word, has a specific function(s). It may often encode an enzyme, or a structural protein. The enzyme causes a specific biochemical reaction to occur (it enables a link, turns it on or off). A structural protein contributes to the structure of a body part – like skin or muscle.

The DNA or RNA that maintains, copies and passes on each specific instruction is a "gene," a unit of inheritance. The message of phylogeny is sustained by copying the DNA code that is carried in the body of each individual cell of every organism, each of the parts in balance with the other parts. The balance of the parts is sustained by evolution and by the ontogeny (development, like an embryo) of the parts during the span of their individual lives.

During ontogeny, every fertilized egg receives two complete sets of genes, one from the mother and the other from the father. The fertilized egg then uses the information in the code to grow an embryo (using the genetic code interacting with other codes) and then a new adult who, as one step in phylogeny, sometimes passes the code to the next-generation embryo. If it has babies.

The DNA code contains instructions about when to turn on and turn off the various genes to make the necessary proteins, and the proteins determine what happens in ontogenesis and phylogenesis and when and where. It knows when and where to turn genes on or off (to make the babies) by recognizing signals (phenotypes, emergent properties, macro-properties) in its environment.

The relationship of the organisms with their environment, that is the exchange of signals, is essential both to ontogenesis (making the babies) and to phylogenesis (passing the code to the next generation) and is sustained/maintained by the processes of evolution (see Chapter 10).

For example, in mammalian embryos, the pattern of gene expression – that is the activation of specific genes and their proteins, is controlled by interactions between the embryo and its environment in the womb. After birth, continued development is controlled by interactions between the baby, youth, adult and its environment. Gene expression is under remarkably intricate control by its environment, and our information about it is at its earliest stage (for example, Xhong-li, 2020).

DNA and RNA molecules are the carriers of the genetic code (the genes).

DNA and RNA have three basic functions in the cell:

1. when the cell (or organism) divides to make another cell, it also makes two complete sets of the genetic code to regulate the life of that new cell. DNA and RNA molecules are the genetic code; their function is to make proteins and the proteins direct the steps of ontogeny;

2. when a cell divides to make a sex cell (an egg or a sperm) it makes one complete set of the code so that, when fertilization occurs and two sex cells (an egg and a sperm) merge to make a fertilized egg (a zygote) the new organism will have two complete sets of cells, one from each parent, all carrying forward the genetic code of LIFE;

3. when the cell is not dividing (making new cells), the genetic code operates the cell, turning on and off specific genes at the right times and places, in response to their environment, to regulate the activities of the cell or organism and their relationships to the whole body and its environment.

Both in ontogeny and in phylogeny, the environment of a system – rather its back-and-forth interactions with its environment -- tells it when to turn genes on or off. We and every other living system cannot survive at all without the cross-talk between our genetic code and its environment.

The Genetic Code – Implications
Everything Works Together in LIFE

The genetic code gives us our inheritance of LIFE. LIFE is the emergent property that results from all the genes coding for the right proteins (micro-components) at all of the levels of LIFE, at the right times and places during development of individuals and of the entire Biosystem. All at the same time over the whole living Earth.

Each individual naturally evolved system has its own emergent properties, and its own emergent functions (often a behavioral response, or a coded action or reaction) that it uses to incorporate itself within and contribute to the whole ontogeny of the Biosystem, and the balance of all that information determines our future.

Climate change? Pandemic? These are not coincidences or evil spirits that we argue over or disbelieve, but the predictable results of our own individual and communal behaviors. And they have been predicted for a couple of centuries. There is nothing wrong with the facts or the science. The facts have not changed and the science has only confirmed more and more clearly the nature of the world of which we are a part, and it is regulated by the same organic molecules that carry the energy/entropy throughout the system. Energy – entropy – information.

For Example - Pigment means color, it is a phenotype; that is, a signal from one system to another system. Many organisms (systems) use pigment to communicate with other systems. And pigmentation is inherited. That means the information is passed on from parent to child using, the genetic code of LIFE.

Pigmentation is inherited using the DNA/RNA/Protein genetic LIFE code. Therefore it can be (and has been) selected for or against by natural selection and also by human (artificial) selection.

That fact makes pigmentation a good model (Lamoreux *et al.*, 2010). The genetics is rather well known, and the functions of the genes can be seen by us in the phenotypes of the systems involved.

For example, in many organisms, including humans and most mammals and birds, there is a gene that "codes for" (that is, it contains the information to make) pigment (color molecules) in the hair, feathers, eyes and skin, and there are other genes that determine what color the pigment will be. And yet more genes that provide the instructions about when, where and how to make the pigment.

Remember, we are still talking about phenotypes. Phenotypes (emergent properties, macro-properties) of naturally evolved living systems are used by the systems to communicate with the specific other systems that can recognize and respond to them.

The aura that I have added to our system diagram represents its emergent property(s). The emergent property of a pigment system is its color.

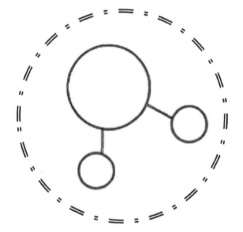

There is a gene that codes for "make pigment." (In my day this was called the *albino* gene). If there is no pigment, probably the albino gene is not doing its job properly. If there is no pigment, the hairs/ feathers/etc. are white.

A lamb has two complete sets of genes – two of every kind of gene – two albino genes, one from the father and one from the mother. All the genes in the lamb are its genome. The pair of genes that determine whether or not it will make pigment are referred to as the genotype of that lamb's albino (pigment/notpigment) gene.

The function of the pair of albino genes is to pass on (from the parents) the gene that carries the code to make the pigment protein. The gene "makes" the protein (actually the gene provides the code to make the protein). If both of the *albino* genes are defective, then there is no normal gene in that lamb and so the lamb has no pigment. (I have never seen a purely albino lamb, but that is what would happen if the code were broken.) The genotype of the lamb – for that particular gene, for the albino gene that we can call c for color, would be c^-/c^- (the normal code is c^+)

The pigment system would be broken.

Now – you do not need to understand what that particular gene is for. It is just an example. The albino gene. We need to know about all the genes (most genes), What they are for.

The genes are the physical instructions for LIFE. They activate LIFE by activating the processes of LIFE, one organic interaction at a time; every one a little different from the others; at the right time, in the right place, over the whole Earth.

It's not magic – it's genetics. Every gene (nearly) carries the instructions for one essential LIFE function. The albino gene determines whether or not there will be pigment. And more importantly, where and when there will be pigment – over the entire living Earth.

The genome of the lamb is all the genes. One pair of every kind of gene that is in the lamb. The genome of the lamb operates the instructions of how to be a lamb. The genome of the pasture grass operates the instructions of how to be pasture grass. Lambs and pasture grasses also can adapt, but I am talking about genetics. Later I will talk about how evolution uses genetics to change the genome of all of LIFE.

The genome of the whole of LIFE:

1. maintains ITSELF by interactions among its parts;
2. reproduces itself in its environment;
3. evolves over time compatibly with its environment;
4. sustains a higher-than-normal level of efficiency;
5. sustains the viable balance among all its naturally evolved subsystems;
6. and communicates the information that is required for all these activities, using many different types of LIFE codes (Chapter 09).

The **genetic code** is written in the DNA and RNA molecules of LIFE and passed forward in time by the cells of LIFE.

In phylogeny, the genome (all the genes) of the whole of LIFE is the genetic code of every living thing on Earth – and the instructions for their interaction at the right places at the right times to make emergent properties happen. In phylogeny, the genetic code is copied and passed forward (often by sexual reproduction).

In ontogeny, the genetic code makes the right proteins at the right time and place to sustain the emergence of LIFE. By making babies. In ontogeny, the emergent properties talk to each other to generate the emergence of LIFE.

The interactions among the emergent properties, precisely when and where they are needed, are what makes LIFE happen.

Every cell, every individual, every species and all their interactions at the right places at the right times. The Earth is one LIFE composed of the interactions (energy, entropy, processes, functions, structures, behaviors, information, BALANCE) among all its parts.

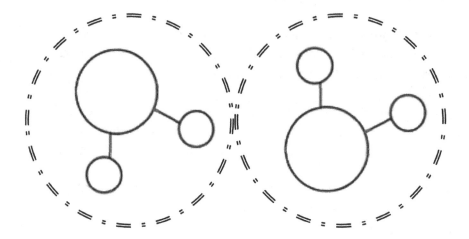

Emergent properties talking to each other.

Phylogeny passes on the instructions in the form of organic molecules.

Ontogeny uses the instructions, those same molecules, to make LIFE happen. It does this, and keeps track of the what, when and where, using the cross talk between and among the emergent properties.

In ontogeny, the functions of most of the genes is to code for a phenotype (emergent property, macro-property). Genes are "turned on." They make proteins or they turn on or off other genes within their own system. The whole system has a particular function that is its emergent property. It "talks to" a receiver in another system. The receiver responds. The whole Earth Biosystem comes alive. It is all connected by its emergent properties turning on and off in the right places at the right times.

Outside my window, in my neighbors' pasture, I see sheep.

I can see pigment in the lambs in my neighbor's property. That little lamb over there is brown. The lamb system is communicating with me, using its pigment phenotype to link with its receivers (my eyes). I love the look of brown mammalian pigment, and this fact has saved two dogs that I adopted partly because I liked the way they looked. The same color as a chocolate Labrador retriever.

They are not albinos, the lamb or the dogs. They both have normal "albino genes." They both have pigment in their hairs. The genetic instructions tell the pigment system how to develop properly in the hairs of the lamb, but that *albino* gene does not tell the pigment what color to be. Other genes carry those messages.

The color of pigment that is in your hair is also an inheritable phenotype (emergent property). The hairs of ordinary people and other animals that have hair (this is also true of bird feathers and the eyes of many creatures) are either black or red or brown. Or some combination of those three colors Or white if there is no pigment. There are other genes that add complications such as how much pigment and where. If they have color – that is if their "make pigment" gene is normal, then the pigment is either red (yellow) or not, depending on the yellow/not-yellow gene. If it is not-yellow, it is either black or brown. Three different genes determine the color in this example. Albino or not-albino. Red (yellow) or not-red. If they have color and it is not-red, then it is either brown or black.

I looked out over the neighbor's pasture this Sunday morning. where beautiful little newborn black lambs, and brown lambs and white lambs, and even a red one, are trying out their wobbly legs, bumping their heads against the mother's udders, asking for their first breakfast:

"More, more, mom, I'm hungry!"

How do they know they should do that? How do they even know they are hungry? The mother stands quite still as she stretches out her near hind leg to encourage the lamb. She turns her head to look in possessive wonder at this new LIFE that has grown up in her womb. All its parts as they should be, because of DNA messages in their ontogenic development (embryology) responding to cues from their environment, which until this morning was their mother – all operating as they must to maintain the balance of their lives.

These qualities have not much to do with the color of the lambs, but behaviors are also inherited using the genetics system. They are instincts that are born into the sheep – "hard wired" into their nervous systems. The mother and child are connected by their phenotypes. The lamb knows better than to bump his little head against a fence-post, and the mother knows not to stand for someone else's lamb. How does she know this? The DNA code tells both mother and child what to do. The information is inherited, but not all the information. The DNA/RNA/protein code of LIFE is nowhere near the whole story. The lambs and their mothers also learn. They get better with practice. Learning can be referred to as one kind of adaptation. The lambs and their mothers can learn, but they cannot change their colors, because colors are controlled by their genetic code of LIFE. Evolution. The *ability to learn* is inherited, but *what you learn* is one kind of adaptation. It can be a choice; it is better to learn about something before trying to do it, because evolution is forever.

As I watch, the farmers are manipulating the acéquia system to irrigate their pastures. They also learn, father to son and simple practice, interacting with their environments. Learning develops their adaptation skills and stores information in their world view codes.

The grass is coming green, and blossoms dangle in their multitudes from the cottonwood trees. The sheep are eating the grass; the farmers are giving water to the grass; there will be a harvest.

Except for the acéquia, all these things are phenotypes (emergent properties) of the lamb's environment, and/or of its environmental systems. For the last seven months, more or less, the lamb's environmental system has been inside its mother. Now its environment is outside of the mother, in the neighbor's yard. That change requires adaptation. The whole of it is connected with the neighbor, and even with me, and with the whole Biosystem itself, which we could say is the mother – the womb of all LIFE.

Each system of LIFE is nested in another (Chapter 03/section Proper Definitions), and each inheritable system and subsystem has phenotypes, whether or not we can see them, and each system uses phenotypes (emergent properties, mostly that we can not see) to communicate with its environments.

And the inheritable phenotypes are generated by and controlled by the genetic code. The DNA/RNA/protein code of LIFE.

And the genetic code is used by evolution to continually improve all of these connections, and also to change all these connections if they must be changed to *benefit the whole Biosystem* or any little part of it.

We are NOT at the center of this LIFE. What is at the center of LIFE is its own need to mold the DNA/RNA/protein code so that it can continue to generate and support all of LIFE.

What is LIFE? LIFE emerges from systems that are able to sustain all these properties:

1. maintain themselves by interacting with their environments;
2. reproduce themselves in their environments;
3. evolve over time compatibly with their environments;
4. sustain a higher-than-normal level of efficiency;
5. sustain the viable balance among all its naturally evolved subsystems;
6. and communicate the information that is required for all these activities, among themselves, using many different types of LIFE codes. (Chapter 09)

There is a naturally evolved lamb system with its different color phenotypes; what does it look like? Like a lamb of course. Brown or black or white or red.

There is a hair system that contains the pigment system, and many links between all these systems. We think of the links between systems as phenotypes, or emergent properties, or macro-properties, or colors, depending whether it is a biologist or a mathematician or the farmer who is thinking about them.

There are also communication links between the lamb and its mother; the mother and the green grass and the water. That kind of thing is what Barabasi is talking about when he says that a system consists of nodes (things) that are linked together by energy and information; in this case by interacting natural behaviors of lambs and sheep and grass and water and hairs and pigment granules.

Naturally evolved systems communicate with their environments using phenotypes (emergent properties, links, macro-properties).

The systems of LIFE -- such as you and me and my dog and the climate and the covid-19 virus, and the tree in my yard and the tree in my Japanese teacher's yard, and the one outside Dot's office that someone cut down because it was inconvenient – these naturally evolved systems are the tiny little parts of the entire Biosystem. In one way or another they are genetically linked with the entire LIFE of Earth, and in that way they are all linked with and balanced with each other. If they lose their necessary balance, we get climate change and pandemics, as the Biosystem struggles to maintain its own emergent property of LIFE, using the natural processes of genetics and evolution, energized by the energy/ information codes that sustain all of LIFE.

The genetic code is transmitted infinitely though time as it is used by evolution to sustain its balance. The same code is used from time to time, as represented by the short arrows, to make new living systems.

It is magnificent; many would say it is the gift of God. A miracle of complexity beyond our ability to understand in its detail.

B – The Human World View Code

The human world view code is more flexible than the genetic code and is outlined below.

I know of no better explanation of the power and reality of a world view, at the personal level, than Tara Westover's memoir (2018) entitled "Educated." Not many people have the courage that Dr. Westover vividly describes in her journey from her primary world view into another, very different environment. It is not trivial. Doing it is scary.

The same two basic American world views that she navigated were vividly displayed at the social level during our most recent election (2021) when American voters rioted against American voters, each "side" apparently believing that it was saving our democracy. Same basic facts, same country, same or similar goals, two opposing world views – one based in dominational behaviors, the other working more collaboratively. My reaction at the time was essentially the same story that I have tried to tell in this book:

BOTH SIDES ARE WRONG IN THE DETAILS! Because we are fighting over something that is not the basic cause of our Problems. It is all about how "terrible" other people are that scares us. But in fact, the threat that we all face is not so much about other people as it is biological. We would have known this if we would TALK ABOUT IT! Discuss the issues and realize that we are all facing the SAME PROBLEM! We are fighting over world views that were, perhaps, appropriate to my grandfathers' pioneer generation, versus world views that have changed to accommodate the growth and hierarchies and morés of rapidly growing cities. All in one lifetime (mine). As the population ballooned beyond the ability of the old world view to support it or the new world view to understand it.

The generations are changing so rapidly that they cannot talk to each other. The solution is to discuss the real Problem (overpopulation) in the context of biological reality (see also Appendix A, the section on blame-placing). And begin to collaborate with the LIFE of our lives -- stop trying to dominate the Biosystem.

It can't be done.

Our world views determine our behaviors, and our behaviors determine our future. Our behaviors are phenotypes (emergent properties) -- links that determine how we will interact with our environments, either for good or for bad. Either to help us humans grow a more comfortable life-style by growing a more fruitful environment, by reducing our populations – or not.

The relationship between our world views and our behaviors is easy to see in any town that depends upon tourists for its survival. And interesting to watch how the tourist interaction with the town environment, and the town interaction with the tourists can be a mutually interactive set of behaviors (phenotypes) that is beneficial to one or the other or both, or harmful to one or the other or both; that is, a win-win or a win-lose interaction (Jandt, 1985). And interesting to apply to our own smaller, everyday interactions. Win-lose; win-win. Win-lose is dominational; win-win leads toward good community.

The human world view code is "written" primarily in our neurons (nerve cells), and of course in the ways the nerves are connected with each other (the connections are called synapses) and with muscles, bones and all the rest of the body. And of course, most importantly as I just said, with our behaviors.

The human worldview is not "written in stone" like the genetic code. Therefore it can be more flexible, responsive to changing conditions in now time.

Reality Number Twenty - *If we want to save ourselves, our species, our safe places, our environment -- the place to start is with something over which we have some control (Chapter 09).*

We cannot change our genetic code; the genetic code is regulated primarily by evolution, not by our opinions and certainly not by our technologies, though the technologies can cause environmental breakdown. Natural changes to the genetic code take generations; artificial changes cannot normally be incorporated into the DNA/RNA/protein code – the instructions that tell all of LIFE where and what to do and when to do it.

On the other hand, we can change our world views if we want to badly enough. The world view code is more flexible and so is more associated with adaptation than with evolution. Not as much involved with long-term evolution for good or for bad, but quick as a nerve to change its behaviors if it sees another way to accomplish a goal that is worth working for.

The world-view code is also more temporary. It sometimes "forgets" things that it should be "remembering." It responds to propaganda. This is one reason that our religions are so important to our survival.

Religion tends to remember what is important, to teach it in our fire circles, write it down, to save it for future generations. Especially it remembers events of our personal and communal behaviors that have caused terrible things to happen, so we should not do that again. Things like crucifiction, or torture, or World War I, or other win-lose behaviors that for example are listed in the Law of Moses, or in the New Testament or the Koran or described in the stories of the Bhagavad Gita or the precepts of Buddhism. Books and stories that bring wisdom to our communities from our far-back ancestors.

Components of a Human World View

There is a sense that our World View Code, similar to the genetic code, is also a dual code (Hoffmeyer, 2008; Tonnessen, 2019). The world view code contributes to our evolutionary future more by our behaviors than by transmitting a hard copy of the code on to future generations. But the two codes work together, of course with all the other life codes.

Our genes and our environment work together in specific stages of our development to create our human world views, using at its base a naturally evolved (genetically encoded) nervous system composed of nerve cells and interconnections of our brain and body that we are born with, that include our instincts, thoughts and subconscious responses, all of which drive our behaviors (Eagleman, 2015).

Our inherited traits (evolved instincts, like the little lamb's search for its mother's milk) combine with our learned experiences (adaptation - the lamb gets better with practice and so does the mother). We are born with naturally evolved instincts that we improve upon as we adapt to our environments. Both the instincts and the experiences are encoded in the nervous system – brain and body, memory, instinct and training, subconscious and conscious.

1. Inherited (evolved) behaviors are genetically "hard wired" into the connections in our nervous systems, and probably are not normally changeable, so I will call them instincts. Clearly, we humans do inherit (and therefore we have evolved over deep time) "hardwired" characteristics such as the ability to take a first breath after birth, and the instinct to go to the breast and nurse, which if you think about it is a truly remarkable behavior. We have many instincts. Our most basic emotions; various physical capabilities that are associated with hormones, the nervous system and other body systems -- and the ability to learn.

2. I believe the instinctual, hard-wired (coded in our genes, evolved), inherited makeup of humans includes a compulsion to make sense of the environment using what we may refer to as "logic," that I think of as cause–and-effect thinking or reasoning, that is one kind of adaptation. Our logic may have originated from the ability of humans and other animals to understand our relationships with events in our environment. This is how we learn. For example, it hurts if we fall out of a tree. Don't do that again. Cause-and-effect.

Making sense of the environment depends both on the inborn capacity to figure out cause-and-effect relationships, and on the environment into which we are born and raised. Some modern environments do not make good sense, but most do, at least within themselves, and it is the nature of humans to believe what we are born into is "normal."

Learning might be (tentatively) defined as the process of cause-and-effect response to our environment by organizing and adding or removing neurons (nerve cells) and/or neuronal connections (synapses, connections among the nerve cells), mostly in our brains.

However, everyone is raised in a slightly different environment (or a lot different, depending on many variables). As a result of different experiences, the world view that emerges through our ontogenic development (our lifetime) is slightly different, or a lot different, from one person to another, depending both on his genes and yet more so depending upon his environment. (And to some extent on her gender.)

> Naturally evolved world views are all different from each other, but at the same time they all make some kind of logical sense of the environment within which they evolved. That is why the scientific method and our religions are so helpful.

The result is that what makes logical sense to me might not make sense to other people. That does not mean that my world view is right, or wrong, only that it is logical in its context. That is why it is so important that we make the effort to align our world views with the universal facts of LIFE. Facts of LIFE do not change to fit our opinions. If we believe in things that are not true, our behaviors may be harmful.

> ***Reality Number Twenty-Two***: *The Facts of LIFE are natural processes that we cannot change. Our long-term survival is not about our tools; our tools cannot change how nature functions. Our survival is mostly about our behaviors; it's about what we do with the tools (technologies). Whether we use them in an effort to dominate the Facts of LIFE and incidentally destroy the balance of LIFE or, holding hands within the community of LIFE itself, use our tools to nourish her healthy abundance (Chapter 09).*

3. A third contributor to our world view is our micro-biome (Chapter 06 in Feldman, 2018). The microbiome is a whole ecosystem of one-celled organisms that live(s) inside us, one-celled organisms that respond to *their* environments (us) in ways that we are just beginning to understand. For one example, they apparently function in our sense of pain (National Geographic, January 2020), and also fear, and I suspect PTSD, though they are not directly connected in obvious ways with the nervous system. The micro-biome, like the world view system is in part passed on to us from our mothers, and in part it invades our bodies from our everyday environments.

   Micro means tiny

   Biome is rather like an ecosystem, but consisting of more different sorts of organisms (in this instance microscopic organisms), that live together in a complex environment (in this case, we are the environment).

Ontogeny of a World View Begins Before Birth

1. During the first few years of development, before and after birth, our brains are very flexible and are changing dramatically in response to our changing environment (Eagleman, 2015; Steingraber, 2011). Neurons are created and eliminated at an enormous rate; connections among the neurons are imprinted on and encoded into the substance of our brains (and in other parts of our bodies in ways we do not yet understand); and the result may be so interconnected with our instinctual "hard-wired" birth brain that, by the end of this early phase of development, there is no essential disconnect between what has been inherited and what has been encoded in response to our earliest experiences. We could call this the primary world view that we were born with and then it grew and changed as we interacted with our early environment(s).

And then of course we continue to add learning (adaptation) and memory and add the new experiences to our primary world view.

2. During adolescence there is another stage of rapid reprogramming of the brain and the world view in response to internal changes and to our environment, removing some parts and adding others, and by maturity each person has grown a world view that is so integrated, and the original inherited brain cells are so interconnected and intertwined with the changes brought about by learning, that it is all one system that can respond to nearly any situation, whether it be everyday humdrum or unexpected crisis.

> ***Reality Number Five A*** - *The first function of evolution of LIFE is to maintain the survival of the whole LIFE system by selecting which subsystems get to survive: that is, those that communicate well with and function collaboratively with the other systems of LIFE in support of the whole of LIFE of Earth (Chapter 02).*

The ability to integrate learning with our basic instinctual system is a great evolutionary advantage for groups of people or other organisms who are living in a relatively unchanging environment. They can become better and better adapted to that environment.

Every generation first learns what the parents understand, and then learns more about the environment, and then they teach what they know to the young generations, so that the entire culture gains in the form of universal facts, metaphors and social "facts" and beliefs and the wisdom gained from day-to-day and spiritual and traumatic experiences. In this way, the whole culture increasingly conforms to the realities of its unchanging environment.

In an unchanging environment, the naturally evolved cultural paradigm becomes more and more specialized and narrowly focused, over the generations, because learning is passed from generation to generation living in and experiencing the same sort of environment.

3. We can and do change our world views later in life by adding more learning to the primary world view, and this kind of information stored, in our brain, seems to be more easily changed (revised, relearned) than the early world view. The later learning, however, is not independent of the primary world view, because it must make logical good sense within the mental foundation that already exists. If new information does not correlate logically with the primary world view, we tend to ignore, discard or deny it, or not even be aware of it, as our brains conform themselves to the early logic that arose from our inborn instincts and our early childhood experiences.

People will go to great lengths to create and maintain a world view that relates logically to their primary paradigm, even when the primary paradigm is wildly out of phase with the real world of now; but even so, change is possible. It may require a significant adjustment of the primary world view; a severe culture shock; an intentional rebuilding or relearning;

but we can change learned behavior if we want to badly enough. We can take control over our world view if we believe we are saving something important.

We cannot as readily change our genetically determined instincts (for example the human capacity for hatred or compassion seems to be hard-wired), but we can learn better ways to express our emotions that are more appropriate to the mature environment.

> ***Reality Number Five B*** - *The second function of evolution, whenever the LIFE system becomes so unbalanced that it is unable to sustain itself, is to eliminate from the Biosystem the systems that cause more harm than good to the sustainable balance of their environments. Or to say another way, to stir the pot, to create more diversity, new "ideas" when the old ones aren't working anymore. (See Chapter 08). Or, if that doesn't restore a balance to the LIFE system, to get rid of the system that is causing the imbalance. That is why occasional extinctions are necessary to the balance of LIFE, so long as they do not further upset the balance Mass extinctions are harmful in the short term (Chapter 02) because they destroy their own environments.*
>
> *In a time of change or crisis, humans do have the ability, at least to some extent, to change or re-organize both the basic world view and the later learned information.*

If we could not change our world views at times of crisis (to adapt), then there would be no way to respond appropriately to the crisis, but such change is difficult, involving culture shock and loss of important social connections. This is happening to us right now, as an indirect result of our overpopulation.

Our environment is one source of our individual development. Our environment, by natural selection and genetics and variability and other mechanisms, in times of change, generates highly variable world views that I describe in Chapter 02 as chaotic.

> *When the environment is rapidly changing, then our world views, and therefore our behaviors, become more diverse, chaotic and stressful.*

This is a natural consequence of the evolution, devolution or dissolution of systems that happens when their environment changes. It is one of the ways that naturally evolved systems function to change themselves when it becomes necessary to respond to changes in their environments. It is probably a form of natural selection. It is also one of the ways that the environment disposes of systems that are not contributing to the welfare of the entire Biosystem or are causing harm.

World View Code – implications

The human ability to 1) increase in specialized wisdom when conditions do not change, or 2) change when conditions do change -- incorporating the two capacities in one developmental system, the world view, that impacts both ontogenic and phylogenetic development, using the processes of evolution and of adaptation, seems to me one of the miracles of LIFE that is as elegant as it is coordinated with the genetic code and informed by its environment, and selected or re-enforced by natural selection.

This is one of the ways that LIFE begets survival of LIFE; by creating new ideas in times of crisis. Many and diverse new ideas, and eventually one or another of these may be preserved by natural selection if it is able to contribute to the welfare of the community of systems of which it is a part at that particular time in history.

This regulation of variability by interactions between feedback mechanisms and natural selection, increasing or decreasing variability among the systems in response to environmental change or lack of change, appears to be a normal property of evolution (Realities 5A and 5B) that is essential to the sustenance of LIFE.

The Logic of World Views

One of the main things humans do is learn to make sense of our environment(s). We are driven to learn; normally we love to learn.

Thus, in my view, making logical sense is a compulsive human behavior, and as a result, most world views are logical. They may be wrong, or inaccurate, they may be as far removed from reality as Star Wars, but they are logical; at least within the fairy tales of their origin.

Therefore, if we want to make the best use our fine logical brain, it is not useful to argue over logic. Every person's logic is correct, relative to herself. Argument is not useful when everyone is "right," especially if the partners do not take the trouble to understand the logic of the other.

What we can do that is useful is to compare our individual world views – not at first with each other, but with the Facts of Life. Because the Facts of Life, the facts themselves, do not change. That is what the word "fact" means – a reality that we cannot change.

Aligning our world views with facts, rather than with opinions or personal experiences, will automatically lead us closer together, because the facts of LIFE are the same for everyone.

And then we must discuss what we can do that is within the facts, if our genuine goal is the welfare of our whole species.

The Tower of Reality

My metaphorical image of a world view is of a tower – maybe the tower of Babel or the leaning tower of Pisa – a tower that lives in my mind. I built it up, brick by brick, insight by insight, from my birth through the rapid changes in my brain during childhood, when vast numbers of unused "bricks" (neurons or their connections) were discarded because they did not "fit" into the emerging logic of the whole in a rapidly changing environment.

This process has continued through my life; bricks are removed, other bricks (ideas) are trimmed and their neurons pruned and connected with other ideas, and new ones added, until the result now I give to you, gloriously logical and mostly accurate, but not totally "right" because once we have built the tower in our minds, we cannot physically think outside that box (tower) that we have created, because we discarded some of the necessary neurons or synapses, or never learned about them.

We move to a different culture with different social truths (BBC, 2020), or a crisis occurs – (WWII, 9-1-1, the covid pandemic). Enter culture shock. The tower of our reality cracks. We hope it does not completely fall apart because that might be insanity if we cannot rebuild it to a new state of satisfying logic, but our old world view no longer makes sense – does not seem to be logical -- in this new environment. That is SCARY for anyone!

But first we are excited by the new experience. Then, about three months into it, we begin to have problems rebuilding that tower and we are drudging through our new environment in a state of depression and discouragement. Our links with our environment no longer comfort and reassure us. They no longer fit our reality. Nothing fits logically together any more, and indeed we are clutching at the remnants of an old view of what we thought was ourselves. This is a time of enormous choice, for good or for bad; great responsibility; and a confused sense of reality.

Is this internal climate change? After all, the world view is also an evolved system.

Do we really exist anymore? Did we ever? As I said, it is scary.

As we carry on, the new environment (or the new learning, or both) begins to make sense, and we start patching up our tower of logic (cause and effect), filling in the spaces where the fallen bricks broke, using bricks that better fit the facts of history and better relate to the reality of now. In the process, which takes about a year if all goes well, we are blessed with new and more beautiful insights and an ever more powerful and useful tower of understanding, and eventually our world view becomes more worldly. If we are lucky and we pay attention to what is happening around us, and if we have the kinds of help and support that we need.

163

It takes time and effort to mold new neuronal and synaptic connections in our brains, and to re-order the bricks of our world views in response to the reality forced upon us by change.

But learning can be fun. Ask any happy child. It often gives us more power to accomplish our highest personal and societal goals and work toward:

> *a reasonably comfortable, sustainable lifestyle for humankind, within a fruitful Biosystem,*

and not only for the "winners" of some competition that may not be relevant to solving our Problem.

Ultimately, however, this happy ending cannot be fulfilled by our modern corposystem world view, because growth by domination for gain cannot align itself logically with factual reality of the universal laws of nature, which require balance by collaboration.

> "No dark fate determines the future. We do. Each day and each moment . . ."
> (Tenzin Gyatso, The Dalai Lama; and Archbishop Desmond Tutu, 2016)

Using our behaviors that emerge from our world views.

The world-view code can and does adapt. It is marvelously responsive to the environment in current time. Also, as adults, we have a good deal of control over it. Thus we could, if we so choose, use our naturally evolved world views – or rather our behaviors – to prevent the disaster that climate change will otherwise become.

LIFE Codes Work Together

The two above codes – the genetic code and the world view code - work together. Actually all LIFE codes work together. The genetic code (the genotype, that we as individuals cannot change) brings information from billions of years of phylogenetic development – information for the future of human kind. The world view code (assuming normal genetic development) primarily responds to our ontogenic experiences during our own individual development and gives us information for our own lifetimes.

> *Reality Number Fourteen – The environment of every naturally evolved system (including us) is literally the other half of the LIFE of that system. The function of every naturally evolved subsystem is not "survival of the fittest." The function of a naturally evolved system is to collaboratively enable the welfare of its environmental system(s). If it does not do this, the environmental system will eventually weed out the unhelpful subsystems. This is how evolution functions (Chapter 03).*

Reality Fourteen is true, but that does not mean that our environment can sit down with our DNA code and our world view and have a pleasant chat over a cup of chai. As always, when it comes to naturally evolved systems, there are rules. Elegant rules and rituals that permit communication between and among naturally evolved systems only in appropriate circumstances, and we cannot change what is an appropriate circumstance.

> ***Reality Number Seven*** - *We, and our parts, and our environments, all ARE naturally evolved systems, as are our social systems and our world views. We are functional, collaborative, complex, adaptive naturally evolved LIFE systems (Chapters 04, 06, 07, 08, 09) that can only partly be described by our human study methods individually, or by all of them together (Chapter 02).*

Again, the world view code – any LIFE code -- must translate into a "language(s)" that can be understood by other systems that are able to respond appropriately. That language has many facets, prominent among them is our behaviors.

> ***Reality Number Four*** - *Our beliefs are not important in the scheme of things except as they inform our behaviors. Our behaviors are recorded in the known and unknown history of all time; both because behaviors (interactions/energy/information) are the universal language of reality, and because we can never undo them (Preface).*

One of the restrictions to communication among systems is that the information in your DNA or in your brain must be translated into emergent properties before the environment can respond to it.

And there appears to be no direct common connection between the micro-components of a naturally evolved system and its emergent characteristics. An emergent characteristic of a naturally evolved system, by definition and in fact, is different from the characteristics of the individual subunits of that same system.

> ***Reality Number Twenty-one*** - *We can not add up all the reductionist functions of every subsystem to understand the whole of a naturally evolved system, because at every step we encounter emergent properties (macro-properties/phenotypes, Chapters 04 and 05) that we do not understand (Chapter 09).*

For the naturally evolved system to communicate with its environment, it must translate (using translation in the general sense of the word) its coded information, both the DNA and the world view, into a format that the environment, or the target system, can recognize, and to which it is physically or mentally or emotionally, instinctually able to respond.

Information	→	Transmitter	→	Message	→	Receiver	→	Information
(source)				(signal)				(Destination)

The human world view code often translates itself into behaviors, including speaking, writing and TV, let's say makeup, clothing, all of our emergent properties and related behaviors.

The DNA code translates itself into phenotypes, behaviors and other characteristics of individuals. It is the emergent phenotypes of the system that interact with emergent phenotypes of its environment. The environment cannot directly contact or recognize the DNA/RNA code because the code is nurtured and protected in the nucleus of nearly every cell. However, the environment can recognize and respond to the phenotypes of the cells, and the phenotype is encoded in the genotype (the DNA/RNA code). That is why we say that the phenotype (the emergent function of each system) is an emergent property that translates the genotype and/or the world view into a form that can be understood by other systems.

> ***Reality Number Twenty-Three*** - *Our world views influence our behaviors; we communicate with our environment primarily with our behaviors, not with our world views. The environment does not "care" about what we are thinking; its primary function is not to care about us, but to sustain itself (see Chapter 04). Therefore, it responds to what we do, but not to why we do it. (Chapter 09)*

We are very unlikely to induce the medical technologies, or the permaculture technologies, as fine as they both are, to generate the necessary combinations of the millions or billions of interacting factors that sustain health and grow food — while at the same time maintaining the efficiency of LIFE systems. What we are doing with our technologies is not joining the stream of LIFE, or improving on LIFE. Rather, we are rearranging the already existing parts of the Biosystem to sustain ourselves. We are not improving on nature's plan; we don't even know what the plan is, and we cannot rearrange what is already a nearly perfect system that we don't really understand – and claim to have made it better.

These parts have already been arranged, each link operating at its own required efficiency relative to the others, by more than four billion years of evolution, looking for the most efficient, or most appropriately efficient, sweet spot for each interaction.

Rearranging the parts works for us — temporarily — but it is asking nature to start over at a lower evolutionary level, a lower level of complexity/information to co-evolve new interactions, combinations, sweet spots among all the parts – if that is possible. We were not a part of LIFE at this lower level. If we force the Biosystem to regroup – very likely – we will not be in the new grouping.

So far, every time the Biosystem has been forced to start over (after each of the great extinctions, the dinosaur extinction is a good example) the Biosystem has come up with a **different** plan, and mathematically that is to be expected every time it is forced to start over again.

C – The Universal Electromagnetic (EM) Code

What could be more important to the LIFE of Earth than its most universal code? That is, electromagnetic (EM) energy that it has used to evolve LIFE itself?

I have said many times that the System of LIFE is basically composed of energy that interacts with matter, but as usual LIFE is more complicated than what we can say. It is W A A A A Y more complex than a simple energy-matter interaction. Appendix E attempts to clarify this difference by giving a very brief and simplistic overview of the current theory of the history of LIFE, beginning with the "Big Bang" that is thought to be the origin of our universe from a state of pure energy smaller than your hand to nearly current size in the "Big Bang" of its origin. The physics of quantum mechanics suggest (Carroll, 2015; Schumacher, 2009) the first subsequent event was the nearly instantaneous condensation of quarks and leptons, the most primordial forms of matter, followed by a few billion years of their subsequent evolution of first simpler and then gradually more complex (containing more information) forms of matter that are studied by physicists.

It took about 10 billion years, give or take, for the universe to generate enough complexity on earth to support the emergent property of LIFE, beginning with the basic unit of LIFE, the cell and then building around those simpler LIFE forms more and more cellular complexity both as aggregations of cells and as specialization of types of cells and other organisms. All able to generate the emergence of LIFE. ALL of them evolved wthin and with a normal field of electromagnetic energy, using information that has its source in complexity (see Chapter 06).

"Only ten billion?" I asked when I first heard that number, but then I stopped to figure out how much years is just one billion compared to my lifetime (I don't really want to reach a hundred, but we can round if off there). How many times the earth would have swung around the sun, if they had been here at the time (Appendix E).

It is impossible to believe that our technologies can have "no effect" on naturally evolved systems when we change the field or the nature or the codes of EMR, to make it carry OUR information, as for example in wifi, as we are now doing, but we actually know very little about even what EMR is, much less what effect is likely to result from slathering the Earth in artificial EMR. We haven't studied that. (But see all of the references listed in the Bibliography under Pall.)

Again, LIFE is defined by its emergent properties. Living things can:

1. maintain themselves by interacting with their environments;
2. reproduce themselves in their environments;
3. evolve over time compatibly with their environments;
4. sustain a higher-than-normal level of efficiency;
5. sustain the viable balance among all its naturally evolved subsystems;
6. and communicate among themselves, using many different types of LIFE codes.

These emergent properties are based upon the balance of all the parts of the living organism all the way up to the whole of the Biosystem. These many systems stay in balance by communicating with each other, using many LIFE codes, and that is what this chapter is about.

Think about it.

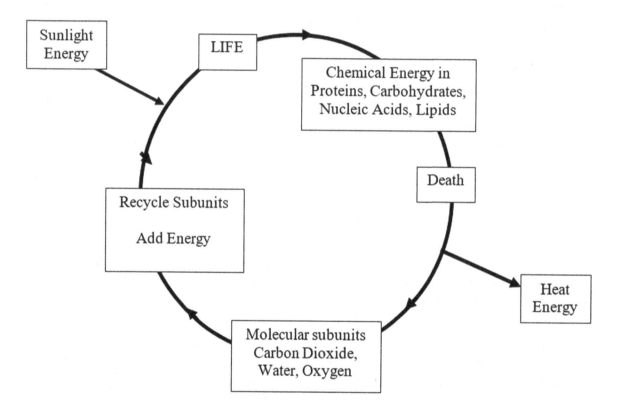

Energy is the essence of LIFE, it is that which makes the information of LIFE -- that informs the emergence of LIFE (Chapter 06). Energy in its many different forms is the source of LIFE.

That makes energy the most basic of all the basic properties of our everyday reality. Energy is what happens; it is what causes other things to happen; in the case of LIFE, it contains also the entropy that tells LIFE systems what to do -- and that balance among the systems, using the information of energy/entropy, is the source of the balance of the emergent property of LIFE.

That means -- among many other changes in our world views -- that we cannot believe rationally or logically that we can save ourselves by diverting the energy that normally sustains LIFE into channels that only or primarily sustain humans. There goes the climate!

Imbalance is imbalance, whether it comes from the sun or from an oil well, if that energy is used to supplement biochemical energy so that we can feed more people – to increase the overpopulation, then the parts of LIFE that are out of balance with the whole will inevitably cause harm to the whole.

The solution to climate change and any other imbalance that human overpopulation has created is to reduce the number of humans on this earth to a level that the earth can support in all of its complexity. It is NOT the energy that keeps LIFE alive, so much as it is the complex BALANCE of the various kinds of energy with and within and organized by and organizing the matter, the nodes of LIFE, that sustains LIFE. Not some fairy tale of dominance or power over LIFE.

And at its core, everything is a kind of energy:

> Matter
> Electromagnetic Energy
> "Dark Energy"
> Whatever else is out there.

Electromagnetic Radiation (EMR) consists of several kinds (wavelengths) of energy that are important to LIFE: sound, sight, touch; heat. These are ways that humans and other life forms communicate with the world outside of our bodies. And there are many more wavelengths of EMR that we identify with our tools and use for our convenience: radio waves; X-rays, many.

To give you an idea of our place within this spectrum go to:
Https://imagine.gsfc.nasa.gov/science/toolbox/emspectrum1.html

These phenomena are studied primarily by physicists – not biologists. We know almost nothing about them biologically; neither their impact on human beings – nor on the "other half" of humans, our environments – especially we do not know how the human body interacts with EMR in terms of communication, but we know that it does.

For starters: we know that it causes sunburn; too much or not enough heat can be lethal; and that it communicates with cells by modifying the calcium channel receptor that is present nearly in all of our cells (Pall, all of his references in the bibliography), is very complex, and influences multiple other cellular processes.

Take heat for a more obvious example. Not enough, we die; just right feels great; too much we die.

It is certain that other wave lengths of electro-magnetic energy, *whether or not our bodies can feel them*, react with human flesh and blood, or with other chemicals in our bodies, either right away, or more likely over (unknown) periods of time.

> Not enough, we die.
> Just right we don't.
> Too much or the wrong kind, we die.

That is why, in my working life, we espoused the precautionary principle. The medical version of this principle can be stated as: "First, do no harm."

The Precautionary Principle

https://en.wikipedia.org/wiki/Precautionary_principle
https://www.Bioneers.org/carolyn-raffensperger-bold-precaution-bioneers/

Check also Carolyn Raffensberger, Environmental Lawyer and Executive Director of Science and Environmental Health Network, and a book she co-edited with Joel Tickner entitled Protecting Public Health and the Environment: Implementing the Precautionary Principle. Island Press, 1999.

The precautionary principle states that we should avoid introducing a new product or process whose ultimate effects are disputed or unknown.

> "When an activity raises threats of harm to human health or the environment, precautionary measures should be taken even if some cause-and-effect measures are not fully established scientifically. In this context the proponent of an activity, rather than the public, should bear the burden of proof. The process of applying the precautionary principle must be open, informed and democratic and must include potentially affected parties. It must also involve the full range of alternatives, including no action." (Wingspread statement on the precautionary principle, Jan 1998).

The precautionary principle recognizes that, if we change one part of any complex adaptive system, like it or not, there are other parts that must also change if the system is to sustain its emergent properties – that is if the system is to survive. And our science has barely nibbled at the edge of the knowledge we require to make harmless changes, if that is indeed possible. Personally, I doubt if it is possible, because of the way systems interact with each other, and because the "codes of LIFE" – all of them – must accommodate any changes we make. They must evolve, and evolution is a slow process.

Everything in a naturally evolved system has a down side (relative to humans) as well as an up side, BOTH OF WHICH are essential to the integrity of the system and other -- nonhuman – systems that are also essential components of the Biosystem. That is how naturally evolved complex adaptive systems work (function).

The precautionary principle warns us to properly test every new man-made technology –to understand the down sides. Everything, from cigarettes to medical technologies, including pills, to automobiles to all chemicals, for example fire retardant chemicals, and fake food and pesticides, and especially cleaning products, including laundry chemicals that are on our bodies most of our lives). Test it before we spread it across the face of the land, because we need to understand that THERE WILL BE A DOWN SIDE TO EVERY TECHNOLOGY AND THE UP SIDE FOR MOST OF US IS ONLY MONEY. That is why the precautionary principle as it is written into international law, is so important to the welfare of our children and grandchildren.

According to the discussion in Wikipedia, there is apparently disagreement about the necessity of and application of the Precautionary Principle. I find this difficult to imagine, because one of the laws of nature is that we humans cannot change time -- history. We can't change what we have done.

We can pretend it didn't happen, the misery caused by our human history -- but we cannot take back what we have done, and the worst thing we can do to ourselves is to unbalance LIFE. Because dead is dead; forever, and on the road to dead is a lot of suffeing. And dead is one of the possible endpoints of our evolution.

Our modern technologists, seem altogether to have forgotten about being careful with the power generated by their tools. We are rushing to fill our environment with artificial, polarized (modified) EMR (electromagnetic energy, wifi, cell phones) and our atmosphere with satellites that emit who-knows what. We study how things work in order to make money that we do not need and would not need if we planned for the welfare of the seventh or the seven hundredth generation to come – at a sustainable level of population. We do NOT study how our technologies are likely to cause harm to our selves – I guess because we as individuals will be gone by then and – who cares about us? As a species.

Rather than argue about so obvious and important a concept as the precautionary principle, I suggest we should use it as a beginning point of our own adaptation to reality and beginning today we should "First, do no harm." It is law in some countries; just because the corposystem doesn't want it, for obvious reasons, is not a reason we should avoid talking and living by such a sensible idea.

What we do know is that EMR, for our example, communicates within our cells, between and among our cells and between our selves and our environments. What we do not know is how EMR communicates and with what messages we are slathering the earth and overwhelming the natural levels of EMR.

What we do not know is how this human EMR, and the chemicals we so carelessly are inflicting upon each other, interfere with the lives of all the other creatures that are subunits of our same environments – how they interfere with the checks and balances that other species – trees for example – use to sustain the flow of organic energy through their bodies and ours.

Implications

The result is that in our age we have massive pollution and a plethora of symptoms that we do not know how to treat and do not try to understand. We have moved on from making pills to cure illness to pushing pills, many of them addictive, that are supposed to make us feel happy. I remember when we were pushing naturally evolved drugs like marijuana and cocaine; that was illegal.

Often our new drugs do make us think we are happy, but apparently with no thought for what they do to the balance of LIFE or the balance of our own physiology. I know that adding more chemical pollution to my own life, or to the LIFE of our world, in an effort to rebalance its LIFE cycle, will not "fix" the problem of EMR or MCS (multiple chemical sensitivity) pollution. It can only make it worse. Because the things we are adding to the cycle of LIFE cannot incorporate themselves into the cycle of LIFE, they will not "fix" the cycle of LIFE, but only muck it up.

It is not possible to cure any problem by administering more of what caused it in the first place, whether it be pesticides, herbicides, cleaning products, dryer sheets, perfume, or EMR or growth. Some people are more sensitive than others. Over-all, we have now reached the level of toxicity that causes severe suffering in some humans and other living things, some deaths, and some suicides. As we keep adding more, of course, higher and higher percentages of our various populations will be affected.

We are making money, by destroying LIFE and the quality of life.

I cannot tell you how EMR will impact human life, because we don't know enough about it. I can tell you what it feels like to be over-polluted by it, but that doesn't help because we have no cures and very wimpy make-shift protections. Alkaseltzer Plus sometimes helps a little. I don't know why.

I can tell you that natural EMR is the most basic Code of all of LIFE, and only a complete fool could believe, after understanding the sustainable nature of LIFE itself, that EMR pollution will make LIFE better than it evolved to be.

Human technologies of any type (other than human birth control and fact-based propaganda) are extremely unlikely to "save" the Biosystem, in a form that is human-friendly, for three reasons at least.

First, just take a look at National Geographic on nearly any month (especially May 2020) to see the levels of pollution in various locations — the ocean, the air, the city dump, the land. The earth, air, water and even the energy that are the human services we require from our environment. Except for energy, the LIFE of Earth requires that its components recycle. The earth, air and water, must be recycled within the biochemistry of LIFE in order to sustain the LIFE of the whole of Earth. Recycling asphalt for example, into any living body, adds to that body toxic chemicals that it cannot process. In other words, it causes illness, as the body tries to excrete the poisons.

Pollution is caused by failure to biologically recycle or otherwise dispose of the products of our technologies. We just simply pollute our earth, air, water and energy. Our most important LIFE services.

Second, we do not know how to achieve the necessary level of efficiency to sustain LIFE, using our technologies. We use our technologies, (that would include technologies meant to dispose of pollutants) in an effort to CHANGE how the Biosystem functions to sustain itself.

Nether the Biosystem nor any inividual can change the laws of physics or the laws of LIFE.

Third, instead of choosing to rebalance ourselves within the body of LIFE, humans have used our technologies to remove the natural, evolutionary limiting factors that normally control our populations. We have not replaced the natural controls with – anything. Not even trying.

The result is massive pollution caused by too many people living in the limited spaces that are available on Earth and discarding their "stuff", that is toxic to LIFE and cannot recycle harmlessly.

The causes of what we now refer to as "environmental illness," of course, have to do with our environments, but the reality is that they are pollution illnesses. A few examples of individual experiences with pollution diseases can be found at the below sources. They were written by only some of the very few people who were lucky or wise enough to figure out what was happening to them, and talented or lucky enough to be able to put it in writing to help others with similar problems. This is not a scam or just a personal opinion. Some of these are people whom I have met and whose homes I have visited.

> www.eiwellspring.org,
> https://soundasacrystal.com/2015/12/31/not-wearing-any-perfume/,
> www.powerwatch.org.uk
> Johnson, Jeromy. TED Talk. https://youtu.be/F0NEaPTu9ol
> Pall, Martin L. 2017. Letter to Governor Brown. http://documents.dps.gov/
> public/Common/ViewDoc.aspx?DocRefId=%7B46F01CB5-ACD8-4888-
> AE61-6563DD19A7CD%7D

> (Baker-Laporte, Paula, Erica Elliott & John Banta, 2008; Evans, 2014, 2019;
> Green, 1991; Pall ML 2013, 2016; Sivan, S & D Sudarsanam. 2012; Stih, 2009)

All these above references discuss only briefly some of the causes of environmental illness.

I mean pollution diseases.

What is Pollution Illness?

Pollution diseases can be an extremely uncomfortable, or even fatal for humans and other sentient beings. The name tries to explain that the conditions are not caused by the direct action of living organisms, like parasites or bacteria -- or by our genes -- or by any human abnormality. It is not like a bacterial cell that invades our bodies and then multiplies; not like a virus, such as the covid-19, that spreads from person to person; or a parasite, like intestinal worms or trypanosomes.

Human pollution diseases are not caused by inherited human abnormalities passed down from generation to generation of humans. They are also not caused by our immune systems. Properly speaking, they are not a "allergies."

Pollution sickness is not caused by abnormalities in our own bodies.

Pollution diseases are caused by the fact that our normal bodies, and all the normal cells and organs in our bodies, are designed to reject poisonous substances, and that is what they try to do. Whether or not those poisons make us sick depends upon how much poison has entered our body and how much poison our body can get rid of through our lungs, urine, feces and skin.

Every normal human body is somewhat different from every other. Some human bodies are more sensitive to poisonous substances than others. I may be more sensitive to toxins than you are, but that does not mean that my body is "abnormal." Any more than my eye color, or my kidney function is abnormal. It is just that every normal person is somewhat different from every other normal person, and some people are more sensitive than others to environmental pollution. But everyone is sensitive to pollution at some level, and the pollution is rapidly increasing. That is why I say that pollution illnesses will probably be the next "surprise" evidence of our increasing overpopulation. Unless on-shore war happens first.

Environmental illness is directly, and indirectly, caused by poisonous phenomena in our environment or poisonous quantities of toxic substances in our environment.

Can we Cure Pollution Illness?

To "cure" a problem, it is necessary to face up to the real cause of the problem and respond accordingly.

Pollution illness, as a generalization, is directly caused by environments that are not normal for normal humans to live in. Because pollution illness is caused by toxins (poisonous conditions) in the environment and not by defects of the human body, therefore it must be treated by maintaining a healthy environment, for example by scrubbing the poisons out of our earth, air and water, or by going someplace away from the poisons.

Giving pills to a person who is suffering from too much toxic chemicals cannot reduce the amount of toxic chemicals in that person's system. To relieve the suffering, to prevent the symptoms and potentially an early death, it is necessary to remove the toxic chemicals. Or not put chemicals into the environment in the first place.

For example, it is unlikely that normal food eaten by a normal person, or normal air breathed by a normal person, will cause an environmental illness. But an overdose of pesticides or cleaning products or perfume in the food or the air can certainly cause illness in a healthy person. As can an overdose of normal or abnormal (artificially polarized) electromagnetic radiation (EM) such as is emitted from wifi and cell phone towers, hearing aids, cell phones, computers and television, and a large number of our other electrical and electronic gadgets.

In order to sustain our normal bodies, humans have always needed from our environment clean earth, air, and water that intricately interact with each other and with normal energy sources ("fire") that living things get from sunlight via the organic energy generated in photosynthesis. That is why I keep saying the most basic needs for human health are NORMAL earth, air, water and energy. Normal bodies in a normal environment, as they were created together by the universal law of evolution to function together.

Abnormal earth, air, water and/or energy can and do cause pollution diseases.

Categories of Pollution Illness

Chemical Sensitivity
Electromagnetic Sensitivity

Chemical Sensitivity is very common, and includes reactions to (usually) manmade chemicals -- especially perfumes, cleaning products such as Lysol or any product with artificial additives, pesticides, detergents, and most kinds of cosmetics, and additives to the food we eat. We wear laundry detergents and dryer-sheet-chemicals on our bodies all day and all night, as though they were natural. They are not. Not only do the detergents and drier sheets themselves smell bad, but also, for many people, the result is: skin outbreaks, unfocused anxiety, intestinal discomfort (we often refer to as "stomach acid"), and that old tired feeling that follows us around all day. These toxins do not "rinse out" of our clothing; it takes about six full washing cycles with normal, nontoxic soap of some kind to get them out. If the cause is toxic chemicals, then it cannot be treated successfully by adding more toxic chemicals to our body.

When did men start wearing perfume? They smelled a lot better clean.

But pollution disease is not a question of how anything smells. The worst culprits do not smell at all, and so we cannot tell that we are being poisoned. It's a question of whether or not we go home with big belly-ache. Or pass out on the bathroom floor. Or cause mental and/or physical developmental harm to our children, before and after their birth.

The "cure" for environmental stress and pollution illness may be to clean all these things out of our homes (Baker-Laporte, 2008; Evans, 2019; Pineault, 2019; Stih, 2009;) switch to "free and clear" products that are not as bad; eat organic foods, but all of our soils are now tainted; use natural cleaning substances such as vinegar or alcohol, with no additives, and stay as far away from pesticides as we can.

Watch for the workers with the spray cans in public buildings and run the other way. Better a cockroach or two than pushing poisons on all the people, many of whom may become ill from exposure to pesticides, depending on how much exposure they have already received. This is also true of perfumes and products associated with automobiles (oil, gas, cleaning products and the "new car smell") because they are harmful in excess and are now nearly ubiquitous.

In our closed homes and public buildings, I believe nearly everyone suffers from exposure to unnamed and unknown artificial chemicals used to make the buildings. For most, it is just a case of the "dreadful draggies," and we blame ourselves. For some, it is a whole life that cannot be well lived because we must stay away from other people in order to stay healthy. Drinking more water or popping the aspirin may help the body to feel better, but it will not help the environment, or our emotional or physical well being. It will not make us OK.

Electromagnetic Sensitivity is affecting more and more people, as we build more towers and joyfully ramp up their power to G4 or G5, and pile neighbor upon neighbor with no way to get away -- and now we even throw untested loads of EMR over the whole earth from our satellites. I have concluded the people who do this believe very directly in "survival of the fittest," but what they must not understand is that this irradiation affects everyone. Not only the fittest, but also the trees and plants and, most obviously, the climate. That radiation (as is claimed by its perpetrators), is polarized. That means they have changed the messages they are sending, without the slightest idea what that change will do in a normal world that has normal communications among all the naturally evolved systems, from bacteria to eukaryotic cells to every kind of organism and ecosystem, and the whole Biosystem.

If you want to fact-check, I recommend you follow the work of Martin Pall that also summarizes other references.

EMR is used by our nervous systems that are specialized for this function, and -- in fact -- every cell on earth probably depends upon EMR for communication with its environment, that is, for its survival.

We also know that the "junk electricity" that is emitted in rooms filled with computer equipment and/or television sets, cell phones, and many other of our gadgets, combined with the toxic molecules that are also emitted by these technologies -- can and does cause physical and mental and emotional harm to those of us who are sensitive to it, and we are all sensitive at some level. That's what "biological LIFE code" means. And we have no idea how these wavelengths affect the biological codes that are essential to survival of whole ecosystems or even the entire Biosystem.

Trees communicate with their environments using EMR and chemical codes. So do birds, and insects, and people. All living things.

Right now, as a generalization, it seems to me that our corposystem, including the medical, energy, activist and economic branches, is simply producing as much pollution as it wants to, in order to generate as much money (or power) as it can. It seems to me that our health and our future is more important than our profit margins or our personal power.

This problem is not trivial; and it is not individual, even though some individuals are more sensitive to pollution than others. I have watched the layers of chemical toxins rise up the levels of altitude in my annual trips back to the Gulf coast, and now I cannot go back home to the Gulf at all, because of the life-threatening pollution from fracking and herbicides (especially Roundup©) that are required to grow genetically modified foods that are also a threat to our human health.

Santa Fe was not so long ago the cleanest city in the country, of its size. Now, I'm sure you have seen what has happened to Santa Fe in only the last 8 or 9 years, and it is affecting more and more people as the concentrations of the pollution increase. I have recently heard people say they are leaving Santa Fe "for their health." I have no idea where they have found to go to.

Our highly trained technicians and technologists, and our governments generally seem to be in denial. That does not mean that we the ordinary people should ignore our suffering caused by the related problems of climate change, chemical and electromagnetic pollution. In fact the suffering of all sentient beings on earth who are exposed to these toxins.

What to do about it?

The first step is to actually TALK ABOUT THE REAL PROBLEM. Read Appendix A and talk about human hubris and human overgrowth and behind all that: human overpopulation. Discuss, brainstorm, learn about the Biology as it is.

Denial, complaining, blame-placing do not change facts. If we want to survive, we must change ourselves, and the most accessible part of ourselves is our world views.

Climate change is real; pollution is real; chemical and electromagnetic sensitivities are what they are; and no person's opinion can change the overall reality, nor can our technologies change the real laws of God and nature that have responded to our attack upon our own environments. How silly it is to stand around arguing about whether or not our well demonstrated biology is real. The real question is how do we respond positively to it?

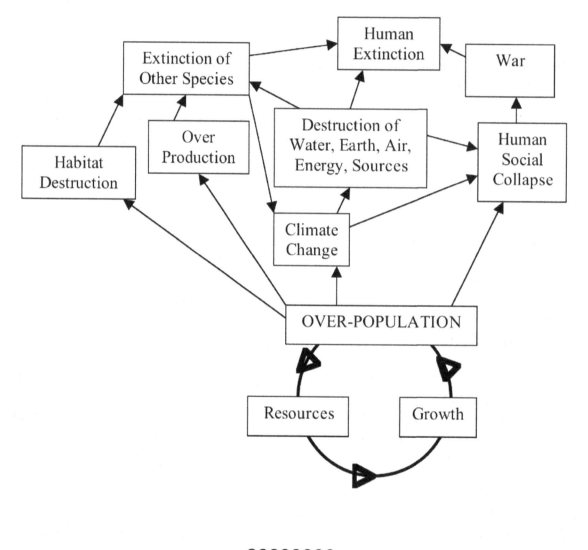

OOOOOOOO

This chapter is dedicated to Sue Windeck, Jane Wood, Fr. Colin Kelly and St. Jerome's Episcopal Church.

"This fantastic difference between information flows
in the biota and civilization
will probably not be eliminated,
however dramatic future progress of civilization will be.
Therefore, people will inevitably face the necessity
of restoring the disturbed biota and preserving the undisturbed biota
to an extent that will ensure, as before,
the maintenance of the global environment and climate
in the state suitable for human life." (Gorshkov *et al.*, 2002)

We might as well start sooner than later.
So far, we are not even talking about it.

CHAPTER 10

FOURTEEN BIG IDEAS

Balance
    Materials
    Energy

Naturally evolved systems (04, 05)
    Emergence
    Phenotype

Self Assembly (Chapter 06, 07)
    Energy
    Entropy
    Information
    Complexity

Evolution (Life Codes - Chapter 08, 09)
    Genetics
    Variability
    Natural Selection

The real miracle of the emergence of LIFE is that the entire tree of LIFE is connected by links of time (phylogeny) and space (ontogeny), a naturally evolved system (Chapters 04, 05) composed of hierarchically organized (that is, organized according to complexity) interacting, naturally evolved subsystems; their parallel systems; and their environmental systems. And the more we learn about the LIFE system, the more we recognize the elegant intricacy of its interdependent functions that surpass any human creation or comprehension.

Both phylogeny and ontology -- that is the history and development of life as a unit, and the individual development of every individual unit of life -- are sustained largely by processes represented by our fourteen big ideas (words). (And more that we do not yet understand.) This chapter focuses on bringing the big ideas together as a whole system generated by the Laws of Nature that regulate the emergence of LIFE within the Biosystem. See also Appendix D.

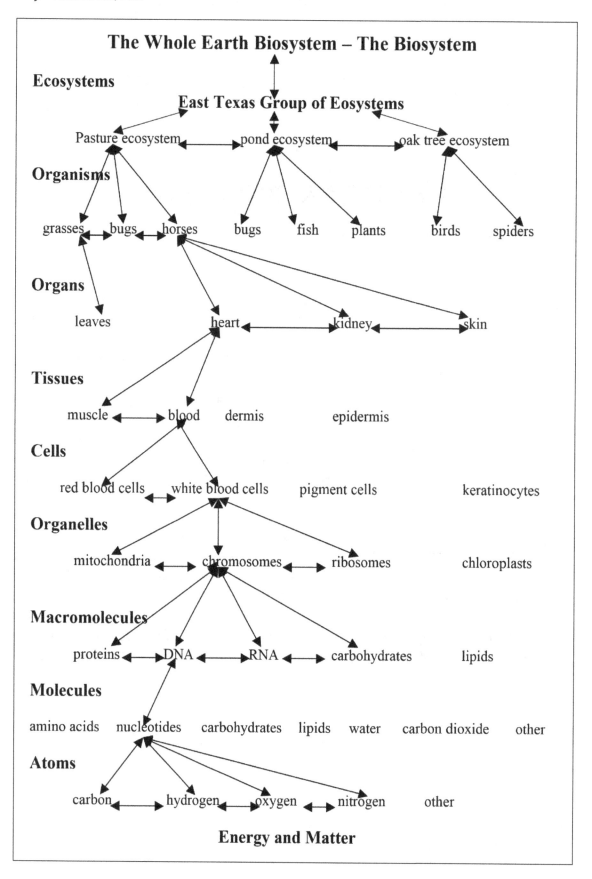

REVIEW

Energy
Entropy
Information
Complexity
Self Assembly

Energy, the ability to do work, operates innately on a range between high to low free energy. Energy cannot be created or destroyed. When I want to think about high free energy with low entropy, I imagine a carbohydrate molecule that is tightly structured with many energy bonds that can be used to do other kinds of work if the energy is diverted to other tasks. People who do not spend time thinking about carbohydrate molecules might better imagine a diamond. Diamonds are made of carbon atoms tightly bonded together, and they do not interact with with other compounds in nature.

Entropy is the natural balance of a process or interaction, on a range between chaos (random behaviors/connections/high entropy) and our tightly ordered, crystalline structure. Carbohydrate, diamond.

Energy and entropy work together naturally. These natural characteristics determine what kinds of natural connections are likely to occur between things. That is, what kinds of "sweet spot" are available by the nature of things.

The level of entropy (amount of chaos) of the partners in an interaction determines how the parts can "self-assemble." Many things do not self-assemble, but if they do have an affinity for each other, then there may (or may not) be a "sweet spot" that describes how they most naturally come together. The relatively most stable state of a given energy/entropy relationship in a given environment, is what I have referred to as its "sweet spot." If the energy or the entropy change, the system can shift into another state, with a different sweet spot and a different way of coming together, with many possible in-between points. Or not. Different combinations have different characteristics. The sweet spot is how the partners interact (if they do) in any given environment. The sweet spot may be different in different environments

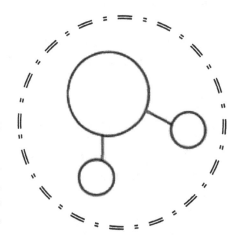

The environment is an equal partner in the energy/entropy relationship. If the environment (or any party to the relationship) changes, the sweet spot may change, and LIFE also uses this property of partnerships to permit important things to happen naturally and save the energy that would be required to *make* them happen. The example we gave in Chapter

06 was of the molecule hemoglobin in the human body that uses two environmentally determined sweet spots to do its two functions. That is, to pick up oxygen in the lungs and then, in a different environment with low levels of oxygen, to drop it off.

The sweet spot depends on interactions among energy, entropy and the naturally evolved environment of the combined *naturally evolved system*. The ways in which they interact can be measured as the *information* (in bits, though that concept is simplistic) that characterizes that interaction, and can be a way of measuring its *complexity.*

The self-assembly (or rejection) relationships among the energy, entropy and environment can apply, at least metaphorically, to naturally evolved link/node relationships at all levels of complex interactions from molecules to organisms to ecosystems. I think of people, whether they like each other a little or a lot, or not. Living things interact, and they interact in specific ways that are determined by their nature.

Self-assembly, then, is the natural formation of link-node relationships. These relationships can be within naturally evolved systems or between them. Links that form within a system connect the "micro-components" (that is, the linked-together parts, components) of the naturally evolved system.

Because naturally evolved systems are also complex-adaptive systems, they have emergent properties (phenotypes, macro-properties). Emergent properties are used by naturally evolved systems to make links (with appropriate sweet spots) between the systems.

Evolution uses the "sweet spots" of organic interactions, to organize the interactions of the Biosystem so that the energy/information flows through the LIFE system from states of high toward low free energy.

**Evolution uses these Natural Interactions
To Sustain the Emergence of LIFE within the Biosystem**

EVOLUTION

> **Genetics
> Variability (including Self-Assembly)
> Natural Selection
> Genetics**

We covered genetics in Chapter 09. Basically, the function of genetics is to preserve the Code of LIFE through time (phylogeny) and use it (in collaboration with the environmental systems) to make the nodes and links that bring the emergence of LIFE to every individual living thing

Variability

Variability means that every naturally evolved system is a wee bit different or a lot different from others, even in the same family. Human systems, for example, differ from each other. This variability is caused by genetics (mutations or different combinations of things) but more so by the variety of interactions between different individuals in the same environments. That is, co-evolution.

Inherited variability is necessary for evolution to happen because:

> If characteristics are not inheritable, then they cannot be passed from one generation to the next in "hard copy"; they would just recombine forever, without causing long-term, directional change; and

> If there were no variability in some population, if everyone were exactly the same as everyone else, then they would inherit the sameness and nothing could permanently change. There could be no natural selection; no evolution.

Most of the variability within species is the result of the normal processes of genetics, including sexual reproduction. Each individual passes on his/her genes to his/her children. In the process, the genes (the DNA code of LIFE) are reshuffled, using sexual reproduction with meiosis (cell division - see your freshman Biology text for the deails) and fertilization of an egg by a sperm. Some people refer to this as recombination. It can be thought of as one kind of self-assembly.

Among different kinds of organisms, many processes contribute to variability, recombination, self-assembly.

Molecules can interact with other molecules in various ways; genes are combined and recombined in different ways in various genetic processes; rarely, cells make new combinations that are able to reproduce, as in the probable origin of the eukaryotic cell from different combinations of prokaryotic cells (Margulis, 1998); and even different species find new ways to work together in more or less the same body, as in the lichens and in human symbiotic "micro-biomes." Micro-biomes are the populations of prokaryotic organisms (bacteria), and other one-celled organisms, that live in the human body and are essential to our health.

Or sometimes, incremental changes over many generations can eventually bring about new capabilities of older systems (wings, legs) that result in the development of new species that have access to new niches and give rise to new species of biological systems.

Anything that is coded in the genetics of an organism can be passed to the children and so into the future. We organisms all have inherited our genomes from an unbroken line of transmission, mixed around a little with every new generation, over four or five billion years, generating the spark of LIFE with every generation. We all are related to each other and to the whole of other living things.

Natural Selection

Using the inherited phenotypes (emergent properties) of the system, natural selection by the environment of each species determines which individuals will pass their genes to the next generation of that species, based on the conditions of the environment at the time of the selection.

If for any reason any naturally evolved LIFE system is not able to pass on its inheritable phenotypes to the next generation, that is natural selection. "Selection against." Survival of the fittest actually means survival of the individual and the species that can do the best job of collaborating with their environment.

Genetics of every "successful" species determines that more babies will be born than can survive in every generation. In normal times, natural selection chooses the best genetic combinations and the others do not contribute to the genome of the next generation.

Limiting Factors in the environment, in normal times determine, which organisms will not pass on their genes. That is, which individuals are selected against. However humans have up to now removed each limiting factor that has threatened to stop the growth of our populations. We believe that is a success story. I believe it is the perfect recipe for widespread misery and suffering. We need to talk about that issue.

Natural selection chooses ("selects for") the best phenotypes and against ("selects against") others. The best emergent properties – best for the existing environment -- are selected for, which means they reproduce and pass on their genes (after being reshuffled by the genetic system) to the next generation.

Evolution chooses the most efficient, collaborative, effective energy/entropy/information link between every system and its environment, at every level, or the best combination of links.

When I say "good" and "bad" and "best," I refer to sustainability. Right now evolution, via genetics, variability and natural selection, is working to eliminate *Homo sapiens* because of our deleterious impact on the Biosystem and its emergent properties. We are not sustainable because we are not contributing to the welfare of the Biosystem, rather we are causing great harm to other species, and so to our own environment.

Evolution

Evolution sustains the LIFE of Earth by perfecting the links (processes) that flow the energy of LIFE through the body of the Biosystem (while at the same time recycling the materials of LIFE), by recognizing and selecting FOR inheritable changes, at any level of organization, that benefit the entire organism, whether the LIFE system be a cell or the whole Biosystem or any level of organization between the two.

Evolution will tend to retain the most appropriately efficient organization of any (and every) interaction -- in the given environment.

Evolution is NOT selection of the "fittest" system as that term is implied within the corposystem. It is not selection against less powerful systems; sometimes less powerful is the most beneficial; evolution of LIFE is selection FOR the COMBINATIONs of systems, at all the levels of LIFE (that is, all the sweet spots of all the systems), that are able to function together at the most viable level of efficiency and other factors involved with viability.

The most useful links survive because they are imprinted in the genetic code, reproduced and regulatd by the nodes (living things) of LIFE, and the combination is passed on to the next generation by natural selection.

That means the links themselves must evolve together, co-evolve – both the phenotype of the system and its receptor in the environment; that is, the ability of the system to make the link and the ability of the environment to recognize the link and respond to it appropriately. (Think of the baby bird crying for food.)

The system and its environment must both participate in any link that forms, and then the response must be appropriate. Therefore, they must evolve together. When the links are firmly established, their functions to some extent protect the complex from entropy.

When links come apart, the entropy of the entire complex may be increased. LIFE begins to fall apart. The second law of thermodynamics then indeed does have its chance to just naturally let the systems fall apart and be lost to LIFE.

How Does Evolution Function?

Stripped to its essence, evolution of LIFE uses variability and the size of the population -- accompanied by natural selection, and applied to genetically inheritable phenotypes/ emergent properties -- to choose the individuals living in today's environment who will contribute their genes to the next generation.

1. Variability, including self-assembly and sexual reproduction, "stirs the pot" of genetics at a very low and stable level, so that every individual is somewhat different from every other, and the information of each is recorded in its genetics.

Actually, of course, not all the information is recorded. For example, scars and most blemishes are not. Only genetic information is passed on to the next generation.

2. Natural selection, including the niche, limiting factors, world views, environmental conflicts, various feedback loops, and other impacts on survivability that we have not discussed (you can research them all), determines which organisms get to pass on their genetic information to the next generation, based upon how well the organisms "get along with" their environments.

3. Genetics preserves the information of those individuals that survive and reproduce. Their genetic information is used in the next following generation to cause LIFE to emerge in every future individual (ontogeny) and over the entire Earth – by turning genes on and off at the right time and in the right place, in collaboration with other LIFE codes and with its environment, all over the entire earth, all at the same time.

4. Any change in a population that is inheritable can contribute to evolution of that population and to other populations with which it interacts.

Consider the Biosystem, tightly linked in all its parts that have (has) evolved over millions or billions of years.

Where did we ever get the idea that we could dictate how we choose to change ourselves in a couple of hundred years while ignoring our own need to sustain our links with our environments?

That kind of change – preventing a system from communicating with its environment -- is how environments get rid of troublesome species. Rather, the environment lets the troublesome species get rid of themselves. The Biosystem, our environment, just carries on, as it must, according to the Laws of God and Nature that we describe with fourteen big words, while we wander off into a wilderness of links and nodes of unnatural technologies of our own making that don't work as well as the original set of links and nodes, thus changing both ourselves and the environment in ways that are not sustainable.

Any system that refuses to support the original flow of energy and information through the Biosystem, that refuses to co-evolve with its environment, DESTROYS ITSELF BY TRYING TO "FIX" or change ITS OWN ENVIRONMENT. That is precisely what we are doing with all or most of our technologies, including the potentially good ones such as permaculture, the internet and the charitable organizations.

We think that we are helping, but in reality (over-all) we are using the technologies to break the ancient links that created us and trying to put them back together in "better" combinations that, however, do not consider their long-term impact on our necessary information exchanges with our environments.

Every generation, because of how its world view grows, believes the time into which it was born is "normal," and unless it is as old as I am it does not see the increasingly rapid toxic changes that are brought about by its own world view.

It won't work.

We humans cannot make organisms that "know" when where and how to do their jobs in a way that enhances the whole of LIFE, and that is what evolution really does require. The last I heard, we were close to making cells, but what good is a cell that is not integrated into the flow of biological relationships? It has no connections with other cells or other species in a way that supports the LIFE of Earth.

That kind of cell cannot survive, and it cannot help LIFE to survive on its own "cutting edge" of efficiency. It simply increases the entropy of the over-all system that requires precise levels of efficiency for specific interactions.

Genetically modified foods, for example, are causing great harm to the Biosystem, not so much because of the nature of the food, though that is also questionable, but more because of how they (the plants and the process of growing them) interact with other species (Crouch, 1990).

For me the greatest miracle of evolution is the way in which it automatically increases or decreases variability depending upon what is most needed. To stir the pot in times of stress; and to sustain, improve, the skill-set in the more quiet times. This can be seen at many levels of LIFE in different sorts of living populations. It is operating right now in our human populations; it operates in the world view code (Chapter 09) and I believe it operates in pollution diseases of many sorts and in our human micro-biome.

During the good times, when the systems are snugly nurturing each other in a consistent environment, they become more strongly linked.

During times of distress or stress, the genetic pot of information – as well as other LIFE codes – the pot is stirred, links break, rearrange themselves or are eliminated, new little ideas come together with the possibility of saving the suffering system. Maybe.

Unfortunately, this kind of change requires many generations of uproar and chaos to find new combinations and recombinations of links and nodes. Billions of years. It is beyond our control.

Right now, our human genetic stew-pot is being vigorously stirred, and if that fails to resurrect a viable human system, then our human system will crash, because there is a limit to what evolution can accomplish in each life time. What we do in this generation will probably make the difference between our survival or our human extinction in the very near future, probably well before the end of this century.

That is why it is so astonishing to me that the majority of people seem to be rejoicing with their unsustainable world views in this time of deep crisis. It reminds me of the flapper generation that ended with the great economic crash of the last century, except this time it is the Biosystem that is now in process of crashing. Along with the corposystem.

We cannot "fix" the Biosystem by propping up the corposystem, as we did with the stock market, because we did not create the Biosystem and we don't really know how it functions. Certainly we are making it worse by expanding our human populations that break more and more links at every generation.

> Think Climate Change, we are responding with technologies. Trying to overpower the symptoms of our overgrowth, by means of technologies, will break more links and make more symptoms and worse symptoms. Of course at this point we have no other viable choice. We must do both – or all – reduce our populations, reduce our impact on the Biosystem, and let the Biosystem begin its recovery before it is too late.

> Think Pandemic, even if we had responded appropriately, its root cause was overpopulation, and we are paying almost no attention to overpopulation. Therefore, it will happen again and worse, as the pollution diseases take hold with no solution available.

> Think Pollution Diseases. We are still pretending they do not exist. Will our populations be reduced by the pollution diseases? Or will we continue our descent into WWIII and reduce the population by means of conflict? Again. The checks and balances of LIFE are intricate and inexorable, but well documented and understood.

> The better choice, our only remaining choice, is to reduce our population with compassion.

Evolution is in charge of sustaining the balance of LIFE, and from the point of view of evolution (if it has one) it is trying to sustain the environment -- not every individual person or other organism in the environment – if it is forced to choose between saving the environment and saving the "fittest" individual, evolution will do the greatest good by saving the environment.

As a generalization, all natural populations produce more offspring than can survive. All of them, including humans.

There is a delicately balanced, apparently genetically controlled relationship between the size of EVERY population of organisms on Earth – all the individuals of every species -- and the niche and feedback mechanisms and other limiting factors in its environment.

You will see that the above scheme – elegant and intricate in every detail – is not what we would prefer that it be. And so we try to save every individual. We would like that every person could survive forever, or at least as long as she wants to survive.

Apparently that is not the will of God for His Creation. At least it is not how The Creation works, and we are assuming that God created the Creation to work the way it works. The Creation will not – can not -- survive human overpopulation (or the overpopulation of any other creature, we are, after all, a part of that system, like it or not).

I speak to God through the reality of The Creation. I do NOT presume to argue with the reality of God's Laws of LIFE. Why, how, who, when is not my affair. It is What IT is (Chapter 01). The reality and the miracle of The Creation.

Our choice now is to fight over it -- or to reduce our own population, as compassionately as possible, in order to avoid the inevitable massive suffering caused by collapse of our unsustainable social system, followed by chaos and the extinction of our species.

God does not destroy The Creation. We do it to ourselves.

And please let us not hear any more of this nonsense that "We didn't know; it was a complete surprise! It's not our fault. We were unprepared!" Etc, etc, etc.

We know how it works; we have expounded The Laws of the Creation and predicted the end points; get prepared now!

It is true that we didn't listen. For one, we refused to listen to me, and I am certainly not the only one. And, without listening, we made a plethora of excuses – I once made a list of all the excuses I ran across -- to look away from at the reality. To ignore it as though it doesn't matter.

In reality, our human overpopulation event is unfolding exactly as has been predicted since before I was born, and I have been talking about it for more than half of my life, as have a lot of other people. Where have you been?

Evolution - Implications

Every time we use our technologies to break the evolved links between ourselves and our environment – which we do every day in many ways, for example driving to the store and buying groceries in small quantities, packaged in plastic – we are forcing the Biosystem to change itself in order to survive. Because every sweet spot of every subsystem must now find a new sweet spot, as its own environment is forced to change. That is climate change.

Evolution (right now, seen as climate change and the pandemic) is necessary because we have forced the conditions to change – the car, the plastic, the supermarket system -- the changes of the conditions cause changes in all the systems, and each of those changes causes changes in other sweet spots of other systems. And all this adjustment requires many generations of all the organisms – ultimately the entire Biosystem -- if it is possible.

If the Biosystem can adapt, and if it contains the variability that is required for natural selection, then it will evolve. And if it cannot evolve, perhaps because the changes happen faster than it can respond, or there is not enough food to put IN those little plastic containers, it will crash as surely as any Ponzi scheme.

Evolution is not adaptation. Adaptation can change back again. Evolution is forever.

And your new President *cannot change these laws of nature, no matter how pitifully you beg him to.*

But he could start to talk about them and explain to the people what we could be doing to save ourselves.

When I slip over into poetical political thinking, I can imagine evolution of the sweet spots at all the levels of LIFE: sweet spots of molecular actions and interactions inside of cells; sweet spots of behavioral interactions between organisms (for the fun of it, think of teenage courtship rituals); sweet spots of ecosystems adjusting to change. Sweet spots of all the citizens talking to each other about our Problem (Appendix A) and how we will all work together to fix it while at the same time helping the sweet spots to sustain themselves – with long-term compassion for the welfare of our species within the Biosystem.

I think of climate change as the effort of our Biosystem to adapt itself to a new overall sweet spot. And because we have destroyed the old one – it is not there anymore. We can't go home again. But at the same time we are reducing the population, we have great compassion for the entire Biosystem and all sentient beings. We help each other over the tough times coming and we help the Biosystem and all sentient beings TO BE WHAT THEY ARE – in service to the whole – not just in service to us.

If we could find just the basics of wise compassion for it all, we might be able to help us all survive within a new and compatible Biosystem environment. Try again to grow a richly productive code of LIFE that is based at its root on wise community and is able to sustain the root all the way to the fruits of its collaborative LIFE style to the end of its time.

Whatever that may be.

Does that sound a bit spiritual to you? It does to me, except that I use biological terminology.

Fourteen Big Words – Implications

If you have gotten this far, you already have way more information than you need to interact respectfully and collaboratively with the processes of the Biosystem.

These are difficult concepts, at least the interactions are, because so many variables are involved, but that is the reality of LIFE. Without that complexity the processes of entropy would indeed overwhelm the emergent properties of LIFE.

However, the ancients understood our Problem, perhaps better than we do, without taking a class in physics; good farmers also understand (Jacke & Toensmeier, 2015a and b), as do many or most of our religions and some of our authors (Antal, 2018; Denkmal, 2009; Diamond, 1997, 2011; Dowd, 2007; duBoys, 2011; Emmott, 2013; Everett, 2017; Loy, 2018; Spring, 1996; Trioir A Films, 2011).

Fortunately, we do not need to understand the details of how the Biosystem functions in order to recognize that we must adapt ourselves to the requirements of the Biosystem. That we are more than likely to blink out the emergence of present-day LIFE if we insist upon trying to make the Biosystem jump to our tune. That the whole of the Biosystem has a physiology in the same way that we do, and like us it must adapt to the reality of its own physiological change -- or it can die.

All we really need -- to understand the most basic fact of LIFE -- is to recognize that naturally evolved systems communicate with each other because they need each other. And nothing could be more obvious.

So if we don't need all these big Words/Ideas, Why are we Using Them?

We are discussing the big words with their big ideas, because we need them to answer the fake debates of the corposystem propaganda mill, because if the corposystem can win a debate, right or wrong, relevant or not, it will simply try harder to do what it has always done – to cure the problems it has caused, using the same thinking that caused the problems.

That won't work.

Because we do need to discuss the FACTS of LIFE that we cannot change so that we can answer the corposystem mantra of infinite growth-by-domination, not only with the observation that neither growth nor domination has ever worked in human history for longer than a few generations before the population hit another limiting factor – and to continue by explaining WHY growth by domination does not work.

Why?

Because the emergence of LIFE is based on sustaining the *collaborative BALANCE* among the naturally evolved systems of the Biosystem using communally beneficial interactions. Because neither domination nor growth can be balanced indefinitely.

LIFE is based upon the ability of naturally evolved systems to:

1. maintain themselves by interacting with their environments;
2. reproduce themselves as a component of their environments;
3. co-evolve over time compatibly with their environments;
4. sustain a higher-than-nonliving level of efficiency;
5. sustain the viable balance among all their naturally evolved subsystems (Chapter 06).
6. that can communicate among themselves, using many different types of LIFE codes. (Chapter 09)

From page one, I have stressed the factual nature of the *balanced* interactions among the *materials* and *energy* of which the universe (and spectacularly, the emergent property of LIFE) are composed; Chapters 02 and 03 and Appendix A describe their biological relationships to our major problems of today.

In Chapters 04 and 05 we describe *Naturally Evolved Systems*.

In Chapters 06 and 07, we *"assembled" energy, entropy* and the environment to generate the *complexity* of our *information* as an emergent output of energy enabled by entropy, and function enabled by structure.

We don't really need to say more than that. However, we did.

In Chapters 09 and this Chapter 10, we are using that information to put all that information together in its interactions – to intellectually imagine how evolution sustains the ongoing emergence of LIFE.

The sweet spot of each interaction, combined with its receptor, acting together, dictate the links of LIFE. Every sweet spot is necessary to the whole – each is different from the others, all together they range from the highest form of biological energy input to the lowest form of biological energy output in such a way that the energy flows itself (with the essential help of the structural information) through the LIFE system.

The "nodes" of LIFE are necessary to direct the flow of energy/information through the "links" of LIFE.

The links of LIFE, the complexity of the links, are/is necessary to bring together and sustain the various processes that must interact; otherwise the Biosystem would all fall apart into chaos, and without all those connections The Earth, like all those other planets, would carry on spinning around in space, but, like Mars, or the moon, there would be no LIFE emerging.

The essential integrative functions – what is necessary to bring together the information of LIFE so that every thing happens at the right time and place during ontogeny – is communication among the systems. Evolution stitches the links together and sustains and distributes their flow of energy and information, using the codes of LIFE.

In principle, the codes of LIFE are necessary to transmit (distribute) the information of LIFE so that all its parts are able to function appropriately: at the right time in the right place in space (ontogeny) and time (phylogeny).

In practice, the codes of LIFE are organized by evolution, for every sweet spot (every link/node/environment interaction) individually -- and as a whole biotic system.

This fact is my miracle. It is too complex to describe in writing, and if you have gotten this far, congratulations. But there is no need for us to understand it, so long as we know enough to defend it and honor it with our behaviors. DO something about it.

DO WHAT? We all ask.

The solution is to rebalance *ourselves* within the whole Biosystem.

The solution is to stop spinning our energy into physical and biological and technological fairy tales and START TALKING AMONG OURSELVES ABOUT THE REAL PROBLEM.

To even begin rebalancing, we need to stop throwing around human memes, as though they were the whole story. We must steep ourselves in good information – we need to begin relevant, collaborative discussion within our supportive communities, such as family, church groups, fraternities, etc.

We all know that the alphabet and the numbers – and no doubt the lists of vitamins and wiring diagrams and the like are essential to our modern education. However, we also need both the liberal arts version and the basic science version of human problem-solving skills, and both versions require discussion among ourselves; not head-bashing. Not rote memory, outdated, so-called solutions.

The solution to a problem is to first understand the problem. Or the problem will just keep on getting worse -- whatever we do.

> "If you want to get rid of painful effects, you have to get rid of their causes."
> Wisdom is: "analyzing the facts and discerning the actual situation."
> (His Holiness The Dalai Lama, 2009)

Our only viable solution will be, if we ever get serious about actually fixing our Problem, to challenge our own personal world views. Educate ourselves. I give you a remarkable body of knowledge in the References section that follows Chapter 11. A university of information, and more, is waiting there for you.

Our culture is rich with information and it is information that tells the energy what to do! But running off in all directions at the same time will not solve our Problem, and we do know what the Problem is. And the solution. We just don't yet know how to accomplish the solution, SO THAT IS WHAT WE SHOULD BE DISCUSSING.

In a biological social group, such as the corposystem or your church or your family, the power is with the group, not with your personal expertise; and if we do not share and sharpen and fact-check the information available to the group, then we abandon our group power to its individual leaders (Janeway, 1981).

Which is, of course, exactly what some of our leaders want us to do.

Or to the power of evolution.

> **Reality Number Nine** – *As citizen activists, we should learn the rules before we try to fix the game (Chapter 02).*

OOOOOOOO

This chapter is dedicated to Erica Elliott and Sylvie Eyrval.

"Many others before Darwin had suggested that all life on earth was interrelated. Darwin's revolutionary insight was to perceive the mechanism that brought these changes about. By doing so, he replaced a philosophical speculation with a detailed description of a process, supported by an abundance of evidence, that could be tested and verified, and the reality of evolution could no longer be denied."
(Attenborough, 1979, and please do watch the PBS videos
that are narrated by Dr. Attenborough)

"I realized that I had to change
my world view.
But how do I do that?"
(Feldman, 2018)

"One life, serving all beings."
(Kaza and Kraft, 2000)

CHAPTER 11

LIFE

My first biology book was a fine, fat 940-page "Handbook of Nature Study" that was published "for teachers and parents" by Cornell University in 1921. It describes the whole of our living environment including its non-living components ("Geology"). It is illustrated with hand drawings of children, decked out in pinafore and short pants, rather like the Alice in Wonderland prints or Christopher Robin as portrayed in the early British children's books. Not like today's nature books, or even the first "nature-study" photo books (for example, The Encyclopedia Brittanica True Nature Series, in the 1940's; Walt Disney's Living Desert, 1954; and certainly not like our more accurate, up-to-date nature series and documentaries on TV – notably the BBC series narrated by David Attenborough) that I so loved and still do.

I definitely planned to be a wildlife photographer for Disney nature movies, but by the time I was old enough Disney stopped making them. I still have some film of a marten somewhere that I photographed for practice in Yosemite National Park; I hope y'all don't trash that wonderful place. It was the only time I ever came face to face with a Marten. A gorgeous creature. I was so excited that I nearly forgot which buttons to push on the 16 mm movie camera.

The "Handbook of Nature Study" may have been more realistic than either today's science or my daydreams, in the sense that it presented a holistic view of the basic science of the day, rather than today's more popular reductionist, technological view of LIFE.

By 1953, my university textbook was dry, precise, and focused on structure/function relationships in anatomy, physiology, embryology and genetics; very technical, heavy with terminology and precise descriptions, definitions and hand drawn pictures of biological structures: leaves, internal organs, teeth. By that time, the definition of LIFE was something like: "LIFE has the ability to replicate itself," which is a description rather than a proper definition (Chapter 03). We knew it; we thought learning more about the reductionist details of LIFE would eventually lead us to a complete definition of LIFE. We didn't understand the connectedness of naturally evolved systems. We did not understand that the natural world is based on an interacting flow of communication so much more elegant than our human books, movies or documentaries.

My first biology professor back then did not have a clear understanding of how LIFE maintains itself through time and space. He followed that reductionist text in describing living things as more or less separate from each other. He described the universe and the Earth as background, as though LIFE were an autonomous phenomenon that was popped onto a pre-existing ball of Earth, rather than an ongoing interactive deep-time collaboration within a universe that, from the time of its origin (presumably in the big bang, see appendix E) has consistently increased both in complexity and in entropy. (Lloyd, Seth. 2016. Lecture One at Santa Fe Institute).

https://www.youtube.com/watch?v=5He7bYM7beM&list=PLZIVBTf7N6Gp1GlndwLny S44OqJoRphOK&index=1

By the 1970's, Margulis and Lovelock (1978); and Odum (1971); and others, were describing emergent properties (see the discussion of systems in Appendix B), systemic interactions and levels of complexity of LIFE, not necessarily using those terms.

By 1975 I was teaching from the college freshman Biology textbook by Curtis, my favorite. It had the perception to say that: "Life does not exist in the abstract," on the page that described the mystery of "emergent properties."

I spent a great deal of brain energy trying to understand what she (Curtis) meant by that statement, until now I claim with some confidence that: "LIFE is an emergent property," and with that insight I began to arrange our science into a world view that is more realistic, fact based and relevant to today's social issues than the one I was taught more than half a century ago.

For a time after that, most of the biology texts descended into a liberal-arts descriptive approach to science, emphasizing the individual parts of the LIFE system as though they were separate and equal, rather than collective and individual, and providing a plethora of what we now know to be irrelevant (but very profitable) metaphors. And then, as we left the 20st century, the physicists and mathematicians got their teeth into complexity and systems analysis, so now we are beginning to understand the work initiated by Margulis,

Lovelock, Odum, in the 70's, and others, as we reflected on the "earthrise" image that nearly everyone understood at gut level with our first gasp of recognition.

LIFE has taken its place in the cosmos as one of the great miracles of The Creation (Smith, 2001), and it has flourished, specialized and diversified, until now the whole earth is our one big blue emergent living marvel.

> "Every single part of the Earth reacts with every other part.
> It's one thing. . .
> If I could get every Earthling to do one circle of the Earth,
> I think things would run a little differently."

> Astronaut Karen Nyberg, IN: Beyond the Blue Marble, by Nadia Drake, beautiful photographs by Martin Schoeller, National Geographic, March, 2018.

They won't get me inside that capsule, but that is what we now need, in this time of multiple human and biological crises. A fact-based path toward the reality of how the Biosystem sustains LIFE, so that we can align our spiritual understandings with the basic science; our technologies with the true needs of our suffering Earth system; and the spiritual wisdom of our ancestors with the reality of our biology.

It is time for us to stop quibbling over the trivia of LIFE and align ourselves in a meaningful way with its realities (Antal, 2018; Armstrong, 2009, 2014 and others; Campbell, 1986; The Dalai Lama *et al.*, 2016; Smith, 1976; 2001), and when we do this, the spiritual and the religious can help to guide the technological; the bare facts can help us understand the philosophies; the beauty of LIFE can help us appreciate the necessary logic of the facts of LIFE; and the Facts of LIFE can illuminate the spiritual so that we can face our own future with a common goal to:

> *help grow a future with wise compassion within a Biosystem that blooms*
> *again with LIFE.*

LIFE is not a human power trip at any of those levels of understanding; it is an emergent property; we are responsible to maintain it, not to usurp its power, as if we could. We have known the answers all along. Now we need to align our education, especially our technologies, with our responsibility to the future, and align our behaviors with ordinary human kindness. Wise compassion is compassion only when it makes a sincere effort to consider the probable future implications of its own behaviors.

Many people are deeply committed to one opinion or another about how LIFE got here on Earth, some people cannot tolerate not knowing and instead of drawing on their faith, they choose to fight or argue over their opinions. It takes a higher level of courage – and faith -- to recognize that we simply do not know very much about LIFE.

But in fact we don't know, and can never know all the details of how exactly LIFE got here or how exactly it functions to maintain itself and us, and that realization is one of the ultimate realities with which we all must cope.

> **Reality Number Twenty-Five** - *It does not matter how we got here; what matters is how we behave, and how we treat the other sentient beings that already were here, now that we are here (Chapter 11).*

Fighting, arguing, debating, does not and never will change the facts of LIFE or the real facts of history. Humankind cannot know everything; therefore we cannot control everything, and that is a good thing. What we do now know can help us catch sight of the true relationships of LIFE and their meanings for humans, who are not its CEO, but only the caretaker.

The first cells may have been popped into an inorganic environment of Earth, all those billions of years ago (see the timeline in Appendix E). I wasn't there; but I suspect LIFE arose *in situ*, beginning with interactions among the nonliving parts, until the "breath of LIFE" - - - we are not omniscient and we could use a little humility, because we don't really know the details; neither our science nor our religions know; and it is better that we do not, because someone would surely use the information to enhance the destruction of our human/environmental complex.

The fundamental requirements for LIFE of the Biosystem have not changed, of course. We described a good many of them in Chapters 04, 05 and 06 and (Barlow, 1991; Feldman, 2018; Lovelock, 1988, 2009; Margulis, 1998; Nyberg, 2018; Sagan C, 1996; Sagan D & Feldman, 2018; Smith, 1976, 2001) every part communicating (more or less emphatically) with the other parts at all times, from at least two miles underground, to the satellites hovering above. The LIFE of Earth is an emergent property of the whole naturally evolved Biosystem. It is, to us, a miracle.

Some people still disagree with this concept (Schneider *et al.*, 2004), but in fact it does not matter what we believe, because there is no reason to argue about the universal facts of LIFE, because we can't change them -- or the origin of LIFE, because we can't know.

What we need to understand is the nature of LIFE, and ITs needs, and more importantly our place in IT, and the only reason we need to know that is so that we can collaborate in nurturing the rich productivity of the miracle. For its own sake and ours, not to cause harm to other people or to the miracle Itself. Not to make money.

It seems that we want to know LIFE more intimately, not so much the details of muscles, bones and cells and how they work together to cause an arm to bend or an eye to see, as to understand, perhaps, Who it is.

But the fact is clear that neither the Biosystem nor LIFE, its major emergent property, is human, and we would be better off trying to understand the holistic glory of the Biosystem, as it is, not what we wish it were in our fuzzy-bunny dreams of human dominance.

And that could be a description of the basic science (not technology) of Biology, if we were willing to listen to the reality. Basic biology, the study of LIFE using the scientific method, is one of the best ways to learn about the fact-based reality within which we spend our own lives. And we are doing this. Especially in the past century or so, we humans, using our naturally evolved corposystem, have gathered an immense body of data about the detailed functions of the biological miracle.

Unfortunately, we have mostly used this reductionist information to generate self-serving technologies that are fun and useful for humans and harmful to the Biosystem. In so doing, we have seriously disturbed our relationships with the whole of LIFE and generated great suffering at a time when we could have been folding our reductionist biological science into its holistic, emergent reality and using both to further embed ourselves within the collaborative processes of the Biosystem with a goal to the welfare of others indefinitely into the future. Each life serving LIFE.

At the same time that we have mis-used the power of science, we have also re-interpreted it, using all sorts of other disciplines, from the humanities to the technologies, that are not basic science.

This effort to clarify the science by re-interpreting it, though well meant, unfortunately adds to our mis-understandings by blurring the realities of all the disciplines -- both the fine art of being positively human, and the unchangeable factual realities of the basic science, and most of all the potential positive uses of technology, leaving the majority of people, or so it seems, confused and unable to sort out the cause-and-effect realities.

For example, in our corposystem world view, LIFE systems are compared with technologies, as though the systems of LIFE were copied from our human drawing board, rather than the other way around.

We have modified the biology texts to fit inside a humanities frame, as though LIFE were a child of the humanities, rather than its source, rather than broaden the reductionist science to encompass and illuminate its emergent realities.

Do we forget that our humanity is born from our human biology? Yes, we often do, and to the extent that this approach to education prevents us from understanding the reality of universal facts, it teaches a false and therefore harmfully homocentric world view.

Some "creationist" world views explain the complexity of living systems using the argument that: "If you saw a watch lying on the ground, you would have to believe in a watchmaker."

I do not see a simple watchmaker in the patterns of LIFE. I believe it is presumptuous human *hubris* to pattern God or The Creation after a human technologist, a watchmaker: and the tree of LIFE (or any part of it) after a human technology. To the contrary; human technologies are crudely patterned after what little we know about LIFE (Principe, 2006).

And no, I am not dissing the humanities, nor our religions, nor even technology. It is how we use our basic science and our technologies that makes all the difference, and for that we definitely need to pay more attention to our religions and our humanity and recognize that our human technologies disturb the balance of the Biosystem that is their source.

In my day, all university undergraduates were required to study two full years of humanities subjects, before they were permitted to take science courses. I think that was an excellent plan. Science is more useful when it is approached as science and not disguised as something else, and if it is not to be useful to humans, rather is used in harmful ways, then what's the point of that? If humans are special for a Godly reason – our big brain and our handy hands, our emergent properties -- of course we are special – then we are special for a reason, and that reason is NOT to destroy the emergent LIFE of Earth. That is not a reason for our creation – it is choice that we make independent of reason. The Creation itself, the emergent reality, is the miracle that we are dissing.

And ourselves with it.

Earthrise, courtesy of NASA

OOOOOOOO

To LIFE

"There are some things in the world we can't change – gravity, entropy, the speed of light, and our biological nature that requires clean air, clean water, clean soil, clean energy and biodiversity for our health and well being. Protecting the biosphere should be our highest priority or else we sicken and die. Other things. Like capitalism, free enterprise, the economy, currency, the market, are not forces of nature. We invented them. They are not immutable and we can change them. It makes no sense to elevate economics above the biosphere."
(From the web, attributed to David Suzuki)

"To conserve (anurak) nature (thamachat) therefore translates as having at the core of one's very being the quality of empathetic caring for all things in the world in their natural conditions; that is to say, to care for them as they really are rather than as I might benefit from them or as I might like them to be."

". . . the ontological realization of interdependent co-arising."
(Donald K Swearer, 1997)

SELECTED REFERENCES

I have made an effort, when choosing references around basic science, to select secondary sources, that is, not the original technical research "papers," but good information intended for the general public. I have also referenced The Great Courses, which are university-level courses straight from the instructors' mouths. I referenced only a few technical research publications from the scientific literature where these are relevant and important and are perhaps not available to the general public. And of course people who are especially interested in the sources of any of these can fact-check their questions by following the reference trails to their sources.

I have tried to select authors, whether or not their works are "easy to understand," who are well-informed, well educated within their specialties, and "translating" information from their specialties, rather than spewing propaganda that may not be true. Certainly, I have not included all such references, as there are many, and my goal is to describe the logic of a world view that could be used to grow a *viable human presence on a fruitful earth* -- something that our current human corposystem world view cannot accomplish.

I am not interested in debating facts, but in describing a viable world view that is firmly based in fact. The facts are the same for everyone. There is nothing to debate, unless your references or your interpretation of the same facts are better than mine.

I have not included or for the most part have not referred to any activism that I believe to be innately destructive. These are also abundant, and they of course need to be discussed, but the discussion must have its base aligned with facts: both the facts of science and the facts of accurate history, if we are to evolve a viable future. I have focused on the facts and their implications.

One of our most pressing needs is public conversation and discussion around the Facts of LIFE. Therefore, this book tends to be a bit intellectual toward the end. Because LIFE is complicated and ordinary words are not always quite up to the task. However, I hope it is clear in every chapter from beginning to end that my theme is the way in which LIFE is embedded in and different from non-LIFE, and we humans are embedded equally within the Facts of LIFE.

207

Much of the world view described in this book is metaphorical, because you and I are not in a position to talk about it mathematically: and I doubt if mathematics is up to the task of describing LIFE anyhow. But I do not deal in fairy tales. Just this morning I saw a corposystem advertisement claiming that "our dreams are more powerful than the pandemic." This is complete nonsense.

We can not dream our way out of real problems; it requires informed action to resolve real problems. But our children of today have grown up believing that our technologies are more powerful than the biological reality; that we can eliminate disease and death; that if we just try a little harder we can be the gods we believe ourselves to be. Most people know this is not true, about being gods, but in fact most people behave as though it were true. The reality is that our behaviors now will determine if humans survive within LIFE, and we are long past the time when we could dream a future into LIFE itself. The Biosystem has run out of resources for homocentric corposystem headgames. Humans are not at the center of the Earth or of LIFE.

The Teaching Company DVD courses that I studied for this book include:

-Carroll, Sean. 2015. The Higgs Boson and Beyond, The Great Courses; course number 1205.

-Gates, S. James, Jr. 2006. Superstring Theory. The Great Courses; course number 1284.

-Gimbel, Steven. 2015. Redefining Reality: The Intellectual Implications of Modern Science. The Great Courses; course number 4140.

-Grossman, Jefferey C. 2014. Thermodynamics: Four Laws that Move the Universe. The Great Courses; course number 1291.
     This course guidebook is particularly helpful.

-Hazen, Steven. 2001. The Joy of Science. The Great Courses, course number 1100.
     This course, together with Sutherland, 2013, and Strauss, 2009, and a good Biology Text, such as the latest edition of Curtis or Freeman, would add up to a good broad education in basic science with emphasis in evolutionary and ecological biology.

-Martin, Anthony & John Hawks. 2010. Major Transitions in Evolution. The Great Courses,

-McWhorter, John. 2004. The Story of Human Language. The Teaching Company, course number 1600.

-Page, Scott E. 2009. Understanding Complexity. The Teaching Company, The Great Courses, course #5181.
     This one is especially helpful.

-Principe, Lawrence M. 2006. Science and Religion. The Great Courses; course number 4691.

-Roberto, Michael A. 2009. The Art of Critical Decision Making. The Great Courses, course number 5932

-Schumacher, Benjamin. 2009. Quantum Mechanics. The Great Courses; course number 1240

-Schumacher, Benjamin. 2015. The Science of Information. The Great Courses, course number 1301.

-Starbird, Michael. 2001. Change and Motion. The Great Courses; course number 177.

-Strauss, Eric G. 2009. Earth at the Crossroads. The Great Courses; course number 1720

-Strogatz, Steven. 2008. Chaos. The Great Courses; course number 1333.

-Sutherland, Stuart. 2013. A New History of Life. The Great Courses; course Number 1520. This course, together with Hazen, 2001, and Strauss, 2009, and a good Biology Text, such as the latest edition of Curtis or Freeman would add up to a good broad education in basic science with emphasis in evolutionary and ecological biology.

-Tyson, Neil deGrasse. 2012. The Inexplicable Universe. The Great Courses; course number 1816

-Wolfson, Richard. 2007. Earth's Changing Climate. The Great Courses; course number 1219.

College Freshman Biology Text Books

-Curtis, Helena *et al*. 2018. Invitation to Biology.
    My favorite version was 1979, third edition. A lot has happened since then, but the facts of Biology have not changed.
        This text is also available in Spanish.

-Freeman, Scott *et al*. 2019. Biological Science. Pearson.

Other References

- Antal, Jim. 2018. Climate Church Climate World: How people of faith must work for change. Rowman & Littlefield Publishers.

- Armstrong, Karen. 2009. The Case for God. Alfred A. Knopf.
   2014. Fields of Blood. Random House
      And other good, well researched, books on related topics.

- Asselin, Mathieu. 2017. Montsanto©: A Photographic Investigation.
   www.verlag-kettler.com

- Attenborough, David. 1979. Life on Earth. Little, Brown and Company.

- Attenborough, David (narrator). 2007. Planet Earth. BBC Worldwide, Ltd. (DVDs)
   2011. Frozen Planet. BBC Worldwide, Ltd. (DVDs)

- Atwood, Margaret. 2019. The Testaments. First Anchor Books Edition.

- Baker-Laporte, Paula, Erica Elliott and John Banta. 2008. Prescriptions for a Healthy House. New Society Publishers.

- Barlow, Connie (ed). 1991. From Gaia to Selfish genes. MIT Press

- Barabasi, Albert-Laszlo. 2003. Linked. Plume.

- Bartlet, Albert A. 2012. https://www.youtube.com/watch?v=sl1C9Dyli_8

- BBC. 2007. Planet Earth. BBC Worldwide, Ltd. (DVDs)
   2011. Frozen Planet. BBC Worldwide, Ltd. (DVDs)
      2020. Civilization.

- Bateson, Gregory. See Hoffmeyer. Also see Tonnessen, and the below.

- Bateson, Nora. 2010. An Ecology of Mind. DVD. BullFrog Films.com
   Also see https://norabateson.wordpress.com

- Berne, Eric. 1961. Transactional Analysis in Psychotherapy. Ballantine Books.
   1964. Games People Play. Grove Press, Inc.

- Berry, Wendell. 1990. What are People For? Counterpoint.
   1992. Sex, Economy, Freedom and Community. Pantheon Books.
      And many other elegant commentaries.

- Black Elk, Nicholas. 1932. Black Elk Speaks. Told through John G. Neihardt, University of Nebraska Press.

- Brown, Lester R. 2004. Outgrowing the Earth. W. W. Norton & Co.
  2008. Plan B 3.0. W. W. Norton & Co.
  2012. Full Planet; Empty Plates. W. W. Norton & Co.
  Dr. Brown kept meticulous statistics on these subjects for over half a century, and frequently consulted with political and industrial leaders.

- Bryson, Bill. 2002. African Diary. Broadway Books.
  2003. A Short History of Nearly Everything. Broadway Books.

- Butler, Tom (ed). 2015. Overdevelopment, Overpopulation, Overshoot. Goff Books (An exceptionally nice book made available to the Chama Library by www.Population Connection.org, and on display next to Audubon's beautiful birds.)

- Campbell, Joseph. 1972. Myths to Live By. Viking Press.
  1976. The Masks of God. Viking Penguin
  1986. The Inner Reaches of Outer Space. Harper & Row
  2011. Mythos. Joseph Campbell Foundation. JCF.org. DVD
  The web site of the Joseph Campbell Foundation is http//www.JCF.org

- Campbell, Joseph and Bill Moyers. 1999. The Power of Myth. PBS. DVD.
  A fine introduction to Joseph Campbell and his many books.

- Capra, Fritjof and Pier Luigi Luisi. 2014. The Systems View of Life. Cambridge University Press.

- Carroll, Sean. 2015. The Higgs Boson and Beyond, The Great Courses, course number 1411.

- Carson, Rachel. 1962. Silent Spring. Houghton Mifflin Company.

- Catton, William R. 1982. Overshoot: The Ecological Basis of Revolutionary Change. University of Illinois Press.

- Chacour, Ilias. 1984. Blood Brothers, Chosen Books/Zondervan Corp.

- Chodron, Pema. 2007. Practicing Peace in Times of War. Shambala Publications

- Chogyam Trungpa. 1973. Cutting Through Spiritual Materialism. Shambala Classics.

- Craven, Greg. 2009. What's the Worst that Could Happen: A Rational response to the climate change debate. A Perigree Book.

- Crouch, Martha L. 1990. Debating the Responsibilities of Plant Scientists in the Decade of the Environment. The Plant Cell, vol. 2:275-277.

- Cullis-Suzuki, Severn, 1992. https://www.youtube.com/watch?v=oJJGuIZVfLM

- Daly (GynEcology, 300-31); Eisler 1989, chapter 7

- Darwin – https://en.wikipedia.org/wiki/Chales_Darwin.

- Darwin, Charles and E. O. Wilson. 2005. From so Simple a Beginning: Darwin's Four Great Books.

- Dear, John. 2008. A Persistent Peace. Loyola Press.
    2013. The Nonviolent Life. Pace e Bene Press

- deBuys, William. 2011. A Great Aridness; Climate Change and the Future of the American Southwest. Oxford University Press.

- Denkmal Film. 2009. Percy Schmeizer – David Versus Montsanto. DVD. www.denkmalfilm.com.

- Diamond, Jared. 1997. Guns, Germs and Steel: The Fates of Human Societies. W.W.Norton & Co.
    2011. Collapse: How Societies Choose to Fail or Succeed. Penguin Books.

- Disney, Walt. 1955. Vanishing Prairie. Simon and Schuster
    "We are snatching a dwindling opportunity to record on film—and here in book form—a kind of native American life which within two human generations has been all but crowded out of existence." (Walt Disney)

- Douthwaite, Richard. 1999. The Growth Illusion. New Society Publishers.

- Dowd, Michael. 2007. Thank God for Evolution. Plume
    2007. https://youtu.be/IrkQUGUKa64

- Dunning-Kruger effect. https://en.wikipedia.org/wiki/Dunning%E2%80%93Kruger_effect

- Eagleman, David. 2015. The Brain; The Story of You. Vintage

- Easwaren, Eknath. 1984. Love Never Faileth. Nilgiri Press.
    1991. God Makes the Rivers to Flow. Nilgiri Press.

- Ehrlich, Paul R. and Anne H. Ehrlich. 1996. Betrayal of Science and Reason. Island Press.

- Eisler, Riane. 1987. The Chalice and the Blade. Harper Collins.

- Emmott, Stephen. 2013. Ten Billion. Vintage Books. (LL)

- Evans, Jerry. 2014. Chemical and Electrical Hypersensitivity. McFarland & Co,, Inc.
  2019. The Healthy House Quest. www.TurquiseRose.com

- Everett, Caleb. 2017. Numbers and the Making of Us. Harvard University Press.

- Feldman, John. 2018. Symbiotic Earth; How Lynn Margulis rocked the boat and started a scientific revolution. Hummingbird Films. DVD.

- Gates, S. James, Jr. 2006. Superstring Theory. The Great Courses; course number 1284.

- Gell-Mann, Murray, Nobel Prizewinner, The Quark and the Jaguar, 1994. A.W.H.Freeman/ Holt Paperback.
  This fine, authoritative, and challenging book, written by a Nobel Prize winner, is available at the Chama Library.

- Gere, Richard. 2020. Narrator. Https://feedbackloopsclimate.com/

- Gimbel, Steven. 2015. Redefining Reality: The Intellectual Implications of Modern Science. The Great Courses; course number 4140.

- Gladwell, Malcolm. 2011. Outliers. Back Bay Books.

- Goldsmith, Edward. 1981. Thermodynamics or Ecodynamics? The Ecologist: vol. 11 No.4, July-August.
  An important work before its time.

- Goodall, Jane. 2010. 50 Years at Gombe. Abrams
  Goodall, Jane with Phillip Berman. 2000. Reason for Hope: A Spiritual Journey. Warner Books.

- Goodenough, Ursula. 1998. The Sacred Depths of Nature. Oxford University Press.

- Gorschkov, V. V., V. G. Gorshkov, V. I. Danilov-Danil'yan, K. S. Losev and A. M. Makar'eva. 2002. Information in the Animate and Inanimate Worlds. Russian Journal of Ecology, Vol. 33 No. 3: p155.
  Another important work similar to Goldsmith.

- Gore, Al. 2006. An Inconvenient Truth. Rodale. (LL)
  2017. Truth to Power; An Inconvenient Sequel. Rodale (LL)
  The videos, on DVD, and the audiobooks, are also excellent.

- Green, Nancy Sokol. 1991. Poisoning our Children; Surviving in a Toxic World. The Noble Press.

- Greer, John Michael. 2011. The Wealth of Nature. Economics as if survival mattered. New Society Publishers.
  2015. After Progress. New Society Publishers.
  2016. Dark Age America. New Society Publishers.
  And others.

- Grigg, Russell. 2010. Creation 32(4):52–54—October 2010.

- Grossman, Jefferey C. 2014. Thermodynamics: Four Laws that Move the Universe. The Great Courses; course number 1291.
  The Course Guidebook is particularly helpful.

- Gulen, M. Fethulla. 2011. Essentials of the Islamic Faith. Tuhra Books.

- Harris, Thomas A., MD. 1967. I'm OK--You're OK. Avon Books.

- Hartmann, Thom. 1998. The Last Hours of Ancient Sunlight: The Fate of the World and What We Can Do Before it's Too Late. Three Press.
  2007. Cracking the Code. Barrett Koehler Publishers. And others

- Hawking, Stephen. 2011. A Brief History of Time, and The Universe in a Nutshell. Bantam Books.

- Hazen, Steven. 2001. The Joy of Science. The Great Courses, course number 1100.

- Hedberg, Trevor. 2020. The Environmental Impact of Overpopulation: The ethics of procreation. Routledge.

- Heinberg, Richard. 2007. Peak Everything. New Society Publishers.

- Heinberg, Richard and Daniel Lerch, eds. 2010. Post-Carbon Reader. Watershed Media.

- Heisenberg, Werner. 2007. Physics and Philosophy. Harper Perrenial.

- Hertsgaard, Mark and Mark Dowie. April 23 2018. How big wireless made us think that cell phones are safe: A special investigation. The Nation

- Heylighen, Francis. Lecture notes 2017-2018. Complexity and Evolution. That were shared on the web and extremely helpful.

- Heylighen, Francis, Johan Bollen, Alexander Riegold, eds. 2010. The Evolution of Complexity.

- Hesse, Herman. 1922. Siddhartha. https://en.wikipeia.org/wiki/Siddhartha_(novel)

- Hoffmeyer, Jesper. 2008. A Legacy for Living Systems; Gregory Bateson as Precusor to Biosemiotics. Biosemiotics 2. Springer.com
     See also Tonnessen *et al.*, 2019

- Hopfenberg R. 2003. Human carrying capacity is determined by food availability. Popul. Environ. 25(2):109–117.

- Hopfenberg R, Pimentel D. 2001. Human population numbers as a function of food supply. Environ, Dev. Sustain. 3(1):1–15

- Hopkins, Rob. 2008-9. The Transition Handbook. Chelsea Green.

- Horan, Daniel P., OFM. 2019. https://www.ncronline.org/news/opinion/faith-seeking-understanding/christmas-all-godscreatures https://www.ncronline.org/news/earthbeat/faith-seeking-understanding/climate-change-mostimportant-life-issue-today

- Jacke, Dave and Eric Toensmeier. 2005b. Edible Forest Gardens,Volume I: Ecological Vision and Theory for Temperate Climate Permaculture. WWW.Chelseagreen.com
     Box 1.1 from this book does an exquisite job of explaining an Intervenor; that is, a person who "Stands outside an existing system and doesn't respect or understand how the system works. The intervenor therefore interferes with the system's healthy functioning, sometimes unknowingly or for fun or profit, but often in an attempt to "fix" perceived problems."

- Janeway, Elizabeth. 1980. Powers of the Weak. Morrow Quill Paperbacks.

- Jandt, Fred E. 1985. Win-Win Negotiating: Turning Conflict into Agreement. John

- Johnson, George. 1999. Strange Beauty. Vintage Books.

- Johnson, Jeromy. TED Talk. https://youtu.be/F0NEaPTu9ol

- Johnson, Osa. I Married Adventure. https://en.wikipedia.org/wiki/Martin_and_Osa_Johnson

- Johnson, Steven. 2003. Emergence. Scribner.

- Klein, Naomi. 2014. This Changes Everything. Simon & Schuster.

- Kolbert, Elizabeth. 2014. The Sixth Extinction. Henry Holt.

- Lamoreux, M. Lynn; Veronique Delmas, Lional Larue and Dorothy C. Bennet. 2010. The Colors of Mice; A Model Genetic Network. Wiley-Blackwell.

- Lamoreux, Lynn. Bare Bones Biology.
  https://factfictionfancy.wordpress.com/2017/01/13/bare-bones-biology-349-in-the-beginning

- LessEMF.com

- Lewin, Roger. 1992. Complexity: Life at the Edge of Chaos. University of Chicago Press.

- Lloyd, Seth. 2006. Programming the Universe. Vintage Books.

- Lloyd, Seth. 2016. Lecture One at Santa Fe Institute.X
  https://www.youtube.com/watch?v=5He7bYM7beM&list=PLZlVBTf7N6Gp1GIndwLnyS44OqJoRphOK&index=1
  "Information edge is when you have a small number of bits of information that can influence a large number of bits of information in the future." probably I would call this an information bottleneck.

- Lloyd, Seth. 2016. Lecture Two at Santa Fe Institute.

- Lovelock, James. 1988. The Ages of Gaia; A Biography of Our Living Earth. W. W. Norton & Co. (and other publications).
  2009 – The Vanishing Face of Gaia: A final warning. Allen Lane.

- Loy, David R. 2018. Ecodharma. Wisdom Publications.

- Lyons, Oren and Bill Moyers.
  http://traffic.libsyn.com/fff/OrenLyons_with_Bill_MoyersAccountabilityB.mp3

- Lyons, Oren and Amy Goodman
  http://traffic.libsyn.com/fff/AmyGoodman_OrenLyons_DN130809-clip.mp3

- Maathai, Wangari. 2006. UnBowed. Anchor Books.
  2009. The Challenge for Africa. Doubleday
  2010. Replenishing the Earth. Spiritual values for healing ourselves and the world. Doubleday Religion.

- Macey, Joanna and Molly Young Brown. 2014. Coming Back to Life: The updated guide to the work that reconnects. New Society Publishers.

- Makhijani, Arjun. 2010. Carbon-Free and Nuclear-Free; A Roadmap for U.S. Energy Policy. IEER Press, Takoma Park, MD

- Margulis, Lynn. 1998. Symbiotic Planet. Basic Books.

- Margulis, Lynn and Dorian Sagan. 1995. What is Life? University of California Press

- Martin, Anthony & John Hawks. 2010. Major Transitions in Evolution. The Great Courses,

- Martenson, Chris. 2009. Crash Course. ChrisMartenson.com. A biologically accurate video set available free on line and at UTube. CMAL, LLC

- Martin, Anthony and John Hawks. 2010. Major Transitions in Evolution. The Teaching Company, course #1518. www.TheGreatCourses.com. DVD

- McKibben, Bill. 2010. Eaarth. read by Oliver Wyman. www.Macmillanaudio.com.DVD
  Also available in print from Times books, an imprint of Henry Holt and Co.

- McWhorter, John. 2004. The Story of Human Language. The Teaching Company, course number 1600. DVD.

- Meadows, Donella H. 2007. Thinking in Systems. Chelsea Green Publishing.

- Midgley G. Four domains of complexity. Emergence: Complexity and Organization. 2016 Jun 30 [last modified: 2016 Aug 21].
  Edition 1. doi: 10.emerg/10.17357.6ffd4f1cee07b1eab0d5e11f6522261b.

- Miyazaki, Hayao. 1997. Mononoke Hime. Studio Ghibli. DVD.
  1989. Kiki's Delivery Service. Studio Ghibli. DVD
  These are available in English as well. I think of Kiki as the dream – Mononoke we hope might be the reality as we live through it, if we care enough to do that -- but Miyazaki's later films suggest it might not be so easy.

- Morrell, Michael and Kristin Wood. 3/27/2020. The Tragedy is that we Knew This was Coming. https://www.washingtonpost.com/people/michael-morell/

- National Geographic, March, 2018.
  January, 2020

- Newitz, Annalee. 2016. The Urban Species: How Domesticated Humans Evolved. Lecture at Santa Fe Institute. http://santafe.edu/gevent/detail/public/2346/

- Nilsson, Lennart, in collaboration with Jan Lindberg. 1973. Behold Man: A Photographic Journey of Discovery Inside the Body. Little, Brown and Company.

- Norberg-Hodge, Helena. 2000. Ancient Futures. Rider

- Nyberg, Karen, Astronaut. March, 2018. IN: Beyond the Blue Marble, by Nadia Drake, beautiful photographs by Martin Schoeller, National Geographic.

- Odum, Eugene P. 1971 and following. Fundamentals of Ecology. W. P. Saunders.

- Odum, Eugene P. and Gary W. Barrett. 2004. Fundamentals of Ecology. W. P. Saunders.

- Orwell, George. 1950. 1984. Penguin Publishing Group.

- Page, Scott E. 2009. Understanding Complexity. The Teaching Company, The Great Courses, course #5181.

- Pall ML 2013. Electromagnetic fields act via activation of voltage-gated calcium channels to produce beneficial or adverse effects. J Cell Mol Med 17:958-965.
  2016 Electromagnetic fields act similarly in plants as in animals: Probable activation of calcium channels via their voltage sensor. Curr Chem Biol 10:74-82.
  2017. Letter to Governor Brown. https://electromagnetichealth.org/wp-content/uploads/2017/10/Pall-Martin-Ltr-to-Gov-Brown-092317.pdf
  2018. https://peaceinspace.blogs.com/files/5g-emf-hazards--dr-martin-l.-pall--euemf2018-6-11us3.pdf

- Pang, L., et al. 2016. Vortical fluid and Λ spin correlations in high-energy heavy-ion collisions. Physical Review

- PBS – 2020 - Civilization

- PBS - 2007 – Planet Earth. DVD

- Peck, M. Scott. 1978. The Road Less Travelled: A new psychology of love. Simon & Schuster.
  1983. People of the Lie: The hope for healing human evil. Simon & Schuster,.
  1987. The Different Drum Community making and peace. Simon & Schuster, page 109 "Flight"

- Patrul Rinpoche. 1998 translation by Padmakara Translation Group.. The Words of my Perfect Teacher, Shambala.

- Peters, Karl E. 2002. Dancing with the Sacred; Evolution, Ecology, and God. Trinity Press.

- Pineault, Nicolas. 2019. The Non-Tinfoil Guide to EMFs: How to fix our stupid use of technology. NSG Media, Inc.

- Pollan, Michael. 2007. The Omnivore's Dilemma: A natural history of four meals. Penguin.

- Population Connection. https://www.populationconnection.org

- Population Matters. https://www.populationmaters.org

- Principe, Lawrence M. 2006. Science and Religion. The Great Courses; course number 4691.

- Raffensperger, Carolyn and Joel Tickner, eds. 1999, Protecting Public Health and the Environment: Implementing the Precautionary Principle. IslandPress

- Rawlence, Ben. 2016. City of Thorns. Picador.

- Redford, Robert. (Mandarin language narrated by Jackie Chan). 2017. Earth: One Amazing Day. BBC Earth Films. (DVD)

- Rifkin, Jeremy. 2009. The Empathic Civilization. Penguin.

- Ripple, William, *et al.* 2017. World Scientists' Warning to Humanity: A Second Notice. Bioscience: vol. 67: December; pages 1026-1028.
  This is an ongoing set of papers written by scientists in a large number of disciplines. Written for and by scientists and very accessible.

- Robb, J. D. 2018. Leverage in Death. St. Martin's Press. Page 256.

- Roberto, Michael A. 2009. The Art of Critical Decision Making. The Great Courses, course number 5932.

- Robertson, Bruce A. and Daniel T. Blumstein. 2019. How to disarm an evolutionary trap. Conservation Science and Practice. 2019;e116 https://doi.org/10.1111/csp2.116

- Ryerson, William N. 2010. The Multiplier of Everything Else. Chapter 06 IN: Post Carbon Reader. PostCarbon Institute and Watershed Media.

- Sagan, Carl. Cosmos, #13, https://youtu.be/WnAQQ4StnEg

- Sagan, Carl. 1996. The Demon-Haunted World. Ballantine Books.

- Sagan, Dorian, ed. 2012. Lynn Margulis. Sciencewriters

- Sagan, Dorian and John Feldman. 2018. Symbiotic Earth; study guide. Hummingbird Films.
  See also Feldman, John.

- Salmony, Steven Earl. 2004. The Human Population: Accepting Earth's Limitations. Environmental Health Perspectives • VOLUME 112 |NUMBER 6 | May 2004 a339s.

- Shantideva (2008 translation by Padmakara Translation Group). The Way of the Bodhisattva. Shambala.

- Scientific American. July, 2018, page 37. "The Science of Anti-Science Thinking." authored by several professors at Arizona State University. (This journal is mostly about technology, not basic science. It swings with the corposystem without overtly misquoting the facts. So I cannot say I recommend it. National Geographic does a more straightforward and readable job of presenting our problems in an understandable way.)

- Schrodinger, Erwin. 1944. What is Life? Cambidge University Press.

- Schumacher, Benjamin. 2009. Quantum Mechanics. The Great Courses; course number 1240

- Schumacher, Benjamin. 2015. The Science of Information. The Great Courses, course number 1301.

- Seife, Charles. 2006. Decoding the Universe. Penguin Books.

- Selak, Joy H. and Steven S. Overman. 2013. You Don't LOOK Sick. Second Edition, demosHealth.

- Shiva, Vandana – Her Message - https://youtu.be/6yfzSvTRPIY UTube

- Sivan, S and D Sudarsanam. 2012. Impacts of radio-frequency electromagnetic field (RF-EMF) from cell phone towers and wireless devices on biosystem ad ecosystem – a review. Biology and Medicine (4):4:202-216)

- Smith, Huston. 1976. Forgotten Truth: the primordial tradition. Harper & Row
    "Strictly speaking a scientific world view is impossible; it is a contradiction in terms. The reason is that science does not treat of the world; it treats of a part of it only."
    2001. Why Religion Matters. Harper One.
    2001. The World's Religions

- Snyder, Gary. 2000. Blue Mountains Constantly Walking. IN: Dharma Rain: Sources of Buddhist Environmentalism. Ed: Stephanie Kaza ad Kenneth Kraft, Shambala.

- Spring, Janet Cedar. 1996. Take up your Life. Charles E. Tuttle Co., Inc.

- Starbird, Michael. 2001. Change and Motion. The Great Courses; course number 177.

- Starhawk. 1979. "Witchcraft and Women's Culture," in Womanspirit Rising, Ed: C. Christ & J. Plaskow, Harper & Row

- Steffan et al., 2018. Trajectories of the Earth System in the Anthropocene. PNAS www.pnas.org/cgi/doi/10.1073/pnas.1810141115

- Steingraber, Sandra. 2011. Raising Elijah; Protecting our Children in a Time of Environmental Crisis. De Capo Press. And other writings.

- Stewart, Ian. BBC. Earth: The Biography. DVD

- Stih, Daniel. 2009. Healthy Living Spaces. ISBN 13:978-0979468-3

- Strauss, Eric G. 2009. Earth at the Crossroads. The Great Courses; course number 1720

- Strogatz, Steven. 2008. Chaos. The Great Courses; course number 1333.

- Stuever, Mary. 2009. The Forester's Log: Musings from the Woods. Univ. New Mexico Press.

- Sutherland, Stuart. 2013. A New History of Life. The Great Courses; course Number 1520. I especially like this one for integrating concepts from various specialized fields.

- Suzuki, David. 2007. The Sacred Balance: Rediscovering our place in nature. Third Edition, Greystone Books.

- Suzuki, David, 2012. https://www.youtube.com/watch?v=bsd1

- Suzuki, David and Peter Knudsen. 1993. Wisdom of the Elders: Sacred native stories of nature. Bantam Books.

- Swearer, Donald K. 1997. Theravada Buddhism and Ecology: The Case of Thailand. IN: Buddhism and Ecology, Eds. Mary Evelyn Tucker and Duncan Ryuken Williams. Harvard University Press.

- Tainter, Joseph A. 1988. The Collapse of Complex Societies. Cambridge Univesity Press.

- The Bhagavad Gita

- The Dalai Lama, 1999. The Path to Tranquility. Ed. Renuka Singh. Viking Arkana.
    2005. The Universe in a Single Atom. Harmony Books.
    2009. Becoming Enlightened, translated, edited and read by Jeffrey Hopkins, Simon & Schuster. In print by Atria.
    2010. Toward a True Kinship of Faiths. Doubleday Religion

- The Dalai Lama and Geshe Thupten Jinpa. 2009. The Middle Way. Wisdom Publications, Somerville, MA.

- The Dalai Lama, Desmond Tutu, and Douglas Abrams. 2016. The Book of Joy. Random House.

- The Koran

- The New Testament

- The Old Testament
  "The Bible." The Old Testament and the New Testament, Revised Standard Version. I could take similar parallels between religion and reality from any of the major religions, because each religion is a social system, a logical world view that is meant to guide the people in their relationship with factual realities of their particular environment, that they cannot control, as understood by the people who lived them. The Holy Bible happens to be more readily available and accessible for discussion with others in this community. And indeed – elegant.

- The Pope
  It is worthwhile to search the web for Laudati Si, a serious, fairly new project of the catholic church to address the problems of climate change.

- The Teaching Company. http://www.TheTeachingCompany.com, and see above.

- Tiroir A Films. 2011. Mother; Caring our Way out of the Population Dilemma. DVD.

- Thomas, Lowell and Lowell Thomas Jr. 1950. Out of this World, Across the Himalayas to Forbidden Tibet. Greystone Press.

- Thunberg, Greta, 2019. https://www.youtube/watch?v=KAJsdgTPJpu&t=144s

- Toms, Michael. 1990. An Open Life: Joseph Campbell in conversation with Michael Toms. Harper Perrenial, ISBN 978-0-06-097295-0

- Tonnessen, Morten, et al. 2019. Jesper Hoffmeyer's Biosemiotic Legacy. Published on line @ Biosemiotics (2019) 12:357-363https://doi.org/10.1007/s12304-019-09369-5
  "Hoffmeyer's key concept in treating this subject (evolution) is code-duality."

- Tutu, Archbishop Desmond. 2016. The Book of Forgiving; the fourfold path for healing ourselves and our world. HarperOne.

- Tyson, Neil deGrasse. 2012. The Inexplicable Universe. The Great Courses; course number 1816

- Tyson, Neil DeGrasse and Donald Goldsmith. 2004. Origins: Fourteen Billion Years of Cosmic Evolution. W. W. Norton.

- Wolfson, Richard. 2007. Earth's Changing Climate. The Great Courses; course number 1219.

- Weinhold, Barry K and Janae B. 1989. Breaking Free of the Co-Dependency Trap. Stillpoint Publishing, Walpole, NH

- West, Geoffrey. 2017. Scale. Penguin Press.

- Westover, Tara. 2018. Educated. Random House.

- Wilson, Edward O. 1992. The Diversity of Life. W. W. Norton & Company
   2002. The Future of Life. New Millenium. DVD.
   2006. The Creation. W. W. Norton.
   2016. Half Earth, Our Planet's Fight for Life. Liveright.

- Witt, Ulrich. 2017. Capitalism as a complex adaptive system and its growth. Journal of open Innovation: Technology, Market, and Complexity 3:12.

- Wolfson, Richard. 2007. Earth's Changing Climate. The Great Courses; course number 1219.

- Woodruff Paul. 2001. Reverence. Oxford University Press.

- Xanthopoulos, Drew. 2017. In Filmmaker magazine.
   https://filmmakermagazine.com/102311-tribeca-2017-drew-xanthopoulos-on-the-sensitives/

- Zhong-Yi Wang, *et al.*, 2020. Transciptome and translatatome co-evolution in mammals. Nature. DOI: 10.1038/s41586-020-2899-z

Web Links

http://FactFictionFancy.wordpress.com/bare-bones-biology

https://factfictionfancy.wordpress.com/2012/10/24/bare-bones-biology-129-community-iii/

https://www.washintonpost.com/opinions/2020/03/27/tragedy-is-that-we-knew-this-was-coming/

http://scientistswarning.forestry.oregonstate.edu/

http://columbiaclimatelaw.com/.../epa-science-panel-disband.../...

https://youtu.be/JRPmLWYbUqA

http://www.pnas.org/content/115/44/11262?fbclid=IwAR1NsxKIHvRN9bo9vzXoi7N4n

9J5VstO7yT7tfD3KhQe1k8Om-0Raw7oOzg

http://www.ipcc.ch/report/sr15/

https://filmmakermagazine.com/102311-tribeca-2017-drew-xanthopoulos-on-the-sensitives/

https://doi.org/10.1111/csp2.116

www.eiwellspring.org

http://annmccampbell.com/sample-page/story/

https://nca2018.globalchange.gov/downloads/?fbclid=IwAR2hHW1mxmK_Z_x2Uw2NLT3SkcID4xpqdySmjKc4xi6SfT2mLQygILkrZPdE

https://www.ipcc.ch/sr15/

https://www.ncronline.org/news/opinion/faith-seeking-understanding/christmas-all-godscreatures

https://www.ncronline.org/news/earthbeat/faith-seeking-understanding/climate-change-mostimportant-life-issue-today

https://www.youtube.com/watch?v=5He7bYM7beM&list=PLZIVBTf7N6Gp

1GIndwLnyS44OqJoRphOK&index=1

https://soundasacrystal.com/2014/12/07/canaries-in-the-coal-mine-multiple-chemical-sensitivities-myth-vs-reality/

https://en.wikipedia.org/wiki/Precautionary_principle

https://soundasacrystal.com/2015/12/31/not-wearing-any-perfume/

https://branchbasics.com/blog/2015/01/fragrance-is-the-new-secondhand-smoke/

www.powerwatch.org.uk

https://www.youtube.com/watch?v=5He7bYM7beM&list=PLZIVBTf7N6Gp1GIndwLnyS44OqJoRphOK&index=1

https://en.wikipedia.org/wiki/Martin_and_Osa_Johnson

http://columbiaclimatelaw.com/.../epa-science-panel-disband.../...

https://youtu.be/JRPmLWYbUqA

http://www.pnas.org/content/115/44/11262?fbclid=IwAR1NsxKIHvRN9bo9vzXoi7N4n

9J5VstO7yT7tfD3KhQe1k8Om-0Raw7oOzg

http://www.ipcc.ch/report/sr15/

https://en.wikipedia.org/wiki/Dunning%E2%80%93Kruger_effect

http://www.undp.org/hdr2003/indicator/indic_38_1_1.html.

http://www.undp.org/hdr2003/indicator/indic_38_1_1.html

https://www.ncronline.org/news/opinion/faith-seeking-understanding/christmas-all-godscreatures

Dr. Albert A. Bartlet, 2012. https://www.youtube.com/watch?v=sl1C9Dyli_8

Dr. David Suzuki, 2012. https://www.youtube.com/watch?v=bsd1

Severn Cullis-Suzuki, 1992. https://www.youtube.com/watch?v=oJJGuIZVfLM

Greta Thunberg, 2019. https://www.youtube/watch?v=KAJsdgTPJpu&t=144s

http://columbiaclimatelaw.com/.../epa-science-panel-disband.../...

https://youtu.be/JRPmLWYbUqA

http://www.pnas.org/content/115/44/11262?fbclid=IwAR1NsxKlHvRN9bo9vzXoi7N4n

9J5VstO7yT7tfD3KhQe1k8Om-0Raw7oOzg

http://www.ipcc.ch/report/sr15/

http://www.undp.org/hdr2003/indicator/indic_38_1_1.html.

http://santafe.edu/gevent/detail/public/2346/

https://www.washingtonpost.com/people/michael-morell/

https://www.youtube.com/watch?v=5He7bYM7beM&list=PLZlVBTf7N6Gp1GlndwLnyS44OqJoRphOK&index=1

APPENDIX A

OUR COMMON PROBLEM

We can not contribute to our human future on our living earth until we can discuss our Biological problem, and that discussion will be helpful only if it is based on biological reality, because it is a biological Problem. We know that is not impossible, because we have a model – difficult as that is to believe – in our own government. NASA.

> "We all have different backgrounds. We all have different projects. But we all have the same goal." (Moodgaga Cooper on NOVA, Search for Life on Mars, 2021)

And look how well we did with our response to the pandemic, once we finally decided to face the facts of LIFE and base our behaviors on our science.

It's not that we can't. Both the thinking and the doing of NASA seem sometimes beyond belief. It's that, for some reason, we aim our gifts at other goals than our own survival. When we get together around well-defined goals that are based in good science, as we have done with NASA and, eventually, with the pandemic, we tend to succeed.

Now we just need to reach a little higher, because both of these examples are technological triumphs, but they do not take us to our final goal,

> *To grow a common culture that respects the needs of a fruitful and reasonably comfortable Life of humans within our Earth environment.*

I know that our dream is possible, because I have seen it.

But we have lost our way; we have lost sight of our goal, in favor of a technological profit cult. We can't see beyond the technologies of our cities (West, 2017). I remember when some basic scientists were worried about what would happen when more than half of our best and our brightest were born and raised in cities. Now we know. We could deal with that, but we cannot solve communal problems that we can't talk about with each other.

Perhaps we should stop playing around with biologically impossible work-arounds, and get down to the nitty-gritty Problem, as it is presented in this book and start facing up to real solutions. Talk good science before we jump on every new idea that seems logical.

Then last year I connected with Jim Antal, author of Climate Church/Climate World (2018) whose work is within the religious communities, and now I have been introduced to the work of Trevor Hedberg (2020), an academic philosopher whose book is subtitled "The Ethics of Procreation." Certainly, all three of those books give us a great deal to talk about in our search for our human place within LIFE and our responsibility to it.

Science – basic science – grew out of the religious/philosophical tradition. Both of those books, and, for example, the PostCarbon Reader (Heinberg & Lerch, 2010), and Chris Martensen (2009), that is free on line as a DVD and on Utube – all these books and more seriously face our Problem, and can help bridge our discussions and expand them to include the human reality, because in my opinion neither the basic science nor the humanities is in service to us without the other, and the discussion seems to have finally begun.

Our Problem clearly does relate to our ancient and modern human belief systems, as well as to the facts of LIFE that those older wisdom traditions try to explain to us, every generation in its own way (Diamond, 2011; Gulen, 2011; Loy, 2018; Lyons; Macy & Brown, 2014; PBS, 2020; and most of the holy books: The Bible; The Koran, etc.).

The separation between science and the humanities, for humans, is artificial and in fact is largely due to the reality of overpopulation and its effect upon our social structures (Campbell, all; Diamond, all; Heisenberg, 2007; Johnson,1999: McKibben, 2010; Miyazaki; Newitz, 2016; Smith, all: Steingraber, 2011; Salmony, 2004; Suzuki, all; The Dalai Lama, 2005, 2010; A Trior Films; West, 2017).

Also: Dr. Albert A. Bartlet, 2012. https://www.youtube.com/watch?v=sl1C9Dyli_8
Dr. David Suzuki, 2012. https://www.youtube.com/watch?v=bsd1
Severn Cullis-Suzuki, 1992. https://www.youtube.com/watch?v=oJJGuIZVfLM
Greta Thunberg, 2019. https://www.youtube/watch?v=KAJsdgTPJpu&t=144s
Daniel P. Horan, OFM,
https://www.ncronline.org/news/opinion/faith-seeking-understanding/christmas-all-gods-creatures
https://www.ncronline.org/news/earthbeat/faith-seeking-understanding/climate-change-mostimportant-life-issue-today
Jeromy Johnson TED Talk https://youtu.be/F0NEaPTu9ol

In our effort to control the realities most important to ourselves, we are all describing the same biological/human jigsaw puzzle in different ways, using different kinds of definitions, descriptions, metaphors, propaganda and personal opinions (based in our different world views). What we have not yet done is verbalize our common goal. Mostly we are not even thinking about it, but relying on a homocentric use of technologies that cannot save us long term.

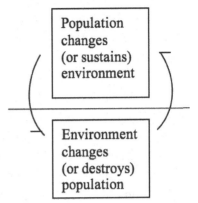

We need our ancient wisdoms and our modern science -- our religions, philosophies and world views – to guide our discussions as we learn to talk together about the real Problem, and its do-able solution.

No one person can speak to and for all our religious/philosophical traditions, but nothing is stopping us from talking to each other decently and with a common goal. We need a great many people to take the initiative for defending us from our own ignorance, not of math or technologies, but of how those achievements relate to LIFE. The solution will come through our many individual behaviors, not our individual intentions, because it is with our behaviors that we communicate with the other systems of which LIFE is composed and with the natural laws that sustain the balance of LIFE.

Our basic modern Human Problem is not so much a problem of science and technology, or whatever we like to do, or who-ever we like to be better than. Certainly not a problem of happiness, or who has the biggest stick. It is a problem of corposystem growth. More importantly, it is a problem of the apparently universal natural law of The Creation that includes the natural law of evolution (see Chapters 08 and 09) and requires, for survival of the whole, a balanced Biosystem.

That is the basic fact.

The human Problem is what to do about it.

We now are experiencing climate change and a pandemic that could or would not have happened or become so threatening in the normal LIFE system (the Biosystem) if our corposystem had not been pushed so far out of its biological balance (its sweet spot as described in Chapter 06 and beyond) by our over-growth.

> ***Reality Number Two*** *– The property of LIFE emerges from our Biosystem that consists of nested, naturally evolved subsystems. We humans cannot change how they evolved or how they function to sustain LIFE. Just as the growth of the human embryo requires the womb, and the mother cow feeds the calf, so do all the mothers and all the species require the appropriate environment for their survival. (Preface).*

LIFE itself is an emergent property of the Biosystem.

The Biosystem is the living Earth system, including all of Its parts (also known as micro-components) that the Biosystem uses to sustain Its emergent properties (Chapter 04).

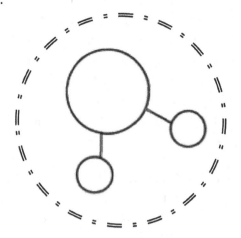

The basic balance required for the emergence of LIFE on Earth is maintained by interactions among the subsystems of which the Biosystem is composed. It is maintained by natural law; specifically by evolution interacting with the processes of communication (LIFE codes, Chapter 09) among the systems. Most of these interactions we do not understand. Or even know about. Therefore we cannot replace them with our lower-efficiency technologies. We cannot change the need for this over-all balance (Chapters 09, 10) because it is a very basic Law of Nature (or at least of LIFE). We *Homo sapiens* must rebalance ourselves within the Biosystem if we truly want to survive. That is the bottom line, and now is the time.

> The corposystem is our human naturally evolved corpo-political-economic-military-medical-educational-religious-charitable social system.

> The corposystem is actively and effectively promoting the growth of itself, and we are collaborating with that effort, even though the corposystem is already way far out of balance with the rest of the Biosystem. The corposystem is, after all also a system – systems normally do promote themselves. That's why evolution has generated so many checks and balances among its parts.

Our Problem is that the growth of the corposystem has escaped the checks and balances. It has unbalanced the Biosystem. Our human corposystem is now causing immense harm to the Biosystem, as the Biosystem attempts to change itself – to rebalance itself in such a way that the flame of LIFE -- its own emergent property -- can be sustained. Currently, we experience that rebalancing as climate change and pandemic.

I do not see any group, neither the good guys nor the bad guys, discussing the real Problem, that is the *conflict* between the corposystem technological world view and the reality requirements of LIFE.

I tried to find a group that I could join to help with this essential effort, and could not. Possibly PostCarbon.org. (Richard Heinberg); LocalFutures.org. (Helena Norberg-Hodge); TransitionNetwork.org. (Rob Hopkins); Perhaps, Population Connection, but they keep dropping me off their mailing list; or now, Population Matters is not afraid to face right off to the heart of the reality with regular, authoritative newsletters that are fact-based and for the most part do not bother with the fluff. But I couldn't join because of some glitch in money exchange. And of course there are many that I don't know about, but there is no point spinning my wheels in organizations that deny the reality of over-population, no matter what good they otherwise try to do. Extinction doesn't care about human rights,.

I finally concluded the only way I could contribute to a viable world view was to write this book.

Meanwhile, the climate change that is caused by this conflict between the corposystem and the Biosystem, since about the hippy generation, until very recently has been progressively pushed out of the news, even as the technological approach becomes rapidly more threatening to our existence, while we horribilize over a variety of other things that are actually symptoms – not causes – of climate change. Climate change is by far our largest threat. Climate change, including the pandemic, is the Biosystem reacting to our imbalance within its own emergent LIFE. Climate change is a biological problem, and our technologies are not more powerful than the Laws of LIFE.

> Too many people: not enough food; only the Biosystem can sustainably make food for us, and only if it is in a healthy balance.

It is late to try to save it ourselves. I have lived to see half of Africa turn from green to yellow, as photographed from the satellites, since well after the publication of that wonderful early photo book by Osa Johnson (https://en.wikipedia.org/wiki/Martin_and_Osa_Johnson) and the eye-opening reports of Lowell Thomas and Lowell Thomas Jr. (1950) from the mysterious heights of the Himalaya, both reports that opened my teenage eyes to the fact that there is a real world out there. That we are part of it, not the other way around.

Late or not, however, there is no valid reason to wait for later. We did not have the solution in those earlier days. Now we do, and now that we have technologies that could be used to help the Biosystem, we won't even talk about it.

> The basic solution, of course, is birth control. The solution is to reduce human growth as compassionately as possible while we do the best we can to repair the symptoms of our overgrowth. The question is NOT what we must do; that question has been answered by the basic sciences and written into this book and discussed by many.

> The question now is how to do it compassionately, rather than wait until the Biosystem does it to us, which is already happening, and which is NOT compassionate. That question requires discussion now.

The enormous difference between now and the hippy era, when we actually did try to deal with the overpopulation Problem (I remember these things), is that we now have birth control technologies to do it with, and quite a few ideas that we have not even tried.

Something as simple as modifying the charter of every dot-com and dot-org, so that they are required to work for human welfare rather than requiring them to work for profit or growth, could make a very big difference. An example of this is Newman's Own©, which appears to be very successful, without spending vast amounts of money trying to move our attention away from the Problem.

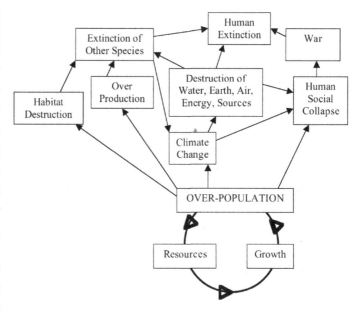

Birth control should be in the hands of every person who wants it -- free -- and its use should be a normal part of our everyday conversation in our homes, in our relationships, and especially in our media. What is the point of "empowering" a few women at the top of the social scale, people who have solutions in any case, leaving everyone else ignorant?

We don't talk about such possibilities publicly anymore, and yet they are possible solutions to climate change and, if we know what we are working toward, all the other symptoms that are associated with and caused by our overgrowth.

The vast majority of technological solutions that we are actually talking about -- predictably will not work, because of the way energy flows through LIFE (Chapter 06), but they are profitable, and so we choose profit and fun over LIFE and ignore the cities of the dispossessed (Rawlence. 2016), or we just send them food – while there is still enough – without sending them solutions.

We try harder and harder to make solutions that will work for the corposystem, but the harder we work in that direction, the larger the population grows, because projects that are funded by the corposystem always involve growth, because that is how the corposystem makes its money. More refugees is good news for the corposystem. It means more profits -- using growth.

And so our proposals – even at the international meetings and the dot-org community that wants our money and especially the dot-gov that already has our money -- in this country at least, all contribute to climate change, because growth at the present time is toxic to the balance of the Biosystem.

Growth is not necessary; sustainability is necessary. What we require is to find a population level within which we can sustain ourselves without destroying the balance of LIFE, and let the population descend to that level while at the same time readjusting the corposystem to its new restraints. Growth at this time goes into supporting the inequities that are built into the corposystem's dominational ethic. Growth is not required for sustainability, unless we are trying to sustain growth, and that is biological suicide.

Climate change is the irreversible *evolution* of our living environment. Loss and change of the actual genetic code of LIFE (Chapter 10).

> Evolution of the Biosystem is not reversible. It is not adaptation; it is a permanent change in the information of LIFE – the DNA/RNA code of LIFE information that took billions of years for evolution to bring to near perfection.

The solution to our problem(s) – the only solution over which we have control -- is to stop the human growth that is killing the Biosystem; we have chosen instead to make money using human growth, and now, with that as our excuse, we have hit the wall of environmental depletion.

What is Our Common Problem?

THE PROBLEM IS OVERPOPULATION

Our most threatening human social problems of today do not have separate fundamental causes. That is why they all become worse at the same time that the root cause becomes worse. They are all symptoms of the slow collapse of the corposystem, as it continues to overgraze the resources of the Biosystem, and the Biosystem responds to this attack in the only way that it can. By changing LIFE itself. The only way it can change, as discussed in this book -- using the Laws of LIFE to change our environmental relationships. If evolution cannot accomplish this fast enough, the Biosystem will again crash, just like it did during the dinosaur era, but for a reason this time that we could have controlled.

And the reason is THE SAME FOR EVERYONE.

It has happened to humans before on smaller scales and many of our pre-scientific ancestors were aware of the Problem (Diamond, 2011). This time it is worldwide. Growth (corposystem) versus balance (LIFE). The Biosystem requires balance of its parts to generate the emergent property of LIFE, so that it can make more LIFE; the corposystem requires growth, for profit, so it can provide technological services to make more growth/profit.

Growth of the human population at this time when we have overgrazed the resources, is dangerous to our own future welfare (Catton, 1982; Douthwaite, 1999; Ehrlich & Ehrlich, 1966; Roberto, 2009; Shiva, Vandana, all; Steuver, 2009; Tainter, 1988: Trior A Films, 2011:

Wilson, 2002, 2016; and others) and to all the subsystems of LIFE that generate its "human services."

There is no doubt, nor do well-informed persons who have seriously considered the Problem proclaim any doubt, that overpopulation is the primary cause of many of our human difficulties in this age. But if you want to do some fact-checking, that is good. I admire fact-checking, and here are a few good, easily available references to get you started; a short list of those I used in writing this book (Brown, 2004, 2008, 2012 and more; Butler, 2015; Catton,1982; Diamond, 1997, 2011; Gore, 2006. 2016; Martenson, 2009, look for the free DVDs of his lectures, which are excellent; McKibben, 2010). Check out a few recent scientists' contributions at the below web sites, and go from there.

http://scientistswarning.forestry.oregonstate.edu/
http://columbiaclimatelaw.com/.../epa-science-panel-disband.../...
https://youtu.be/JRPmLWYbUqA
http://www.pnas.org/content/115/44/11262?fbclid=IwAR1NsxKIHvRN9bo9vzXoi7N4n
9J5VstO7yT7tfD3KhQe1k8Om-0Raw7oOzg
http://www.ipcc.ch/report/sr15/

And no, it is not getting "better" just because the growth curve is leveling off. Runaway growth curves, if they are not dealt with, ALWAYS level off just before they crash.

A well informed British politician recently was quoted as saying:

> "There's no point bleating about the future of pandas, polar bears and tigers when we're not addressing the one single factor that's putting more pressure on the ecosystem than any other — namely the ever-increasing size of the world's population." (Chris Packham, PM)

Mr. Packham is correct, except for two things. (1) There is always a point to community discussion of our mutual problems, because we cannot solve them by ignoring them. (2) There is always a point in maintaining the diversity of the earth, because it carries forward the DNA of the Biosystem in the form that we need -- but not if we let our LIFE on earth blow away while we are doing it.

I would say this in a different way: there is no point promoting the things that we love about humanity while ignoring the progress of our own extinction. Bleating about side issues (the symptoms of overpopulation), is necessary, but it will not solve the root issue, which IS overpopulation. The Biosystem would begin its recovery tomorrow if we were not here.

Because we have stopped talking about overpopulation does not change the reality. It just looks a little different with each generation of humans, and humans always tend to believe that whatever they were born into is normal. Today is not normal, wherever you are.

The solution is to consider the side issues as they relate to their own cause: the solution is NOT to prop up the corposystem that created the *cause* that then created the side issues. The solution is to maintain a sensible level of ethical behavior and use that sensible behavior to sustain ourselves with minimum suffering while removing the cause of the Problem. The solution is to STOP promoting impossible money-making dreams that will inevitably result in another crash. G5 for example. What would all that money have done if invested in birth control for everyone who wants it? And G4 was already sufficiently harmful to our citizens and biological resources who suffer from EMR sensitivity. The corposystem is backing itself into a lethal corner from which there is no escape (Robertson & Blumstein, 2019).

We have had a recent spate of heart-rending anxiety over the sperm counts of human males that someone says is dropping worldwide. If true, this would not be surprising, in view of the worldwide slather of pollution: poisonous substances and toxic overloads of polarized EMR (electromagnetic radiation) that we are spreading throughout the Biosphere, but these sob stories do not mention causes or solutions, so what's the point of all the heart-rending?

I think the point of modern heart-rending is to make money (or otherwise win something) – not to help people, but to pull our attention away from the unfulfillable needs of nearly half our populations.

Frankly I'm tired of hearing sob stories that are disconnected from discussions of cause, rational solutions, and the effects of our proposed solutions on future generations. You and I have more important responsibilities than someone else's sperm count, or even your own. If that particular bit of corposystem propaganda was even true?

Propaganda that makes people upset but does not contribute to a solution just stirs the pot, makes some profit for someone, or merely distracts our attention from something that actually is important

How can we possibly get upset about what happens to sperms while we ignore the primary cause of the death and suffering of living human beings? I don't know. It seems incredible to me, but this kind of illogic is plastered across the internet until we actually begin to believe in it, and it has even crept into the executive wing.

Our Problem cannot be solved by knee-jerk, juvenile junk propaganda. We require collaborative, collective discussion in an atmosphere of wise compassion.

> "If you want to get rid of painful effects, you have to get rid of their causes."
> Wisdom is: "analyzing the facts and discerning the actual situation."
> (His Holiness The Dalai Lama, 2009)

We need to understand the universal facts (such as, nothing can grow forever in this world), and not only as a reflection of what the corposystem wants us to believe. We already know what it wants us to believe. It wants us to believe that growth can save us, when in fact growth today can only increase the biological imbalance that is at the root of most of our currently worsening problems. And not only in the big city in which you may have been raised. Big cities are not sufficiently efficient to support LIFE without a healthy Biosystem to provide resources (West, 2017).

That above statement always makes me remember the first time I ever realized that some children literally believe eggs come from, are generated by, supermarkets. That we pay the markets to make food for us.

We don't. Nobody can make food and insert it into the cycle of LIFE of the Biosystem, for reasons explained in this book.

We need to understand the universal facts within the context of LIFE of the entire Earth – not in the context of the corposystem view of life as a means to profit. We need to make propaganda that is reality based.

There is no point arguing over which view of our common Problem is more logical – the corposystem view or the LIFE view. We must aggressively propound the reality view, and for all of our behaviors discuss the reality view of LIFE. The corposystem view is logical within the corposystem, but it assumes an outside source of both food energy and machine energy, neither of which exists. The Biosystem view is logical within the Biosystem, and that is where we all live (See Chapters 01 and 03). We can argue to doom's day about which is most logical and only keep arguing in circles, going nowhere, because these world views are all logical, each in its context. What we need is not argument. Or logic. We need to grow a common world view that is based in unchanging universal facts, because that is the same for everyone.

All world views are logical within their context, but supermarkets DO NOT MAKE EGGS. That is a fact. Some things we have been raised to believe are NOT ACCURATE or RELEVANT to our Problems. Those are the things we need to discuss.

Survival of the Fittest?

And for those of us who cannot move our thinking away from "survival of the fittest" -- no shame, it's not easy – Gary Snyder (2000) said it very well:

> "It would appear that the common conception of evolution is of competing species running a sort of race through time on planet earth, all on the same running field, some dropping out, some flagging, some victoriously in front."

That is NOT what evolution is, and I even agree with his descriptions of the nature of LIFE, though they are expressed in a very unscientific fashion. He elegantly describes more or less what I have tried to say in the chapters of this book, using his words in a more Buddhistic fashion. Biologists, Christians, Sikhs, Muslims, Jews and earlier belief systems have recognized the same truths, each it its own way.

So we have many views of nature, but the universal facts are true of all of LIFE. We can observe and use the facts of LIFE to benefit ourselves, but *how* we do that is what makes the difference. Whether we tromp on through life with an "I win/you lose" attitude, or use our belief systems to understand the difference between fact, fancy and fairy tales and then use the facts to the benefit of both ourselves and our environment.

We cannot just ignore the parts we don't want. We cannot ignore the requirement for balance, or not for very long in evolutionary time; we cannot ignore the requirement for collaboration; we cannot ignore the fact of overpopulation and pretend that our technologies can compete with the reality of the Biosystem's elegant use of both energy and entropy. Or we can, but we will be booted out of the Biosystem. And it seems to me that people who run around touting their prowess without bothering to find out what is needed have been in charge longer than is necessary, and never did deserve our respect.

And this is Our Common Problem:

> The corposystem is killing the Biosystem – or at least forcing it to change away from the conditions that we require for our survival. And we as individuals mostly are not aware that our support of the corposystem inevitably causes harm to the Biosystem because our support generates corposystem growth. The whole point of the corposystem is to generate growth. That is what it does. It is time to stop letting it do that if we want to work for the benefit of our grandchildren.

Center of the Universe Thinking?

Meantime, this book wonders how the human species has become so arrogant as to espouse a world view that places humans at the center of the universe to the exclusion of the Laws of LIFE that generated -- or at least sustain LIFE. Anthropocene indeed! What nonsense.

Didn't astronomers try, earlier in our Western history, to prove that the earth, with its human population, is the center of the universe? And in the end, they could not make the whole Earth— never-mind *Homo sapiens* — even be the center of the solar system. Because it is not. No matter how hard they wanted to believe it. We laugh at them now.

So I wonder why do we, as responsible citizens of the Biosystem, avoid analyzing the real facts and recognizing that we are making precisely the same mistake. Only biologically much worse, because we involve the welfare of all of the LIFE of Earth. All sentient beings. All creatures great and small.

When we could be collaborating with the entire glorious miracle of the LIFE OF EARTH to save the whole shebang.

In fact, there are many ways to look at our common human Problem, from the simplest to the most complex valid modern science, and they all agree:

1. The self-evident approach - nothing can grow forever bigger; we have arrived at the crunch.
2. The straight-forward approach -- the bathtub model. This simplistic linear view of human life is the bathtub being filled with water. When it is full, it is full, and no more water (people) can be fitted in, and technologies are temporary (flawed, see Chapter 06) fixes. The overflow is the victims whom we now are for the most part ignoring (Rawlence, 2016).
3. The agricultural model. Anyone who understands livestock also understands that we must not put too many cows, or horses, or sheep or goats on one piece of pasture land, and leave them there, because if we do they will die of starvation, competition, or some associated symptomatic disease state. They die because the pasture, which is their environment, sooner or later dies of over-grazing.

Overpopulation of livestock -- not giving them enough to eat -- leads to their death because they can no longer live and reproduce without the organic food that they require. Human food does not come from the supermarket or the corner grocery. It comes from earth, air, water and the energy/information combination that is required to make organic molecules, which are the body and blood of LIFE. Of course we could try to "make" real food by putting together organic molecules in giant factories and then eating the molecules, but the energy to do that project far exceeds the nourishment we would get out of it, because LIFE is so much more efficient than giant factories, and so the whole system would go yet more off balance. We are neither God nor evolution to put a few billion years into doing the project properly, and neither are our computers.

Organic energy is a component of things that grow and live, just as we do, by eating or otherwise consuming the energy of LIFE and using that organic energy to create and re-create their kind, that is to reproduce themselves, using the codes of LIFE (Chapters 09 and 10). LIFE uses the organic energy to recycle (maintain the balance of) the matter, the systems that LIFE is made of (Chapter 04) -- the cells of which your body and all other forms of LIFE are composed. Overgrazing the whole earth will have the same effect on us as overgrazing the pasture has on sheep. Except that we will have no other place to go to.

4. Answers (excuses) in this generation tend to be based on the assumption that humans can manipulate something or other, using our innate capacity for tool-making, and if we find the right thing to manipulate, we can overcome the straightforward, obvious reality of the Problem. Maybe. The fact is we cannot save ourselves with tools as we use them to create growth, for reasons covered in Chapter 06 to end of book. Briefly, humans cannot make tools that are sufficiently efficient to replace LIFE processes. Not that we could if we try harder. We can't; there are too many LIFE processes and they are all unique; and our very best scientists do not know what they all are.

Our technologies are mechanical solutions that do not recognize and cannot mimic the multitasking efficiency of LIFE that evolution has already generated – that generate LIFE. Adding inefficiencies does not increase the ability of LIFE to balance itself "on the edge of chaos." Adding inefficiencies increases entropy which increases chaos (Chapters 06 and 07), just exactly as the laws of thermodynamics says it should. We cannot make technologies that balance LIFE on the cutting edge of chaos. We cannot make eggs. We cannot make LIFE sustainable. Only the balance of LIFE can do that – but we could stop making LIFE unstable.

How does LIFE work?

LIFE is real, and it operates by real rules, and if we really want to help support:

> *a healthy and reasonably comfortable human presence within a flourishing Biosystem,*

then we cannot do it by overpowering the laws of God and nature. That's why we call them laws, not opinions or "social facts" (see the Preface and Chapter 02).

If the divine created LIFE, then LIFE functions as it was created to function, using the Laws of LIFE. If the divine did not create the Laws of LIFE, then LIFE still functions as it was created to function. Humans cannot "fix" or improve LIFE, or the Laws of LIFE (Chapters 06 onward and Appendices B and D) using technologies or using overpopulation. We cannot change how the facts of LIFE function to sustain the reality of LIFE, but we could fix a lot of our problems, including climate change if it's not too late, by changing our behaviors.

> ***Reality Number Twenty-Four*** - *The primary requirement of the Biosystem is to balance every part of itself around sustainably regenerating resources of our whole biological system, so that the energy and information of LIFE can flow automatically through its self from high energy/low entropy toward low energy/high entropy (Appendix A). High entropy is chaos.*

A balanced system goes unbalanced if we add too much to one part of it – any part, even too much of a good thing. That is the most basic Law of LIFE. "Survival of the fittest" is only valid if we imagine that fitness is the same thing as responsive balance among the processes.

We already knew that. What we did not know is that technologies, as we are using them, do not and can not rebalance the earth. Not by themselves. Because of the way the organic molecules of LIFE flow all four necessaries of LIFE through the substance of LIFE, as described in the body of this book.

The four basic substances of LIFE, as recognized long ago, by primitive peoples all over the earth are: earth, air, water and fire. Or, as we now can think of them: earth, air, water, and the "sweet spot," as described in Chapter 06, of energy *including information* that arises from natural selection (evolution) of complexity.

That is why our modern science, and the technologies derived from it, are not sufficient to support LIFE. Technologies are not alive because LIFE requires more complexity of information incorporated in the organic energy that flows through its own body -- which is the entire Biosystem -- than we can possibly replace with human technologies, and because LIFE balances every organic interaction individually, and we do not understand every organic interaction. We don't even know how many interactions there are, and it would take some billions of years to figure it out using our current linear, bottom up research methods.

This is difficult to explain, it takes time to imagine, and it is impossible for humans to replicate without understanding all or most of the interactions of the Biosystem.

> We do not understand all or most of the interactions of the Biosystem.

> We can't wait that long to learn to behave in positive, LIFE-affirming ways.

Even with a quantum computer that Seth Lloyd (2016) is working to devise. As he says, it would take as long for such a computer to replicate and explain how the Laws of LIFE (particularly evolution/natural selection) gave rise to, and continue to perfect, the balance of the LIFE of Earth -- and maintain it -- as it took for evolution to actually do the job, which was somewhere in the neighborhood of thirteen billion years (Appendix E). Or five billion plus, if we only count the time of LIFE of Earth. Evolution is doing its job right this minute, all the time, no matter what happens -- and we still don't see it.

Our viable solution is to use our remaining resources to BALANCE OURSELVES, reduce our populations to a sustainable level and let the Biosystem restore itself.

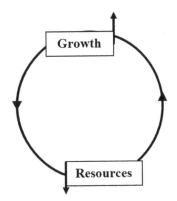

Humans understood this reality long before we had science (Campbell and Moyers, 1999; Huston Smith, 1976). It is still true. It will always be true, so long as there is LIFE.

Every naturally evolved system is organized (because that is how it evolved) around its own particular set of emergent properties (see Chapters 04 and 05).

Naturally evolved systems have emergent properties. The emergent properties connect each system with appropriate other systems in the environment within which it evolved, like the teat connects the baby with its source of milk. As a result of its requirement for connection, the functions of all or most of the parts of the system represent a tightly woven set(s) of interactions that sustain and support the emergent characteristics and functions of that system. As time goes by, if the system is a success, it grows to be more and more specialized to perform its own emergent self-properties — unless and until it becomes disconnected from its environment to such an extent that one or the other (the environment or the system) must change or collapse.

> The environment is not the one that collapses. The environment changes so that its subsystem collapses within the environment in which it evolved. The over-specialized naturally-evolved self-focused system kills its own self by damaging its own environment using its own emergent properties, carried to their extreme.
>
> That is what is happening to us now.
>
> The environment is changing: the corposystem is collapsing.

That is my fifth way of saying that our basic Problem, that evolved out of our human specialized skills of thinking and making technologies, is over-population plus over-production. Humans have become too clever at our specialized skills. Or not clever enough. We have become so good at it that we, via the corposystem, are destroying our own place in LIFE

> ***Reality Number Two*** *– All of the Biosystem, and its emergent properties including LIFE, consists of naturally evolved systems. We humans cannot change how they evolved or how they function to sustain LIFE. Just as the growth of the human embryo requires the womb, and the mother cow feeds the calf, so do all the mothers and all the species require the appropriate environment for their survival. (Preface).*

What Can we Do?

We can begin by discussing the real Problem and its relationship with the symptoms.

To do this, we must recognize LIFE for what it is; not for what we want it to be.

LIFE is the emergent property of a naturally evolved Earth system that uses complexity — collaborative, responsive complexity guided by evolution -- to balance itself -- to sustain itself between the natural forces of energy and entropy; of chaos and inflexibility (Hawking, 2011; Heylighen, all; Lewin, 1992; Midgley, 2016; Lloyd, 2016; Schumacher, 2009, 2015; Seife, 2006; Strogatz, 2008; and see Chapters 04 through 07).

What I see is many people, many heartbroken people, working to "save" the Biosystem using methods promoted by the corposystem. The corposystem uses the media to prevent us even from thinking about the real Problem, much less talking about it. That is one reason that -- whatever we do within that system – it is more than likely to cause more suffering by promoting more growth. Whether or not we know it.

I see other people who are spending vast amounts of effort and money promoting technological cures that will no doubt be useful for something, but not unless we reduce the population to a level that the processes of LIFE can sustain.

We cannot fix LIFE. We must fix ourselves, so that LIFE may live. How to do that is our Problem. How to fix ourselves. Instead, what we are now doing, centers around blame-placing, head-butting and another half-true meme, "I'm OK; you're OK." None of these addresses our biological Problem.

Blame-Placing

Our Problem is not primarily caused by specific, behaviors of individual people, because it is a corposystem Problem, caused by growth of the corposystem, which is a different system from people as a whole (our species, *Homo sapiens*) or as individuals. Growth is an emergent property (macro-property, phenotype) of the corposystem itself. Individually, we are micro-components of the corposystem. There is no apparent direct connection between the micro-components of a naturally evolved complex adaptive system and the macro-properties (phenotypes, emergent properties) of the same system. There is no apparent direct connection between the micro-components (us) and the macro-properties (growth by domination) of the corposystem (Chapters 04 and 05).

Don't get me wrong. I know the rule of our appropriate human law and our individual behaviors is essential to this effort and therefore we must enforce an appropriate rule of law; and we are not. That is a different problem, and inappropriate blame-placing is very likely to drive us to war with each other without demonstrating any law breaking; and, in that way or other ways, make our Problem worse.

To resolve our relationship with the Biosystem, we need to understand the real needs of the Biosystem and use that understanding to HELP the Biosystem fill those needs. Not to dominate the Biosystem, and definitely not try to force it to be what we want it to be, because that is impossible. The Biosystem operates by the laws of God and Nature, and the corposystem operates (more or less) by the constitution, the rule of law, and the worship of growth and profit.

We can use propaganda and advertising and blame-placing to try to get certain things accomplished within the corposystem, for example electing a President. However, fairy tales and fantasies that differ from the biological reality we face -- cannot be used to change the reality. And blame-placing, usually, is not directed at the source of the Problem.

Fixing something else that is not the primary Problem -- will not solve the primary Problem. It will probably make the Problem worse.

Our wisdom traditions have known these things all along. They just say it differently.

That is why this quote from The Dalai Lama is so appropriate.

> "If you want to get rid of painful effects, you have to get rid of their causes."
> and Wisdom is: "analyzing the facts and discerning the actual situation."
> (His Holiness The Dalai Lama, 2009)

Blame placing that is not directed at the cause of a Problem does not resolve the Problem; it makes it worse.

My bigger concern, however, is that we non-presidents and presidents alike, waste enormous amounts of energy on "ain't it awful" and "who's to blame" human social games (Berne, 1964), when that effort (and money) could be used to actually solve the real Problem.

The president is not the corposystem. The president must be held responsible within the rule of law for his or her own behaviors, but if the corposystem is the cause of climate change, then it is unlikely that a president can solve it. Therefore, if we spend our lives fighting against the president, believing that we are "fixing" climate change, there is a sense in which we are wasting our lives. Or at the very best, we are only delaying the crash.

Yes, it is necessary to deal with the *symptoms* of overpopulation -- climate change, war, poverty, ignorance, illness, and so on -- but if we don't ALSO deal with the *cause* of climate change, what's the point? Quite soon we won't be here to care about the other things and we are just reinforcing a positive feedback loop of a runaway system, and the Problem will never stop getting worse until that system crashes.

That is our Problem. In our world views, most of us believe we are trying to fix the biological Problem, but at the same time our own behaviors re-enforce the corposystem paradigm that caused the biological Problem in the first place. The harder we work using the same belief system that caused the Problem (growth by domination) the more we harm the Biosystem, no matter our good intentions.

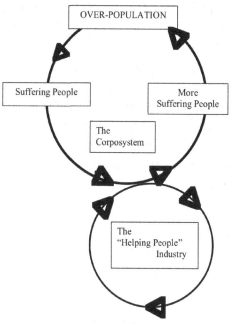

That is how evolution gets rid of species that cause harm to the entire system.

That's how it works, and that's what we must talk about if we want to fix it for the future more than we want the easy life and/or fame and fortune for a few of us, for today.

Blame-placing is a fun game because it relieves us of our own sense of responsibility. A sense of responsibility is a good thing, but we are not responsible for things over which we have no control. We have very little control over the emergent properties of other systems. We are micro-properties of one system trying to use the emergent properties of our system to talk to or repair other systems.

We human citizens of Earth have in common the vision and goal of helping to regenerate a healthy earth that can comfortably support a human presence; the resources we have to work with are the unchanging and unchangeable Facts of LIFE that are based in the universal natural laws of energy, entropy, information, complexity, evolution, self-assembly and natural selection — all of our fourteen big ideas that all work together, that are listed in Appendix D and described briefly in Chapter 10.

And time.

But not much more time. Most people already understand that.

But we have wildly varying opinions about how to use our same natural laws (Facts of LIFE) to get to that goal of a healthy relationship with the Biosystem.

There is one that we know is the cause; we haven't even yet tried to slow down the cause.

> "Insanity is when we keep doing the same thing and expect to get a different result." (unknown)

> "If you want to get rid of painful effects, you have to get rid of their causes." Wisdom is: "analyzing the facts and discerning the actual situation." (His Holiness The Dalai Lama, 2009)

Headbutting versus "I'm OK/You're OK."

If we are old enough to have seen several turns of the wheel of the corposystem, we know that the symptoms we are trying to heal are not improving. In fact, the harder we try to fix the symptoms, the same symptoms – poverty for example – hostility, war, greed, crime, starvation, sickness -- the worse the problems get -- because we are not addressing their root cause, which is growth beyond resources.

The corposystem tells us these symptoms are getting better, or will get better if we do one thing or another, and for some reason we believe this, even though the data and our own eyes do not support that claim. Poverty, war, education, human rights, even human courtesy as a measure of compassion. If you have lived as long as I have, you know that these are not getting better (Bryson, 2002; Butler, 2015) and there is a reason for that – a reason that also is confirming fact-based predictions, and in fact surpassing them (Gore, 2006, 2017; Heinberg, 2007; Heinberg & Lerch, 2010; Makhijani, 2007; Martenson, 2009; McKibben, 2010; Ryerson, 2010; Orr, 2004; and many others).

And we are responding to the changes in the corposystem, often in one of two corposystem-approved modalities:

1. I'm OK/You're OK; or
2. with classical dominational arguments of various kinds that I refer to as "headbutting."

The Biosystem functions by collaboration, as explained in the text of this book. Neither of these human social games is an effort to collaborate with the needs of the Biosystem.

The first is akin to shunning, prevents discussion, and results in something like: "each man is an island, condemned to be himself alone."

Headbutting includes confrontations of many kinds from arguing or debate through war. It does not include partnership, discussion, mutual analysis or win-win negotiation. Even better, win-win-win. I once managed a four-win solution, and I'm not even very good at that style of relationship! If everyone would think win-win, and consider the differences among the needs of the various systems, we would lick this thing fairly quickly.

The Biosystem requires collaborative relationships that support its need for high efficiency (Chapter 06). And so the situation worsens for another turn of the wheel of human life and its impact on its mother, the environment.

I'm OK/You're OK

The "I'm OK/You're OK" model for citizen action, references a meme that was popular some decades ago (Harris, 1967).

Based on this meme, the presumption seems to have arisen in the corposystem culture that every human opinion is equally valid, that my view is almost as good as yours, and vice versa, that all opinions are good if our intentions are good.

I read the book. Dr. Harris did not mean that it is OK to stop considering the short term and long term consequences of our behaviors.

It seems to me that good intentions, if they really are, would follow the advice of His Holiness (2009) and take the trouble to deeply inform themselves and then to determine what systems are primarily involved with the Problem, before taking actions that affect other living systems (for systems see Chapters 03, 04, 05, and Appendix B).

And -- here is the difficulty -- if we each take on one problem (symptom expressed within the corposystem), for example if you do poverty and I do compassion – we tend to believe that our work will together add up to the emergence of our common goal, and it's all good. The harder we work, the better it will be for everyone.

This additive philosophy is very attractive and is useful in many situations, but unfortunately naturally evolved systems do not work that way (Chapters 04, 05, 06), because they are systems. The emergent results of manipulating systems, especially their down sides and especially as we usually do not evaluate the down sides, are not predictable unless we consider the needs of the system(s) that we are impacting.

Just as you can't help another person unless you consider what she really needs, it is even more true that you can't help other non-human systems unless you consider what they need. What they need will be related to their primary emergent property.

In reality, the harder we ignore the root Problem while trying to fix the symptoms – the WORSE the symptoms become, and the less we understand each other. Or an apparently unrelated problem will pop out in a different sub-system that is worse than the one we are trying to fix. We can see this in our relationships with other people. It is even more so in our relationships with non-human systems.

Our Problem is not a linear, additive challenge. Our Problem revolves around the symptoms of the down-side (from a human perspective) of a naturally evolved nonhuman system, the Biosystem, that is struggling to retain the balance of its own LIFE that the extreme of modern corposystem "success" has disrupted, and so the harder we work using the flawed additive corposystem reductionist model that caused the symptoms -- the worse become the symptoms, unless ALL (or enough) of us ALSO address their root cause.

I'm OK/You're OK cannot resolve human social problems because it represents compassion in absence of discernment:

1. It assumes that mommy and daddy will take care of us. Or maybe Trump. That will not happen in any human society. That's what a competent and well-educated youth is for. To carry forward the culture. Not necessarily by means of sperms.

2. It assumes that our works, our charitable efforts within the corposystem, are additive. They are not. We live in a world composed of systems that interact with each other at every level, as they modulate their responses to our behaviors.

3. Within the corposystem, we are not collaborating. We are competing, which is a dominational style of relationship. We might find our viable niche within the collaborative system (the Biosystem) by competing against each other within the corposystem, but not by competing against the Biosystem, which is far more complex and powerful than most people, especially technologists, understand. The corposystem will not help us any longer – can't because we have overgrazed its resources; furthermore, as a system, it functions primarily to perpetuate itself.

   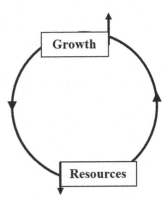

   Its method of controlling us, in part, is to train us to WANT to compete for the goals that the corposystem needs us to accomplish so that it can grow. As good citizens of the corposystem we may not, perhaps cannot, even think about the root causes of our Problem -- and so we no longer talk about causes. We simply apply for the money and work for the recognition, and better the fame. If we succeed, we work harder in our efforts to undo the after-effects (symptoms) of overpopulation, that are caused by our own hard work!

4. The symptoms of human overgrowth are felt within the corposystem as human suffering. However, the root cause of all the symptoms is human overgrowth so massive that it unbalances the whole Biosystem. The cause of our human Problem is our attack upon the balanced welfare of another system, the LIFE System/ Biosystem.

   The corposystem demands that we adhere to its mantra of growth by domination/ competition or it will not fund our work; the Biosystem requires a sustainable, collaborative balance within its entire system (the entire LIFE of Earth) -- not growth -- in order to maintain the environment that we humans require for our survival. The modern corposystem (a Ponzi paradigm) cannot survive as it is today without growth, and its environment (the Biosystem) cannot support more human growth. It is the Biosystem, not the corposystem, that supports all of LIFE on Earth, including human life. The solution is not to keep trying to change the Biosystem, but to change the corposystem.

5. The result of I'm OK/You're OK -- that is, everyone doing something helpful to address the symptoms of today without addressing the common root cause of our Problem – the result is not so much a common solution, as it is common chaos. A shattering of our storyline into diverse and competing paradigms. Each with the same good intentions, but none (or few) collaborating with the others toward that goal. We are competing against each other in nearly every aspect of our lives. This is not a wise or compassionate or practical way to solve Our Problem.

I'm OK-You're OK, live and let live is not wise; not even responsible. We must expect and receive from our fellow humans, and enforce, behavior that is responsible to the whole of LIFE.

We of the corposystem generations were raised, trained and brainwashed (imprinted) in the corposystem mantra (growth by competition or domination for gain). That paradigm, therefore, seems very logical to us, and in fact it is logical if growth is what we need.

Many things are logical that are not sustainable, or even not true, and the corposystem paradigm was quite successful as long as the Biosystem could give us more resources than we needed to maintain the growth of the corposystem. The illusion of success on our terms.

But logical does not mean accurate. And that was then, and now humans have overgrazed the earth to the extent that we are laying waste the Biosystem itself. That means there is not enough food to support the other living creatures – the other micro-components of the system of LIFE – and when we change the micro-components, then we change both the DNA program that regulates LIFE (Chapter 09), and the emergent characteristics of the Biosystem, in ways that we cannot predict. Currently that is climate change along with a pandemic that would not have occurred or spread exponentially over the whole earth, without overpopulation.

We are "eating up the seed corn." In this metaphor, the "seed corn" is the species that maintain the LIFE of the Biosystem. More attacks against the symptoms within the corposystem (poverty, starvation, war, etc.) without reducing their cause (human growth) will not make more seed corn within the Biosystem; it will simply make more profits for the fewer number of people who control the corposystem by destroying more resources that the Biosystem needs for its own balanced welfare.

The harder we work to help the corposystem grow -- in order to achieve a good life for all the people – our wonderful progress in human rights and all the other good things -- the closer we drive the corposystem toward collapse because there are no longer enough resources for all the good things for everyone, bcause every generation has more or less twice as many people in it; and in our efforts to get and continue to get enough good things, we are destroying the other species; that is, the nonhuman species that generate earth, air, water and manage energy in the form that the human physiology can use it. That is our Modern Problem.

> **Reality Number Eight** -- *Within the systems, there is no dichotomy between a "glass half full" or a "glass half empty." If a glass is half full it is also half empty. Every action has both up sides and down sides, yin and yang, good and bad results. Good is here defined as sustainable, relative to the needs of the particular system. If we do not anticipate all the possible good and bad outcomes of our behaviors, we will continue to have many unpleasant surprises in our future. If we "understand the rules" (Carroll, 2015), that is, the Facts of Life, we have a better chance of anticipating all the possible outcomes of our behaviors, before we do actions out of ignorance, that we come to regret. Our behaviors for any reason are equally as bad as they are good – and they cannot be reversed. (Chapter 02, Appendix A).*

By using the I'm OK/You're OK model, we are choosing to ignore the rules of nature in favor of a human meme that is not even accurate – to look the other way and let Mother Nature decide which among us happen, often by chance, to grab the gold ring of riches, while the corposystem crashes. The up-side of this choice is that everyone gets to do whatever she feels called to do if she can find the resources. This is fun for the winning few, and makes them feel important in a culture that is based in competition and growth, but there are at least two negative results for those of us who would rather work for a comfortable human presence in a healthy Biosystem:

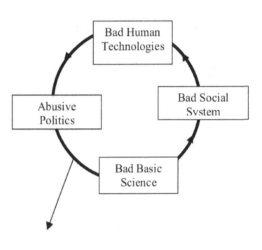

1. The net result of I'm OK/You're OK is that everyone who is successful is, by default supporting the corposystem ethic of growth by competition or domination for gain, and the more we support that failed system -- the worse will be the inevitable crash when it comes. It is inevitable because nothing on Earth, nowhere, nohow, can grow forever. This is not tomorrow that I am talking about. It is yesterday and today.

2. We are (it is fascinating to a basic scientist who is trying to learn how to look at the naturally evolved systems from the Biosystem point of view, or better yet a human religious point of view) we are actually leaving our survival choices to natural selection, even though we are probably the first species ever to have the option of making its own evolutionary choices.

Rather than using our marvelous human brain for its survival function and working together toward our common goal -- I'm OK, You're OK uses it to generate individual perks, leaving natural selection to decide which is best. If any.

Happy, loving people who are doing good work (that is most people) do not want to hear about the down-side of what they are doing, but -- just as there are always more than two choices in a naturally evolving system — there is also always a down side, from any perspective, to all the choices.

Probably that is why human communities evolved. No individual can know everything, and the community as a whole can benefit from the knowledges of all its parts. That is why we need seers, and prophets and wisdom and evil; that is why we need "outliers" of all sorts (Gladwell, 2011). That is why our obligation as normal, responsible people, is to listen to such people, not just pat them on the head, thinking: "you're OK, even if you are wrong." Of course they are OK; that part is easy; they might also be right.

Our part in community survival is to listen to the knowledges of the "outliers," and consider what they know that we do not. And what they do not know. And above all, to discuss this knowledge in relation to each other, so that the knowledge considered can emerge a community wisdom that is greater than the sum of its parts.

And we have the media to help us in our discussion. If we genuinely want to grow a comfortable human presence within a healthy life system, it would be better if we (each and all and preferably together, it's no fun doing it alone) were to also challenge our own world views – to evolve our world views, so that they accommodate the basic Facts of Life and not the unfettered growth paradigm of the corposystem, or someone else's wishful thinking, neither of which is sustainable

The process of self-examination would not lead us all to enlightenment, but it would automatically tend to align our world views, and therefore our behaviors, more closely with the Facts *and with each other*, because the facts are what they are no matter our opinions, and they are the same for everyone. If we want to help each other, there is no point growing a mirage that can never happen, of human technological or spiritual power over The Creation.

I'm OK/You're OK is a human solution to human social problems within the corposystem, not the Biosystem. It is not "bad," but LIFE is not so simple as "bad" and "good," and the corposystem cannot fix LIFE for all the reasons given above, and because LIFE requires for its welfare all the different kinds of sentient beings. Not only humans.

> **Reality Number Nine** – *As citizen activists, we should learn the rules before we try to fix the game (Chapter 02).*

Perhaps your answer to the above is:

"How can we be against I'm OK-You're OK? It is the only possible answer! There is no way we can get together around the root cause because the root cause is population growth, and we can't talk about the population issue. That would require mass debates, and we are already fighting over all the issues mentioned above, plus a few more. In fact. we are at war over these issues ~ even the anti-violence-pro-compassion movement is fighting to dominate the behaviors of the people. We don't need more fighting. We must find ways to get along with each other, or the result will surely be dissolution of our current successful social system. We can't resolve the chaos of our social dissolution by fighting with each other!"

Yes. And no.

Of course you are right, except for three factual realities:

1. The current system is not successful. It is the cause of the Problem. It appeared to be successful when the Biosystem had plenty of extra resources. Now, the metaphorical teat of the Biosystem has run out of milk. It's time we wean ourselves of our fairy tales of omnipotence and omniscience.
2. Facts are real, and one of the facts is that human technologies cannot change facts – and the fact is that nothing on Earth can grow forever. And the more it tries to do so, the more suffering it will cause. (Perhaps I should mention here that I am not opposed to death as a necessary part of LIFE, but I am against the unnecessary creation of suffering and the causes of suffering.)
3. Who says we can't talk to whomever we want to talk to? Who says we only have two choices? We in this country are so very fortunate that others before us have given us better options. And yes, we are losing them now, so we also need to pay attention to that, but not at the expense of our population Problem, because what's the point of having rights if we aren't here?

It is the corposystem, not the reality that tells us we cannot talk about our most critical issue, or that we only have two choices. In a natural system, we never have only two choices – not until the very last choice. We always have at least three choices, and usually way too many. That is probably one of the reasons that nature is built around complex adaptive systems rather than linear, dichotomous either-or choices. It's a very much more resilient situation than we realize when we limit ourselves to two choices. We have many options still, and nature has even more.

Reality Number Ten -- *Every problem gives us more than two possible choices, usually many more than three. Simplistic answers, such as memes and either-or choices, do not solve complex systemic problems. That's why debate is good for the warrior (including our modern politicians) but is not really good for problem solving. Usually, simplistic answers make things worse. Fortunately, we each have a very complex human brain that is capable of understanding our modern biological Problem. (Chapter 02)*

We can agree that arguing, debating, war, within a culture, does not support that culture unless that's what we want – arguing, debating and war. It is what we've got, and some of us want it, or we wouldn't have it. Some of us will do anything to win an argument, a debate or a war. However, most of us, most likely, would rather sustain an honorable rule of law that can give us a reasonably comfortable lifestyle within a healthy Biosystem. And we do not want to fight.

So we do nothing; or we are citizen activists. Those are two relatively easy choices that are available in our social system. There are others.

But life is not easy; and the goal of LIFE is not happiness – it is survival. Preferably with comfort and in joy (The Dalai Lama *et al.*, 2016).

LIFE is not supposed to be easy, and that may be one of our problems; we expect easy, but it never was easy and it never will be easy. The whole point of LIFE is survival of LIFE, and survival is not easy. And it will be much more difficult for more of us if we do nothing and let nature choose our future, because the crash of a Ponzi scheme, especially when the "crash" consists of lives lost through suffering, is not what we want to watch or participate in. And now that we have a worldwide economy, we will, in the end, have worldwide participation in its collapse (Diamond, 2011) unless we work for the welfare of the Biosystem IN ADDITION TO whatever we do that supports the creation of a better social system and/or our own livelihood.

Trying Harder

It seems as though we of the corposystem are not really trying to solve our fundamental Problem. Instead, we are running off in all directions at the same time, with no common sustainable paradigm to guide us. Each person or organization focused upon a different problem; a different symptom of corposystem or Biosystem dis-ease; each according to his own unique and individual world view, without regard to the common goal or the Facts of Life to which we must all adhere or fail. (Peck, 1987, the section on "Flight"; Lamoreux, Bare Bones Biology 024, 025, 026, 317 and others). Thus, our individual self-focused efforts obscure the clear path toward a common world view that might achieve a successful outcome (Craven, 2009).

To me, successful = survival of the Biosystem, with its necessary species. A successful world view is very similar to what The Dalai Lama refers to as a wise world view (The Dalai Lama, 2009). Closely related to a win-win, or even a win-win-win result (Jandt, 1985) with the future as one of our winners.

Instead of using the undeniable basic Facts of Physics and of Biology to save ourselves within the Biosystem, we are living a co-dependent life style in the arms of a false God, the corposystem (Weinhold & Weinhold, 1989).

If everything we are doing is wrong, is there anything that is right?

It is normal for dying systems to fragment into chaos. That's how evolution functions. In the good times, natural selection reinforces the status quo of a system, the cohesion of the system; in the bad times, the system sets up a lot of uncoordinated variability, so that, if the system crashes, then natural selection can choose whichever of the fragments contributes positively to the welfare of the environment that remains -- and let the other fragments destroy themselves. This is a normal part of the evolutionary process.

This is what is happening to *Homo sapiens*. Variability is being generated within the corposystem as a normal step in its continuing crash. There is nothing unusual or surprising about what is happening to our climate in response to our behaviors. So, yes, it is normal for dying systems to fragment into chaos.

It is also normal for humans to want to do something about the chaos.

I'm not proposing that we try to ignore the situation just because it is normal; normal is not always the best choice. But whatever solutions we choose, I am proposing that we base those solutions on good information about their sustainability – not on our own ignorance or someone else's un-tested belief systems or the greed that is embedded in our social system. https://en.wikipedia.org/wiki/Dunning%E2%80%93Kruger_effect

I am proposing, if we choose to do something to "fix" the Problem, then it would be best to choose something that has a chance of succeeding. Something that conforms to universal Facts of LIFE.

Humankind already has everything we need to contribute positively rather than destructively within the Biosystem, whenever we decide to, or are forced to, reduce our populations. We do know the root cause of the problems, and we already know a better way. A way that has a chance of succeeding and has succeeded in similar situations. It is one of the greatest advances of our science and technology; we do this routinely in medicine and in agriculture.

For example, a child is brought to hospital running a high fever caused by a biological infection. The hospital treats the fever and all its symptoms. AT THE SAME TIME, the hospital will give the patient a shot that raises the patient's immunity to the infection. That is, we kill off the overpopulation of some infective organism.

The human medical system and also the agricultural system use this method routinely, with vaccines and other nontoxic (to us) approaches to prevent overpopulation of various species in the Biosystem, from measles to blowflies. As I write this, we are on hold in mid-pandemic, waiting for a vaccine that will reduce the overpopulation of the Covid-19 virus.

But who will protect the Biosystem from us? Evolution will, inevitably and soon, unless we choose to take care of ourselves. There is no reason we cannot use our minds to protect ourselves from ourselves.

There is no point to poisoning the environment to solve a environmental problem that is caused by pollution. GMO (genetically modified organisms), for example, as we use them, require massive applications of herbicides (-cide means poison) to grow massive amounts of tainted food that we would not need if we were not overpopulated. They harm the Biosystem in order to feed us. This is neither tolerable nor sustainable, because it is extremely toxic to the Biosystem. Those poisons are now being recycled within the body of the Biosystem, which includes us, and bees, and Monarch Butterflies. And now it has been found by a court of law to be also toxic to humans. Well, we already knew that, didn't we. The court of law can not prevent past suffering, but the precautionary principle (Chapter 09) could have, and we could have prevented BOTH problems and a great many others, by reducing the population.

Wise compassion would have been to reduce the human population — and suffering — not to make different kinds of food to feed more people and make more profits, when the Biosystem resource "services" are insufficient, causing other necessary species to go extinct, while at the same time causing an increase in the human population that must be fed (or starve) in the following generation and an increase in environmental pollution that is more than likely to be our next "surprise" human illness problem.

If a hospital were to use the same method of treating diseases that we are applying to our larger social and biological Problem – that is, treat the symptoms while ignoring the root cause, when a nontoxic cure for the cause is available — or another example, prescribing toxic designer drugs when the problem could have been cured by saline infusions, or simply by drinking more water — we would call that criminal neglect. If a politician does the same, we call it crimes against humanity.

Even our societal complexity must be sustainably balanced if we are to benefit from its rich creativity:

> "Intensified food production and societal complexity stimulate each other by autocatalysis; that is, population growth leads to societal complexity by mechanisms that we have discussed, while societal complexity in turn leads to intensified food production and thereby to population growth."
> (Dr. Jared Diamond, UCLA, Guns, Germs and Steel, 1997)

That is, intensified food production that is not balanced by the normal checks and balances of evolution, because it is not embedded within the information of LIFE (Hopfenberg R,

2003; Hopfenberg R, Pimentel D. 2001; Salmoney, Steven Earl. 2004 and others; United Nations Development Programme. 2003.)
http://www.undp.org/hdr2003/indicator/indic_38_1_1.html.

Long term, this just makes the imbalance worse.

We know the root cause; we have the necessary technologies to reduce our human population, both physical and educational technologies, are available.

An Appropriate Response Would Be

To first recognize the cycle of Biosystem collapse and human social collapse that we have created, and then cut the cycle of collapse using the same approach that the emergency room uses to prevent or cure infections. By controlling the overgrowth of the organism that causes it, whether it be a bacterial infection, or a parasite, or a virus (covid-19) or *Homo sapiens*.

That is the same advice given by His Holiness, The Dalai Lama in the quote above:

1. Identify the Problem. That has been done.
2. And now, eliminate the cause, beginning with prevention of all unwanted pregnancies. Worldwide. Please do not tell me we are already doing that until you have checked your facts and can support your claim.
3. Eliminate the denial, individually and communally. Explain the Problem to the people, for example as our Governor in New Mexico has done so well in the face of the pandemic -- and begin the discussions.

As compassionately as possible. Before the processes of nature and the Biosystem do it for us with no compassion (because the Biosystem does not have human emotions) and with great suffering.

We should check with history as we try to decide on a method that might work. The Hitler method did not; neither has WWIII, or our modern technologies. And then discuss, discuss, discuss before we jump on the first original but ignorant idea that crosses our headlines.

All the people with any specialty of corposystem expertise – religion, economics, medicine, all those symptoms of our dis-ease – yes I am talking to you also. You should be talking more loudly even than the scientists about the Problem that we face. After all, the scientists already have funding, which means they are now mostly embedded in the corposystem way of thinking. You may have something better to offer.

When I say things like that, usually the first answer I get is:

"I can't stop what I'm doing to jump on your bandwagon!"

DID I SAY THAT?

I DID NOT SAY THAT.!

What I did say is -- if anyone wants to make a truly meaningful contribution to the longterm benefit of human kind -- they should do so using their own expertise, and *at the same time* support and help those who are making available the necessary birth control technologies. Not one or the other; a serious commitment requires both.

Everyone should stop planning for a future that very likely will not happen because we keep planning for it rather than working to ensure that it can happen.

"When we reach the year 2050"

should NOT be part of our vocabulary. We should not be talking fake hope that only creates no hope. With that attitude, we very likely will never reach the year 2050. Here is our reality:

"IF we reach the year 2050."

Why not try for something that is possible?

Why not start thinking about HOW to reach the year 2050. Something that actually has a fact-based chance. And then do it collaboratively. Snipping off symptoms from the branches and blossoms of corposystem dis-ease, while the engine that causes all these problems is still churning at its base, cannot change the toxic effects of our over-growth. Why not stop lying to our children with platitudes and start planning to stop the growth at least by discussing the issue in all possible venues.

The corposystem does not require growth to sustain itself where it is now, and growth now is very toxic to the Biosystem.

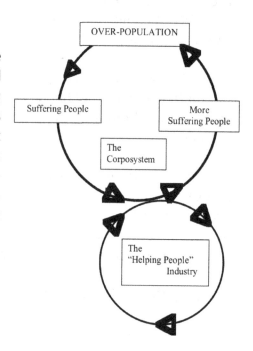

256

Stop the growth in numbers of human bodies; stop the growth in GNP or any other way of measuring economic or organic growth; stop the growth in complexity that is generated by the growth in population (Diamond, 1997). Stop the growth in food production. (Salmony, 2004; Diamond, 1997; Hopfenberg, 2003; Hopfenberg and Pimentel, 2001; United Nations Development Programme, 2003) or gradually reduce it while making available universal birth control. Stop writing growth into dot-com and dot-org charters; require them to show that they are not adding to the Problem. At least that might make them think.

And most especially, stop the suffering of unwanted babies by preventing their birth before they have a chance to suffer for their whole short lifetimes.

Start thinking and talking about the connection between unwanted babies and the sex industry, child labor, slavery, war, wherever they end up. You will find plenty of references in older issues of National Geographic and other honest magazines and news media. Lately, our corposystem apparently is trying to silence this kind of information, but I am sure these situations have not improved.

And while we are doing that, we can start talking about population reduction toward a stablizable economy at a level that the Biosystem can support.

Why?

BECAUSE THAT IS OUR JOB! That is why we were put on this earth at this time. That is how we can contribute to human welfare – not by making more people to justify the growth of the compassion industry by generating more suffering because the resources of the Biosystem are being destroyed because there are too many people.

But to require our own social systems to adapt to the reality of LIFE.

Stop thinking about survival of the fittest. It won't work, as we imagine it, because —

> **Reality Number Twenty-Five** - Evolution is not about "survival of the fittest." It is about the flow of information and energy through collaborating systems (Appendix A).

Flow the information, not the ignorance!

The only reason an economy needs to grow is to make billionaires and starvation, and then it will crash anyhow. It is a Ponzi scheme, and it is out of resources at its bottom. It will crash in any case; better a transition.

Start to line up the facts that basic scientists can measure to a certainty of, say 95%. Line these up on one side, believe in them at least tentatively, figure out how they work, and begin by adjusting our own individual world views to accommodate the real universal facts -- rather than concentrate primarily on the "social facts" the corposystem has taught us so illogically to believe. That kind of evaluation might help us to devise win-win, partnership-style solutions (Jandt,1985; Eisler 1987) and (Lamoreux, Bare Bones Biology 317), each within our own disciplines, to a serious fact-based biological Problem.

Too often, instead, we waste our time and effort trying to accomplish the impossible using "I'm OK, You're OK" approach to fixing the unfixable. Or blame-placing politics. Or the headbutting "war to end all wars" fairy tale.

Why are we so afraid of talking among ourselves, and not so afraid of starvation, poverty, war, disease and extinction when they happen to other people?

Why would we rather fight or deny or attack the Biosystem rather than address the real Problem?

Is it possible that our chaotic response to our social and biological collapse is not so much about facing up to the Facts of Life as it is about the necessity of getting together to "analyze the facts and discern the actual situation" in an effort to grow some wisdom around the Problem? Is it perhaps that our World Views, rather than informing us about the Facts of LIFE (that are basically collaborative) are pushing us apart, preventing us from getting together even to discuss serious life-and-death issues? Teaching us that we can "win" by trying harder - by domination – by making enemies that we won't talk to?

Do we want to work together toward a resolution of our common biological emergency?

Or not!

That is our final choice.

OOOOOOO

This Appendix A is dedicated to Steven E. Salmony.

APPENDIX B

DEFINITIONS, DESCRIPTIONS, KEY CONCEPTS

I would like to see the story of LIFE consciously told in a myriad of ways, because that is what people have been doing from the beginning. It is all the same story, as it must be if we are to align our behaviors with the requirements of the facts, and that's what human stories are for. It is the same facts, but they arrange themselves into differing world views within different cultural environments. So our understanding of the facts changes, and our modern understanding of systems has dramatically changed since the corposystem grew itself around a mostly false image of "survival of the fittest" that favored growth and grew to be abusively dominational. I mean abusive toward LIFE itself and therefore toward ourselves, though it is very nice for some individuals in the short term. To serve everyone and to involve everyone, we tell stories, and to share the stories we need common words.

There is no perfect definition of any word; there is no perfect human idea. One problem in trying to share our words and ideas is that we often use the same words to support a cluster of different ideas. This Appendix B is an effort to define and describe some of my more important words and ideas.

Please use my definitions while thinking about my ideas. The facts will not change, of course, but our ideas might if we understand each other in the pleasure of our discussion.

CONCEPTS

My intention is to contribute to:

> *a reasonably comfortable, sustainable human presence within a compatible, healthy and abundant Biosystem.*

Sustainability means the ability to continue – to cycle forward in time -- forever. Or, unto the 7th generation and beyond. (Lyons, Oren)

It is possible to destroy everything that we love WITHOUT violence and, in that way, keep the people happy until the very last minute, when the shit hits the fan, and there is no place else to turn. That is not the intention of any publication cited here, nor of most "actions," but I am quite certain there are some very sophisticated organized efforts to "win" the propaganda wars by mis-using the words of our good intentions. (Reality Number Eleven, Appendix C).

Greater evil hath no man if, by working hard to garble the information from 99% of the scientists, he prevents the message reaching the people and destroys human life on earth for his own personal gain.

Evil here applies to human behaviors that involve intentional harm to the systems that we all require for our welfare (Peck, 1987).

Trying to change the unchangeable facts is not where our power lies. We have more important things to do (Reality Number Twelve, Appendix C).

Good/bad – The terms "good" and "bad" in these pages relate to sustainability -- NOT to human world views, ethics or opinions and not to whichever organism can eat the other organisms.

The Creation - I like Huston Smith's (2001) definition: "Everything, as it is." See also Tyson & Goldsmith (2004); and Wilson (2006).

The Creator - For this book, because it is primarily about LIFE, I will accept that The Creator refers to the creator of LIFE of Earth. Or of the entire universe.

God - I will not presume to define God. I will assume that, whatever our image of God, it is of The Creator. The complexity of God the Creator must be greater than The Creation, and so far I have only scratched the surface of understanding the Creation, so I do not try to understand why, who, when, but I think we are beginning to comprehend how. I think The Creation was created and sustains itself using the immutable laws of nature, and I believe that the deep laws of nature do not change. They are the facts of LIFE.

Here are a few publications I have found meaningful: Armstrong, 2009 and others; Attenborough, 2007, 2011 (BBC); Black Elk Speaks, 1932; Campbell & Moyers, 1999; Chacour, 2003; Chodron, Pema, 2007; Chogyam Trungpa,1973; Nilson, 1973; Grigg, 2010; Gulen, 2011; Hesse, 1922; Patrul, 1998; Smith, 2001; Stewart, Ian, BBC; The Dalai Lama, 2005, 2010; The Dalai Lama and Geshe Thupten Jinpa. 2009; Goodenough, 1981, Redford, 2017; Shantideva, 2008 translation; Woodruff, 2001; and various scriptures.

"Science without religion is lame. Religion without science is blind."
This was attributed, on the web, to Einstein; one smart guy.

Hubris = egotistical, individual-centered pride

Homocentric = human centered. If we want to survive, we need to remember that humans are not at the center of anything except *Homo sapiens* and perhaps the corposystem.

Technologies = tools made by humans

The Earth – The third planet out from our sun, The Biosystem, upon and within which the system of the LIFE of Earth arose, about 5 billion years ago, in the form of prokaryotic (bacteria type) cells and evolved, system by system to become the LIFE of the whole Earth.

The Biosystem - the entire naturally evolved living system that now includes the Earth and generates and regenerates the LIFE of Earth that is its emergent property. See systems and LIFE. A primary emergent property of the Biosystem is LIFE.

Ecosystem - is a higher-level naturally evolved LIFE system (higher, more complex, than the cellular, tissue, organ or organ system, or organism levels of complexity). The ecosystems are composed of other systems including cells, tissues, organs, organ systems, organisms. The Biosystem is composed of ecosystems.

The Corposystem - our human naturally evolved corpo-political-economic-military-medical-educational-charitable social system. Two of its sustaining emergent properties are growth and dominational relationships. A third is money.

Human = An individual organism (naturally evolved system) of the species *Homo sapiens*.

Homo sapiens = the human species, a naturally evolved, inter-breeding species. That means that humans can mate and produce fertile offspring. That is the definition of a species. Two well developed emergent properties of humans are tool-making and our sometimes elegant ability to think.

Species - The biological definition is: A group of organisms that are capable of sharing their genes. This means a population of organisms that can mate with each other and produce fertile offspring. The sharing of information is important for LIFE, and sex is one (of many) methods that information is shared and distributed by the species of LIFE.

Mitosis = Cellular reproduction that results in genetically identical new cells.

Meiosis = Cellular reproduction that results in haploid (having half the normal number of chromosomes) sex cells.

zygote = fertilized egg that will grow into an embryo.

Gene = a unit of inheritance. Humans have two complete sets of genes. That means humans have two of every different kind of gene. Every kind of gene has one particular function, which is usually to provide the code for a particular kind of protein.

Genome = all the genes in one particular organism or other unit of LIFE.

Gene Pool = all the genes in all the organisms of a particular species or other unit of LIFE.

Gene Pool of the Biosystem. I use that term in this book because I need to talk about all the genes in the entire Biosystem, at any one time. I do not know of any other word for that idea. The idea is important.

Overpopulation is the growth of any biological population or species beyond its ability to communicate collaboratively with its environment and the environment's ability to support its numbers.

Collaborative Relationships. Other terms for the same or similar concept are "partnership" (Eisler, 1987) and win/win exchanges of information (Jandt, 1985).

Dominational relationships can be thought of as win-lose, competitive, co-dependent etc. Dominational relationships may be hero-victim or villain-victim "co-dependent" interactions. Or they can be more overtly war rather than collaboration, debate rather than discussion. In this book I refer to dominational relationships as contrasted with collaborative (partnership), win-win or win-win-win transactions within which everyone (ideally) eventually benefits. Dominational relationships are win-lose cycles within which everyone eventually loses (Dear, 2008, 2013 and others; Jandt, 1985; Weinhold and Weinhold, 1989).

Dominational relationships are not survival-friendly for several reasons:

> They are narrow and biased and "all stuck in the same rut," and lack diversity, and therefore very easy to outwit as their efficiency can be overwhelmed by complexity.

> They are very powerful, and therefore very destructive, if their power overwhelms diversity and communication.

> They are biologically part of the useful and sometimes necessary yin and yang of existence, but they are subject to overthrow by blowback generated by their own behaviors (Janeway, 1980)

FACTS

Universal facts are realities and processes that we cannot change because they operate throughout the entire universe, for example, energy, entropy, information, self-assembly, natural selection, time, gravity, history. We do not understand these facts perfectly; sometimes our understanding of them changes. But the facts do not change; in reality, it is we who change. Therefore. real universal facts are our most useful support in our efforts to understand the most unchanging reality of our environments.

Our human social facts (Gimbel, 2015), on the other hand, are not universal Facts. They are beliefs or situations or answers that have been imprinted on our common consciousness, during our communal development as a naturally evolving human society. Imprinting is one of the ways that our environment communicates with us during our development. It is perfectly normal (Eagleman, 2017), and probably necessary. But not always perfect.

"The rules by which we determine a social fact are internalized.
We never think of them . . .
sometimes the social facts are there for good reason,
but sometimes they're not. . . . Not all social facts are desirable,
and unless we are forced to confront and justify them,
they will remain of their own inertia, and become worse if not challenged."
(Gimbel, 2015)

History as it actually happened is factual. As with most facts, we do not normally know the whole story, but as they happened, actions, behaviors, events that took place in past time cannot be changed and will affect the future of LIFE. It it is important that we know the factual reality as accurately as possible, rather than a self-serving, homocentric version that does not help us to use our fine brains to benefit from past mistakes and successes.

Facts of Life = The universal facts that the entire naturally evolved system of LIFE must use in Its ongoing imperative to stay alive. Some are summarized in Chapter 10 and Appendix D.

Linear Thinking – thinking like a book, from beginning to end, usually with an artificial (or real) anticlimax, or "arc" to add interest. Being a scientist actually taught me how to think linear, reductionist. Apparently I was born thinking like a system; well, of course, the brain is a system; then, through schooling, the science and the corposystem taught me to classify and sequence and cause-relate, either-or. Then I had to learn yet more to understand that LIFE is not linear, it is systemic.

So I learned to translate my native systems thinking into linear, and then try to translate the linear into some kind of explanation of systems that my readers can understand that is not linear, I mean teach or explain how to swirl one's mind around a biological system rather than just memorize some facts and use them to get what we want. A web site that does a better job of the same thing is NoraBateson.wordpress.com. See also Hoffmeyer, 2008; and Tonnesen, 2019.

I have not found a "best" way to present systemic viewpoints in a book, because the book is limited by its linear structure, but it might be done, using a computer and well designed links. Maybe I'll try that next.

Reductionist thinking studies the small bits of systems and how they function, and tries to figure out how the whole system functions by adding up the bits. This is our reductionist scientific approach and of necessity it also describes much of our technology. Indeed, it is important to identifying basic facts and functions, but beyond a certain point, that approach to understanding naturally evolved systems, that approach does not work very well, if our goal is to understand the naturally evolved functions of the systems, because each naturally evolved system also has emergent functions (emergent properties, phenotypes, macro-properties) that cannot be inferred from adding together functions of the bits and pieces (micro-properties) of which it is composed. See systems and emergent properties below.

Reductionism, as it relates to the Biosystem, is basically the study, usually scientific or technological methods, of the micro-properties of LIFE systems. The individual details rather than the emergent whole. Or the details as they relate to the whole.

Holistic thinking (Holism) in this context tries to understand the functions of emergent properties (macro-properties, phenotypes) of a system and how they relate to the useful functions (processes – the flow of information) of systems and the interactions among the systems.

Logic, as I use it here is very basic, simply cause-and-effect thinking. Not the formal presentation within the disciplines.

Learning = applying the logic of our experiences. Learning can be thought of as one kind of adaptation. Learning might be (tentatively) described as our process of cause-and-effect response to our environment by organizing and adding or removing neurons (nerve cells) and/or neuronal connections (synapses, connections among the nerve cells), mostly in our brains. Using energy to carry, maintain and update the structure/function relationships, the information, encoded in the brain.

Ignorance does not imply inability to think. To be ignorant is to be uninformed. It is fixable. Nobody can stop you from learning to fit more facts into your logical world view. It is not useful to fit in more unsupported propaganda.

Cause-and-effect thinking is for example what a mechanic uses when he tries to understand the relationships between and among automotive problems and the various parts of a car. It is one of the most important (perhaps THE most important) of human emergent characteristics.

When something is made to happen there is a cause. The thing that happens is its effect.

If there is another cause that generates the first cause, then we can follow a trail of causes and effects. A trail of causes and effects that ends with humans is caused by humans and is under human control. A trail of causes and effects that ends in the Biosystem is caused (at its root) by the Biosystem. A trail of causes and effects that ends in an unchangeable fact, a natural law or a mathematical impossibility has its root cause in the fact.

To believe that we can cure anything that we did not cause -- is almost always self-serving, and reminiscent of the argument between the Church, Copernicus and Galileo that took place around the year 1543 and thereafter, when it was eventually agreed that the Earth is not the center of the universe (Principe, 2006). Humans also are not the center of the universe. There are many universal things over which we have no control.

Humans cannot change facts. That's why they are called facts, although I do understand that we have also changed the meaning of that word, "fact," to maintain the false belief that we humans are both omnipotent and omniscient.

We are neither.

The point is that the root cause, if it is a fact that we are facing, will not change no matter what we do. For example, it is not possible to grow forever in any finite space such as the Earth – no matter what we do. This limiting factor that we are now facing is indeed a Fact of Life, and if we do not deal with it now, then we will do as our more recent ancestors have done and pass on a much worse Problem to our future generations. Infinite growth in a finite space is not possible, and our populations have already surpassed the carrying capacity of the Earth. Some time during the last century. It's time we stop trying to squeeze in a few more (I'm thinking of Japanese commute trains, but you may not have seen them push a few more people onto the train.) There is a limit, and there is no reason to wait for the end of human time to deal with it.

How much or who is right or who is wrong or when it happened is NOT RELEVENT.

We need to be studying how to fix US, not how to "fix" the Biosystem. We cannot grow any more without severely damaging other life forms that are our partner organisms within the Biosystem and that interact with us to generate the LIFE of the Biosystem in the form that we require for our own survival. We cannot grow any more without evolving the Biosystem, and evolution is not adaptation. Evolution cannot grow backwards (see Chapter 09) if the necessary information to do so is not available.

We are the top-dominant species. That means we live because of the less dominant creatures and the work they do to make the soil, water, air, alive to us, with us, for us. That fact will not change; therefore, we must change or we will be eliminated by changes that we inadvertently cause among the "lower" creatures of the Biosystem.

The solution to our Problem is to cut the cycle of our human growth, at whatever point it is possible to do so, as we have done with other organisms. There is no point in trying to change the fact or put off rational cause-and-effect behaviors until tomorrow when it will be too late.

Omniscient = all-knowing

Omnipotent = all-powerful

WORLD VIEW

A human world view is a paradigm. A system of thinking that makes logical sense of its environment, or the environment in which it was raised (Eagleman, 2015). I consider a world view as a naturally evolved system of thinking. By logic I just mean simple cause-and-effect thinking. I believe that humans crave logic, and as a result most world views are logical in their context.

Where we make the mistake is in believing that logical is the same as correct, and then being threatened by other peoples' world views, rather than sitting down together and growing a bigger body of more accurate logical information that is more relevant to the fact-based reality. Being logical, does not mean that our world views are necessarily correct or accurate. Because we cannot change facts, the important reaction is to figure out what the facts are and then how we should proceed in a way that accepts the facts while working to sustain ourselves and the environments that secure our lives.

The corposystem world view is based primarily on human technologies and the use of the power of those technologies to dominate other systems, including our environmental system. That is logical within the corposystem world view. Unfortunately, it can not correlate with basic facts of LIFE, and so it won't work long term.

The Biosystem is based in shared information, not growth by domination -- mostly by collaborative communication.

Selectively shared information that has evolved for very precise collaboration, shared with each other and with our environments, is the key to aligning our world views with each other and with our biological environment. Shared accurate information is essential to evolution and to understanding evolution. Every link in the naturally evolved systems -- of our world views, of our social systems and of the whole system of LIFE -- consists of shared information of one kind or another. And without the links – the energy of shared information – there can be no system.

Communication as it is used herein is defined as any exchange of any kind of information.

Information – is discussed in Chapter 06.

Ignorance does not imply inability to think about the information of our lives. To be ignorant of something is to not know about it. Ignorance is something over which we do have control. We know how to fix it. We should.

Wisdom is: "analyzing the facts and discerning the actual situation."
(His Holiness The Dalai Lama, 2009)

SCIENCE = the study of measurable phenomena using the scientific method.

> **Basic science** is not technology. Basic science is about inquiry that informs our world views. It's about expanding our available knowledge within the cloud of our ignorance.

Technology, when it is science, is applied science, and now it is mostly about tools (engineering rather than science) that we of the corposystem use to try to enforce our world views upon our environmental systems. Technology uses the factual realities that are elucidated by basic science to make tools to fulfill human desires. Or at least that is how the current corposystem uses technology.

Our technologies are not more powerful than the Facts of LIFE, and some of the reasons that they are not are the topic of this book. Basically, however, in one sentence, our technologies are not more powerful than LIFE because they are not sufficiently efficient or precise to sustain LIFE (Goldsmith, 1981; West, 2017; Gorshkov *et al.*, 2002).

To sustain LIFE we require a compatible environment, and that means we must be compatible with it – not the other way around. It is what It is. We are famously adaptable.

We are subunits within the system of LIFE. Therefore, to the extent that we damage LIFE, we damage ourselves as a species.

It could be possible to align our technologies with the needs of LIFE, but we cannot do that (or at least we are not) within the corposystem world view. The up-side of the corposystem world view is fun, or power – or what some people call happiness. The down-side is growth by domination for gain. At this time in history, that latter ethic is severely damaging LIFE and the primary code of LIFE (see Chapter 02, Chapter 09, and Appendix A, The Problem). It is time that we use our power to re-enforce the stability of our own environment. Not just to have fun.

"Survival of the Fittest" – an inaccurate corposystem meme that purports to define or describe or represent the essence of the process of evolution.

> "It would appear that the common conception of evolution is that of competing species running a sort of race trough time on planet earth, all on the same running field, some dropping out, some flagging, some victoriously in front." (Snyder, 2000).

Yes, that would appear to be the common conception. It is not accurate.

Evolution – Evolution is not (as it is perceived within the corposystem world view) primarily "survival of the fittest." According to Wikipedia, the latter meme was coined by Herbert Spencer (Creation 32(4):52–54, October 2010) around the end of the 18th century. It's a cute meme, quick, easy to understand, catchy and wrong, because in our culture it assumes the power of dominance.

We have based our social system on a "bad" (unsustainable) meme. Hitler used this meme to support his eugenics (power over human evolution) theories; some others used the meme and the apparently inaccurate theory of polygenic origin of humans to support slavery. Even science, within the evolving corposystem, has used this meme to promote our dominational social system. Even Nobel Prize winners. However, if we want to grow a better social system, that is not how to do it.

The way to grow a better social system for ourselves is to find one that is more realistically aligned with a more accurate view of how LIFE functions – how evolution functions to sustain LIFE.

More realistically, evolution has been viewed as a "dance," of intricate collaborative interactions of the ongoing Creation and maintenance of the naturally evolved living systems among which LIFE has been created and is sustained (Catton, 1982; Dowd, 2007; Goldsmith, 2004; Goodenough, 1998; Peters, 2002; Tyson & Goldsmith, 2004; Wilson, 2006). An incredible, collaborative balancing of interactions between and among the environments; the laws of nature, such as self-assembly, natural selection, (see Chapter 10) and probably some we do not understand; all the systems and subsystems and processes of our universe; and our behaviors within the systems. All is systems. We are naturally evolved systems, we are made of systems, our world views are mental systems (See Chapters 04, 05, 08, 09, 10). Naturally evolved systems are no-where near as simplistic as the idea of survival of the fittest.

Evolution really is about the regulated flow of information (all kinds of information) through systems, and since we do not understand all the kinds of information and we do not understand all the ways that information flows through the Biosystem, it is way past time that we STOP promoting our own omniscience and omnipotence and take our only viable place within the dance of LIFE.

ENERGY AND ENTROPY

Energy is usually defined in dictionaries as the ability to do work. As a generalization, if something is changing, work is happening and energy is involved, and the laws of thermodynamics are also involved:

1. Energy cannot be created or destroyed, but
2. It can be used to drive high-energy work or low-energy work, and/or all the levels in between.

LIFE has used the naturally evolved relationships that sustain IT, particularly the codes of LIFE, to individually and collectively evolve processes that use energy at all levels as it directs its multitasking flow of energy, in ways that are significantly more efficient over-all, and more importantly are specific to each biological interaction, than our man-made technologies and cities can be (West, 2017).

Higher efficiency means more work can be done using the same amount of energy. Given the right information, that is information that contributes to the connectedness of the whole, this efficient complexity can maintain LIFE against the pull of entropy.

Entropy can be defined as the information component of energy, measured in bits (Grossman, 2014; Page, 2009; Schumacher, 2015).

Multitasking of the Cell – As an example of both efficiency and multitasking, the organic molecules of the cell can accomplish work and information transfer -- and other functions -- at the same time, using the same process and the same bits of energy. Multicellular organisms have even more methods of multitasking. These elegant uses of energy differentiate between living systems and technological systems and can be described in a general way by measuring the efficiency of energy use (West, 2017).

It seems to me possible that LIFE on earth originated as a result of the multitasking capability of organic molecules, and it seems likely that the origin of LIFE on earth has to do with a combination of capacities (including their efficiency) that somehow (perhaps by billions of recombination events over a couple of billion years), by recombining the information capabilities of the cells, was able to reproduce itself.

But I don't know. I wasn't there.

Complexity – This book is about the Biosystem, an extremely complex, naturally evolved, adaptive system and its emergent property of LIFE. Complexity is described by Page (2009) as consisting of:

> "interdependent, diverse entities, and we assume that those entities adapt – that they respond to their local and global environments. Complex systems interest us for several reasons. They are often unpredictable, they can produce large events, and they can withstand substantial trauma. Complex systems produce bottom-up emergent phenomena, where what occurs on the macro level differs in kind from what we see in the parts. Emergence takes many forms, including self-organization. Finally, complex systems produce amazing novelty, from sea slugs to laser printers." (Page, 2009).

Because of all the complex and integrated characteristics and process of LIFE, some of which are listed in the Preface, and later in this book, and using organic energy and other characteristics of organic molecules, LIFE systems are able to sustain themselves at a peak of complex efficiency that lies between high free energy and low free energy (Chapter 06). LIFE generates and uses its chemical (organic) energy gradient, regulated by organic molecules, to do the work of staying alive.

That is the answer to the entropy question. LIFE uses the gradient of free energy between sunlight and more entropic forms of energy to drive the processes of LIFE by generating and sustaining its balanced, complex, control over its own complexity. To do this, LIFE forms use their emergent properties – including reproduction in kind, death, and intricate, intimate communication with their environments.

SYSTEMS (see also LIFE)

A system is a group of things, objects or characteristics (the micro-components or subsystems) that are organized so that they interact with each other (using energy) to make a functional unit. For example, I am a naturally evolved system composed of a group of organs that interact to keep me alive. My car is not a naturally evolved system, but it is a system composed of tires, engine, you know all that, which all work together to perform a common function of getting me from here to there. (definition modified from Barabasi, 2003)

Characteristic Functions of Naturally Evolved Systems

1. Each is somewhat unique;
2. They resist change automatically, as part of their system functions;

270

3. Naturally evolved systems are components of (and composed of) other naturally evolved systems.
4. All successful naturally evolved systems must be able to interact in positive collaboration with their environmental systems. Therefore, they must be able to communicate with each other.

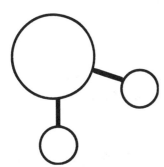 A system is a group of things (objects, nodes, matter) that are linked together as a unit, with or without boundaries, by the processes (energy) they organize. In a system, the nodes and links function together to perform a particular systemic function, each type of system with its distinct functions. The systemic functions of naturally evolved systems are their emergent properties, also known as macro-properties and/or phenotypes. This diagram represents the micro-properties of which the system is composed. The following diagram represents the micro-properties surrounded by the macro-property(s).

A system is a group of interconnected nodes and links that work together (using energy and information) to maintain themselves. The nodes are "things." The function of the things is to organize and direct the "links." The links are behaviors, processes, actions, energy interactions, forms of information, etc. (Barabasi, 2003; The Dalai Lama and Geshe Thupten Jinpa. 2009)

It is not possible to write about all of our environmental systems and parallel systems and subsystems; there are too many and they are too intricately interconnected. But it is useful to learn to think about them as systems.

To avoid confusion in a confusing situation, I will try to limit myself to talking about my main four systems, but there are many more (see Chapter 05). Millions.

My four are:

1. Myself as an organism in my environments. My environments are my essential other half. If you are a physiologist, you will want to think about your subsystems. You need to take good care of them.
2. Collectively, humans as a species.
3. Our primary social system, the corposystem. Your family may be more important to you. Or the poker club.
4. And the one system that is essential to the survival of all of Earth's living systems, Gaia, the living Earth.

It takes a bit of practice to think of ourselves this way, but it's worth it to view LIFE more nearly as it is. And it's useful conversation in the family or the poker club. Or the book club. Better than false memes.

Micro-component. The micro components of a system are its physically interacting subunits (parts) and their individual properties that work together to generate the emergent properties of that same system.

Emergent Properties (Macro-characteristics) of Naturally Evolved Systems

> "Emergence is when the macro-properties of a system differ from the micro-properties, not only in scale but in kind" (Page. 2009).

Macro-property = emergent property = phenotype. The macro-properties of a naturally evolved system are basically its characteristics that are generated by the interactions among its micro-components. Macro-properties function to communicate with other systems.

Emergent properties (emergent characteristics, macro-properties, phenotypes) - are a normal component of complex adaptive systems, including naturally evolved systems. Emergent properties are characteristics of the system as a whole that differ from the characteristics of any of its parts. That idea is central to this book.

It is clear that LIFE, that emerges and from the complexity of systems that make up the Biosystem, could not stay alive if naturally evolved systems were unable to communicate with each other in ways that are sustainable (Chapters 09 and 10) and specifically responsive.

Similar to the inter-digitation of the gut tissues with the internal tissues of the same body, the figurative or literal inter-digitation of the emergent properties of the system with its environment permits communication among the systems so that each nourishes the other (in different ways) and together they help to enable the high efficiency of the living system.

The "codes of LIFE" of which there are quite a few, including the genetic code and the world view code and the electromagnetic code that are provided as examples in Chapter 09, enable communication using emergent properties.

I will assume that emergent properties (the macro-properties of a system, phenotypes) evolve in complex systems because complex system *do interact* with their environments, and because they *must interact* with their environments in order to survive. Because the Laws of LIFE are essential to survival, and natural selection is one of the Laws of LIFE, therefore naturally evolved systems require emergent properties so that they can interact with each other by means of natural selection and other kinds of information exchange.

In other words, I am suggesting that naturally evolved complex systems could not conform to their environments without emergent properties, and that developing systems that express/exhibit emergent properties that are not useful to the environment will be eliminated by the Laws of LIFE because the Laws of LIFE function to maintain LIFE as a whole, not specifically human life.

Types of Systems

Naturally evolved system. A naturally evolved system is a system that was not created by humans. Naturally evolved systems consist of subsystems (micro-components). And emergent properties (macroproperties, phenotypes). LIFE itself – the quality of being alive -- is an emergent property of the whole, naturally evolved Biosystem and of many of its subsystems.

A naturally evolved system is a complex adaptive system that arose by evolution as it really functions (not primarily as "survival of the fittest," but as a result of the interactions of the Laws of LIFE).

I am a naturally evolved system composed of subsystems; the physiological and behavioral functions my subsystems (organs, tissues, cells) perform to maintain me; and the environmental systems within which we all interact.

Naturally evolved systems of LIFE are complex adaptive systems that can reproduce and maintain themselves using information that they contain within themselves -- stored, retained and passed forward in the form of codes of LIFE that are "translated" as emergent properties.

Complex adaptive system

> **Complex systems** are composed of subsystems that differ from each other, that is, the system is referred to as complex because its subunits (micro-components) are not all the same as each other. Their emergent properties also differ.

> **Adaptive systems** are able to respond to their environments.

Complex adaptive systems are composed of a variety of micro-components, each with individual properties (functions, characteristics). The micro-components of a system are its parts. That is to say, all the things that are part of the system, as defined by the emergent property(s) they work together to generate. The parts of the system work together to sustain the system. In living systems these micro-components are often or usually smaller systems. (Smaller complex adaptive systems that interact with each other using their own specific emergent properties). Nested sets. You are not crazy or ignorant if this blows your mind; following up on the plethora of interactions is very confusing. We are interested in the essential components of LIFE. Not the details.

A naturally evolved system is a complex adaptive system that evolved historically and interactively from pre-existing systems (its environment) with which it functions interactively, as a cyclic unit (in response to the natural processes of energy, information and self-assembly, and natural selection) to maintain itself. In our simplistic diagram, the nodes are "things," objects. The function of the things is to organize and direct the "links." The links are behaviors, processes, actions, energy interactions, all the many forms of information exchange. Links and nodes can be and usually are subsystems within a larger naturally evolved system that is their environment. Within which they evolved.

The Biosystem is a naturally evolved, living complex adaptive system. It has the emergent characteristics of LIFE (see below), and specifically it is self-sustaining within its environment. The Biosystem is the most inclusive system of the Life of Earth. Its primary emergent property is LIFE.

The emergent properties that define LIFE, are variously described, but for here we can say that living things are complex, adaptive, naturally evolved systems that minimally can:

1. maintain themselves by interacting with their environments at a very specific level of efficiency (Goldsmith, 1981; Gorshkov, *et al.*, 2002; West, 2017);
2. reproduce themselves in their environments;
3. evolve over time compatibly with their environments;
4. sustain a viable balance among all the naturally evolved subsystems and environmental stystems.
5. and communicate among themselves, using many different types of LIFE codes. (Chapter 09)

An organism is a naturally evolved complex adaptive system, a unit of life that is a subsystem of its ecosystem and of the entire living earth. Organ systems are subunits of some organisms, as are organs, tissues and cells. Some cells are independent organisms composed largely of water and organic molecules.

It is possible to imagine the entire universe as a naturally evolved living system of which we are a teeny-tiny part. Just as we can imagine a living cell as a teeny-tiny part of ourselves.

Organic molecules are little systems inside the cell, but they cannot reproduce themselves outside of the cell, so we do not think of organic molecules (usually) as having all the characteristics that we associate with LIFE. If you think about it, the second half of the definition is a flawed argument, but that does not concern us.

System, subsystem, environmental system – The point here is that organisms are examples of (a) naturally evolved systems (b) that have the emergent properties associated with LIFE. We are human organisms. We contain subsystems (heart, lungs, etc). And similarly, we are subsystems within our environmental systems: our social systems, our ecosystems and the entire Living system of Earth. (See also the answer to the faux Spider Question in Chapter 04).

Subsystem - A system that resides and does its job (emergent property) within another system. For example, a mitochondrion is a subsystem of eukaryotic cells, a kidney is a subsystem of some organisms; an organism is a subsystem of an ecosystem; an ecosystem is a subsystem of the Biosystem.

Environmental system – is the environment in which the subsystem resides and does its job. For example, the cell is the environmental system of a mitochondrion, the organism is the environmental system of the kidney, the ecosystem is the environmental system in which the organisms can function. Just as the organic molecules require a cell to function in, so also the organism requires an ecosystem in which it can function.

Parallel system or partner system – Another subsystem that functions as a partner node within the same environmental system. A partner system to a mitochondrion (in a green plant) might be a chloroplast, which is of the same level of complexity, but with a different function. A partner system to a kidney might be a liver; a partner system to me, as an organism within the Biosystem, might be you, or Bitsy, or a family member, or even Donald Trump – or the cedar tree (ki) outside my window in the canyon that makes me remember my Japanese teacher, another partner system in the Biosystem who taught me what I know of Japanese and much of what I know about compassion.

It is critically important that we realize – half of ourselves, individually and collectively, in very many ways, is our environment; self-assembly depends upon the environment; food energy and information energy depend upon our environment; our ability to adapt to changing conditions depends upon our environment; and remember that is part of the definition of a living thing. We could not be born without our environment; neither embryology (development of a living thing) nor phylogeny (evolution of living things) (Chapter 09) could happen without our environments.

World View - paradigm – A naturally evolved human system of thinking that makes logical sense of its environment, or the environment in which it was raised (Eagleman, 2015, and Chapter 09). I believe humans crave logic, and as a result most world views are logical. Being logical, however, does not mean that they are necessarily correct or accurate. A sad, courageous, memoir by Tara Westover (2018, entitled Educated), vividly describes the tragedy of our time, the irrelevant conflict among world views, in personal terms. The US capitol riot of February, 2021, expresses essentially the same problem, as our system attempts to transition between two diametrically opposed world views. The split between the dominational logic and the collaborative logic within our naturally evolved human social system, the corposystem.

Social System – Our social systems are naturally evolved complex adaptive systems that arise from the interactions of all of our individual behaviors and beliefs as we (the subsystems or micro-systems) interact among our selves.

The Corposystem our modern naturally evolved complex adaptive human corpo-political-economic-military-educational-charitable social system can be characterized by its most troublesome emergent property (expressed by its behaviors as it interacts with other systems) of growth by domination for gain

Balanced Systems – If any naturally evolved system cannot sustain itself – or if its particular unique characteristics cause more harm than benefit to its environmental systems, then that harmful system will be eliminated (by the processes of evolution, see Chapter 10) from the environment of which it is a part. Automatically. Because of the universal Facts of Life. Systems that are balanced within their environments do not cause harm to their environments.

In other words, naturally evolved systems must sustain themselves in balance between the chaos of entropy and the energy required for efficient complexity (Lewin, 1992; Lloyd, 2017). LIFE systems sustain themselves – not against entropy but using the fact of entropy to flow the energy through the system, and the tools of communication and natural selection at specific levels of efficiency that are sufficient to maintain their complexity.

LIFE (See also systems)

Viable – Able to be alive.

LIFE is the most significant emergent property of the Biosystem, at least to us. I use this term CAPITALIZED to refer to the property of LIFE itself, an emergent property, not to an individual living thing such as a tree or a dog or a person that is equally as capable of being here, whether or not it is alive.

LIFE is an apparently unique emergent property of the naturally evolved system of today's Earth. LIFE is an emergent property of a complex adaptive system, The Modern Earth, the Biosystem. See also system, emergent property.

> *Reality Number Two* – All of LIFE consists of naturally evolved systems. We humans cannot change how they evolved or how they function to sustain LIFE. Just as the growth of the human embryo requires the womb, and the

mother cow feeds the calf, so do all the mothers and all the species require the appropriate environment for their survival. (Preface).

LIFE can be defined as an emergent property of the Biosystem, a naturally evolved complex adaptive system that is able to obtain matter and energy from its environmental system(s) that it then uses to sustain the emergence of LIFE. Living systems are able to:

1. maintain themselves by interacting with their environments at a very high level of efficiency (Goldsmith, 1981; Gorshkov, *et al.*, 2002; West, 2017);
2. reproduce themselves in their environments;
3. evolve over time compatibly with their environments;
4. sustain the viable balance among all their naturally evolved subsystems (Chapter 06).
5. and communicate among themselves, using many different types of LIFE codes. (Chapter 09)

Its environment is the other half of the life of every naturally evolved system. The relationship between a living system and its environment is similar to the relationship between a pregnant woman and her unborn child, molding and nourishing the codes of LIFE during ontogeny and phylogeny (Chapters 09 and 10) to ensure the survival of the child and of the whole LIFE of Earth.

> ***Reality Number Fourteen*** *– The environment of every naturally evolved system (including us) is essential to the LIFE of that system -- is literally the other half of the LIFE of that system. The function of every naturally evolved subsystem is not "survival of the fittest." The function of a naturally evolved system is to collaboratively enable the welfare of its environmental system(s). If it does not do this, the environmental system will eventually weed out the unhelpful subsystems. This is how evolution functions (Chapter 03).*

Its environment(s) is the other half of every naturally evolved system, molding and nourishing the response of all its micro-components and of the whole of LIFE, its many emergent properties, to the codes of LIFE and the Laws of LIFE, during phylogeny and ontogeny, to ensure the survival of the whole system of LIFE within its environments.

Ontogeny – Embryogenesis and beyond. The development of an individual organism through its life time.

Phylogeny – The development of the species throughout their "life spans" from their origin to their extinction and/or incorporation into the whole of LIFE. More information about this is found in textbooks on the subjects of evolution and eco-evo (ecological evolution).

LIFE is not a technology or a machine and does not behave as a technology or a machine, although of course all kinds of systems must "obey" the universal natural laws. Machines and technologies are tools that are made by and for humans. Humans did not create LIFE or the living Earth. This is important because human tools are not (and cannot be, Chapter 06) as efficient as LIFE (Goldsmith, 1981; Gorkoshkoff *et al.*, 2002; West, 2017) and therefore may cause more harm than good to humans, depending on how they are used by humans.

LIFE may be sacred (Stuever, 2009, page 105, Logging in on Forestry). However, individual lives are not. Humans are not the center of anything biological -- except *Homo sapiens*. The biological and ethical function of individual humans is to support the whole of LIFE. If we continue to believe that we -- the individual parts -- are more important than the whole -- we may very well destroy *Homo sapiens*.

```
Balance
    Materials
    Energy

Naturally evolved systems (04, 05)
    Emergence
    Phenotype

Self Assembly (Chapters 06, 07)
    Energy
    Entropy
    Information
    Complexity

Evolution (Life Codes - Chapter 08, 09)
    Genetics
    Variability
    Natural Selection
```

LIFE of Earth – is the emergent property of the entire Earth Biosystem that consists of an unimaginably complicated assemblage of nested and parallel sets (levels of organization/complexity, niches, trophic levels) of interacting naturally evolved complex adaptive systems and subsystem of the Earth that have co-evolved (evolved together as a flexible unit), that provides the necessary conditions to sustain LIFE as a whole system.

The Law (or Laws, or Facts) of LIFE – consist minimally of the fourteen big ideas shown here (Appendix D and Chapter 10); that is, the following processes acting within, among and between the systems of LIFE.

All of these processes and more are required, working together and in balance, for the maintenance of Life:

Balanced Systems The systems of LIFE are so tightly organized that, when conditions change, the interactions among the systems are modified in a way that allows the whole of LIFE, and each system of LIFE, to respond to its environments. This subject is vast and is presented here as a background fact that is important to those of us who want to behave in ways that can support the LIFE of earth in a form that can support the human system(s). For now, we just keep the fact in mind and discuss it with friends as part of our decision-making – whatever we do changes LIFE in many ways – both good ways and bad ways, for us.

If any naturally evolved system cannot sustain itself – or if its particular unique characteristics cause more harm than benefit to its environmental systems, then that harmful system will be eliminated from the environment of which it is a part. It will unbalance some part of the system of LIFE and will be eliminated automatically by the processes of evolution -- acting through the universal Facts of Life that are listed in the box above.

As I am using this term, balance refers to the relationships among naturally evolved systems when all the systems function collaboratively and effectively to sustain the existence and the emergent characteristics of all the systems, while maintaining the relationships between the recycling of materials of LIFE and the organic energy that makes the recycling possible. The functions of the natural laws in a viable system is to maintain the balance of the system(s). Or we could say that naturally evolved systems use the natural laws to maintain their balance.

Sustainability = The ability of the individual system to survive without destroying the resources that it requires from its environmental system. Basically this means the ability of a naturally evolved system to find a suitable *niche* within its environment. A niche that is within the *limiting factors* the individual system requires for its survival, while contributing its functions or behaviors to the welfare of its environmental system.

> **Niche -** A system's niche within the whole of LIFE is its particular unique lifestyle (or set of functions) that it has evolved to respond to (or communicate with, using its emergent phenotypes), its environmental system(s).

> **Limiting Factor** – The particular characteristic of an organism's environment that limits its population size, or its niche, at any given time and place. For example, it might be availability of water, energy (food), nesting sites, disease, all these things that are a component of the balance of LIFE. Limiting factors relate to niches; that is, the limiting factor and the specific requirements of the niche balance each other to regulate both the niche and the population size. Unfortunately for us -- up to now we have used our technologies to overcome our limiting factors. Our current limiting factors are the pandemic, and probably (perhaps?) the final solution – climate change.

Resilience = The ability to survive in changing conditions. Resilience is not possible in the absence of diversity and natural selection, but those are not the only necessary elements.

Efficiency - Because of all the complex and integrated characteristics and processes of LIFE that are listed in the Preface, and in the later text, and using chemical (organic) energy and other characteristics of organic molecules, LIFE systems are able to sustain themselves at a peak of complex efficiency that lies between high free energy and low free energy. LIFE uses the gradient of free energy between sunlight and more entropic forms of energy to drive the processes of LIFE by generating and sustaining its balanced, complex control over its own complexity. These factors apply to every interaction individually (every communication, chemical, physical or other reaction) because all or nearly all interactions (links in our model) are different from the others. That is why our technologies are doing more harm than good to our biological system.

This is one reason for the efficiency of LIFE. Each of the functions of LIFE must mesh and multitask so elegantly that they all contribute to the efficiency of the overall whole, within the requirements of LIFE. To cause or permit the flow of energy from high free energy to low free energy – while using the energy and entropy to do the work of staying alive.

A major difference between the "efficiency" of LIFE and the efficiency of technologies is that LIFE requires a particular relationship of energy and entropy (a particular complexity of information and energy) for each of its myriad interactions. Over-all efficiency is important, but not more important than the relative efficiency of every interacting link of every system within LIFE that is balanced to regulate the flow of information/energy through the system.

Communication - Obviously, to accomplish the above complex tasks, the systems must be able to communicate, both internally, within each system, and externally, between systems. They do so using the codes of LIFE that operate via the emergent properties of the interacting systems. Communication as it is used herein is defined as any exchange of any kind of information.

Trophic Level – Refers to the level of energy transfer within the LIFE of Earth as it moves from plants to animals doing the work of sustaining LIFE.

> **Producers -** Plants, of course do not actually produce energy (see Chapter 06, energy cannot be created or destroyed), but they do use sun energy to make organic molecules. They are able to use the energy from the sun to generate biological (organic, chemical) energy that is embedded in organic molecules (such as proteins, carbohydrates, lipids and nucleic acids).

> **Consumers** - primary consumers (herbivores); secondary consumers (carnivores and omnivores); and decomposers get the energy and much of the information they require from eating plant molecules, which are then digested (taken apart and the energy used to sustain LIFE) and the molecules are reorganized according to the genetic code of whatever organism did the eating.

Finally, the information is recycled (the atoms and molecules are used again by plants using their specific genetic code of LIFE to capture more energy from the sun and keep the cycle going indefinitely, so long as we do not interfere by 1 - eliminating steps in the cycle (plants or animals or other species) or 2 - failing to recycle the parts of LIFE back into LIFE. Or to say again, by unbalancing the cycle of LIFE that sustains LIFE.

See a good Freshman Biology text for a great many more details.

Climate Change – Earth is a system; one of its emergent properties is the climate. When the subsystems (the micro-properties) of the Biosystem change, then its emergent properties automatically also change, as the Biosystem tries to sustain the balance of its parts so that its emergent property (LIFE) can be sustained.

EVOLUTION (Life Codes - Chapter 08, 09)

> Genetics
> Variability
> Natural Selection

Evolution, including genetics and the Codes of LIFE -- including the inheritance of our basic physical and emotional makeup in ontology and their transmission in phylogeny -- is responsible for the resilience of LIFE systems and ultimately for their sustainability, as they are able to change when their environments change.

Diversity/variability – In this context of evolution, diversity means that every individual within a species is somewhat different from every other, so that some will be better able to survive when changes occur in their environments. This is also a description of Natural Selection. This is necessary for resilience and sustainability, and all three are necessary to maintain the balance of LIFE in changing conditions. Evolution sustains survivability, using genetics and natural selection.

Natural Selection is a component of evolution, as are **variability**, including **self-assembly**, and the **DNA/RNA Code of Life** (genetics) and other sources of inheritable variability. Natural selection determines which specific organisms get to successfully reproduce (pass on their genes) within the niche and limiting factors of the species.

Evolution of species may be most simply defined as a change in the gene pool over time in response to conditions in the environment.

The **gene pool** of a species is all the genes in the entire species of interbreeding adults. The species is the primary unit of transmission of the genetic code of LIFE in sexually reproducing organisms, but systems interact with each other in many additional ways. I will use the term gene pool in other contexts in addition to gene pool of species. For example, we need to consider the gene pool of the entire Biosystem, which may be more important in our time than only the gene pool of a species.

Reproduction is necessary to pass on the traits of the species. The niche and limiting factors are necessary to nurture the organism. Natural selection is necessary for the species to respond to changes in the environment and to sustain the balance between the species and its environment.

Death is an essential component of evolution. Evolution is a change in the gene pool. The relative balance of the gene pool can not change if all its members survive and reproduce. This is one reason that there can be no LIFE without death.

Or we could say that evolution is the result of the balanced interactions/communications among the emergent properties of a system and selection of the positive ways that it interactions with its environmental systems.

Or we could say that specfic niches that are most useful to the maintenance of the LIFE of the environmental system are most likely to be retained within the community of the systems of LIFE.

All of this describes LIFE not primarily as a set of dominational interactions, but perhaps the deepest collaborations that we know about.

Communication as it is used herein is defined as any exchange of information.

Information – is discussed in Chapter 06. It is obvious that systems could not do their functions, or even generate their emergent characteristics, unless the subunits of the system were sharing information as well as energy, among themselves.

OUR FUNDAMENTAL HUMAN PROBLEM - (see Chapter 02 and Appendix A)

At this time and under today's circumstances, our root problem from which arise most of our political problems, is overpopulation. We have evolved our society to accommodate enormous numbers of humans. The Biosystem, on the other hand, requires a critical balance among its complex parts in order to maintain LIFE. This difference generates an imbalance in the flow of energy through the uncountable subsystems that make up the entire system of LIFE, as the energy that once sustained LIFE is diverted to human uses.

The flow of energy through The Biosystem is critical to its survival and is maintained at every step by the evolution of its parts. Climate change is the response of the Biosystem as it tries to regain a new viable relationship among its subsystems so that it can sustain its emergent properties. If necessary, LIFE of Earth can start over with its most simple subsystem, the prokaryotic or eukaryotic cells, in order to save its own life and all of LIFE, as it has done several times before in response to mass extinctions that were caused by more than one different kind of imbalance of different Biosystems (Kolbert, 2014; Wilson. 2002, 2016). However, that would leave no future for humankind, and the change has already begun.

Overpopulation – The relationship between an organism and its environment when the behaviors or numbers of the organism are not sustainable within the requirements of the environment for its own welfare. The common term might be overgrazing, when the number of organisms of a given species cannot be supported by its ecosystem or by the whole Biosystem, because the organic molecules are being diverted to unbalanced uses, and the amount of energy and other resources that the environment is capable of producing are not sufficient to support the needs of the environment and the overpopulated system.

Overpopulation is our Common Problem, because our human overpopulation unbalances the energy and matter that are required to support the LIFE of Earth and all its living parts and diverts them to human uses.

Ponzi Economics – Basically a Ponzi (money) scheme collects resources from clients and uses the collections to pay back other clients, with an artificially high return that attracts yet more clients. This requires a never-ending and always spreading source of client resources.

When it runs out of clients or resources, the Ponzi system crashes. Always, because there is never an infinite supply of resources or clients.

Our corposystem is a Ponzi scheme, feeding off of Mother Nature more organic energy than she can provide.

THE SOLUTION

What we can do that is useful is to align our individual world views with the Facts of Life. Because, while LIFE changes all the time, the Facts of Life, the facts themselves, do not change. So, if we understand the basic facts as clearly as possible, and plan our lives to conform to the biological Facts of LIFE, this will automatically tend to correlate our world views and our common goals with the reality and with each other. And it can give rise to some very productive and useful discussions – as opposed to the corposystem norm, which is to yell at each other (ref. Facebook, nearly anywhere that science is discussed. Well, usually it's technology, not science).

Chaplain - According to www.gotquestions.org/what-is-a-chaplain.html "A chaplain is essentially a spiritual representative attached to a secular institution. Chaplains may or may not be certified, have a theological education, or be ordained or commissioned by a particular denomination, though many are."

This is good, because I once applied for a certification program and was rejected on the grounds of religious affiliation (the "wrong" one). "Chaplains are expected to serve the spiritual and emotional needs of others. Chaplains may also function as advocates."

The Biosystem is definitely "other." It is not human. It is a different naturally evolved system; it lacks a brain; so far as we know it lacks even a nervous system, though its parts do communicate and organize the whole using electromagnetic, organic and other sources of energy.

It is unlikely that the Biosystem, or LIFE, requires anyone to serve its spiritual and emotional needs. The Biosystem is the origin of LIFE itself, on earth, and so far as I know It doesn't need *Homo sapiens* at all – or me. Or you. But really I don't know about that.

However, the Biosystem clearly does require an advocate, and very specifically the Biosystem requires every human to be aware that we of the *Homo sapiens* system make choices, and more importantly exhibit behaviors, every day, that affect the physical welfare of the Biosystem and therefore the spiritual and emotional and physical welfare of *Homo sapiens*. Ourselves. We require a specific sort of healthy Biosystem climate as a source of food energy; clean earth to support the plants that bring us the food energy, drinking water, and breathable air; and a healthy social environment within which we can effectively communicate to others of our kind without causing harm either to them or to the whole of our environment within the LIFE of Earth. *Homo sapiens* is a subunit of the Biosystem but is not the Biosystem and has many differences from the Biosystem. The Biosystem is not us; it is not our pet; it is not our servant. It has different needs.

Chaplains to the Biosystem, in this age, must be aware of the needs of the Biosystem as those needs are in fact, and as they differ from the needs of the corposystem, and be willing to make their life choices *first* based on the needs of the Biosystem and *second* their personal welfare within the corposystem. Chaplains to the Biosystem serve people by serving LIFE, and they serve LIFE by serving people, not only by saving the human and nonhuman victims of our crimes against LIFE, but also by understanding LIFE itself, not as we wish it were, but as it is.

If we do not understand the needs of the system we are trying to support, we will just end up as "do-gooders," which can be fun and rewarding but is basically what I mean by homocentric *hubris*. It will not help the Biosystem, or the future of our kind, because the Biosystem is not human and because humans do not know how to successfully control all of LIFE. We must, if we want to survive, learn how to help sustain the balance of the whole of LIFE, and that means controlling ourselves, because we, ourselves, is the only part of the equation that we have the power to control. There is enough information in this book to control our human impact on our environments, if we think about what we are doing; but we do not know enough to control the operations of the Biosystem.

If we could dominate the Biosystem we would be gods. If we were gods, we would be *omnipotent*. Or at least we would be more powerful than LIFE itself, because we would have created LIFE itself. We are not more powerful than LIFE. The fact is, we are becoming extinct because of the ignorant homocentric hubris with which we wield our tools and technologies, and I am not referring to only the "bad guys," but also to the "good guys." While we spend our time blaming each other for our basic Problem, we are all engaging in the same blasphemy against The Creation itself, and so its Creator.

OOOOOOOO

REALITIES OF LIFE

"Really, the reason why we devote our lives and our money to . . . (basic scientific research) . . . is because we want to know the answer. . . We want to discover the way the world works. . . We want to know what this nature is that we live in, what are the rules, what are the ingredients."
(Carroll, 2015)

My goal is to use the biological realities to help generate a
human culture that is biologically sustainable.

What is your goal?

Reality Number One - We cannot align our behaviors with the fact-based requirements for all of LIFE if we don't know what they are – or if we believe an alternative, unnatural or homocentric version of the story of LIFE (Preface).

Reality Number Two – All of LIFE is an emergent property of the Biosystem, which is a naturally evolve system that is composed of other naturally evolved systems. We humans cannot change how they evolved or how they function to sustain LIFE. Just as the growth of the human embryo requires the womb, and the mother cow feeds the calf, so do all the mothers and all the species require the appropriate environment for their survival. (Preface).

Reality Number Three – Naturally evolved LIFE systems are fundamentally collaborative, feeding information/energy back and forth. They are not primarily dominational. They mostly function to support themselves in ways that do no harm to, but instead support the whole system that is their environment (Preface).

Reality Number Four - Our beliefs are not important in the scheme of things except as they inform our behaviors. Our behaviors are recorded in the known and unknown history of all time; both because behaviors (interactions/energy/information) are the universal language of reality, and because we can never undo them (Preface).

Reality Number Five A - The first function of evolution of LIFE is to maintain the survival of the whole LIFE system by selecting which subsystems get to survive: that is, those that communicate well with and function collaboratively with the other systems of LIFE in support of the whole of LIFE of Earth (Chapter 02).

Reality Number Five B - The second function of evolution, whenever the LIFE system becomes so unbalanced that it is unable to sustain itself, is to eliminate from the Biosystem the systems that cause more harm than good to the sustainable balance of their environments. Or to say another way, to stir the pot, to create more diversity, new "ideas" when the old ones aren't working anymore. (See Chapter 08). Or, if that doesn't restore a balance to the LIFE system, to get rid of the system that is causing the imbalance. That is why occasional extinctions are necessary to the balance of LIFE, so long as they do not further upset the balance. Mass extinctions are harmful in the short term (Chapter 02). They destroy their own environments.

Reality Number Six - Universal facts are realities and processes that we cannot change because they operate throughout the entire universe, for example: energy, entropy, information, self-assembly, natural selection, time that gives us history, gravity (Chapter 02 and Appendix B).

Reality Number Seven - We, and our parts, and our environments, all ARE naturally evolved systems, as are our social systems and our world views. We are functional, collaborative, complex, adaptive naturally evolved LIFE systems (Chapters 04, 06, 07, 08, 09) that can only partly be described or understood using our human research methods (Chapter 02).

Reality Number Eight -- Within the systems, there is no dichotomy between a "glass half full" or a "glass half empty." If a glass is half full it is also half empty. Every action has both up-sides and down-sides, yin and yang, good and bad results. Good is here defined as sustainable, relative to the needs of the particular system. If we do not anticipate all the possible good and bad outcomes of our behaviors, we will continue to have many unpleasant surprises in our future. If we "understand the rules" (Carroll, 2015), that is, the Facts of Life, we have a better chance of anticipating all the possible outcomes of our behaviors, before we do actions out of ignorance, that we come to regret. Our behaviors for any reason are equally as good – and bad – as their results, and they cannot be reversed (Chapter 02).

Reality Number Nine – As citizen activists, we should learn the rules before we try to fix the game (Chapter 02).

Reality Number Ten -- Every problem gives us more than two possible choices, usually many more than three. Simplistic answers, such as memes and either-or choices, do not solve complex systemic problems. That's why debate is good for the warrior (including our modern politicians) but is not really good for problem solving. Usually, simplistic answers make things worse. Fortunately, we each have a very complex human brain that is capable of understanding our modern biological Problem (Chapter 02).

Reality Number Eleven - It is possible to destroy everything that we love WITHOUT violence and, in that way, keep the people happy until the very last minute, when the shit hits the fan, and there is no place else to turn. That is not the intention of publications cited here, nor of most "actions," but I am quite certain there are some very sophisticated organized efforts to "win" the propaganda wars by mis-using the words of our good intentions. I don't know what they believe themselves to be winning. Therefore, we should be always aware and make every effort to understand each other before reacting to each other (Chapter 03).

Reality Number Twelve - Trying to change the unchangeable facts is not where our power lies. We have more important things to do. Our job is to nourish a sustainable, reasonably comfortable future for our descendants (Chapter 03).

Reality Number Thirteen - Evolution really is about the flow of information through systems (Chapter 03) (see Chapter 07, 08, 09 and 10 regarding evolution).

Reality Number Fourteen – The environment of every naturally evolved system (including us) is essential to the LIFE of that system -- is literally the other half of the LIFE of that system. The function of every naturally evolved subsystem is not "survival of the fittest." The function of a naturally evolved system is to collaboratively enable the welfare of its environmental system(s). If it does not do this, the environmental system will eventually weed out the unhelpful subsystems. This is how evolution functions (Chapter 03).

Reality Number Fifteen - LIFE is an emergent property of the naturally evolved Biosystem. To maintain this emergent property, the Biosystem requires that the naturally evolved living systems of Earth collectively sustain the balance of their collaborative, efficient interactions that took billions of years to evolve to near perfection (Chapter 03).

Reality Number Sixteen - The primary emergent functions of each kind of naturally evolved, complex adaptive system can, in a general way, be deduced by the emergent characteristics (that we will from time to time refer to as the phenotypes or macro-properties) of that kind of system (Chapter 04).

Reality Number Seventeen - The primary function of each naturally evolved complex adaptive system is to perpetuate its own emergent properties. Such systems have evolved and survived because they *can* perpetuate themselves, and they do it primarily by their uniquely efficient ability to balance energy, entropy and information in their relationships with their environmental systems. Not by dominating, changing or destroying their environmental system (Chapter 07).

Reality Number Eighteen - Technology can move food around to serve people. Technology cannot, at the same time do this in a way that incorporates the cycles of energy, information and materials that sustain all the cells and all the organs and all the species that maintain the next higher level of LIFE on Earth, the ecosystems, our necessary environments, and the Biosystem, and their emergent properties (Chapter 07).

Reality Number Nineteen - The function of community is to create safe places for people and their environments. Instead of growing safe communities, evil systems are evil precisely because they destroy safe places (Chapter 08).

Reality Number Twenty - If we want to save ourselves, our species, our safe places, our environment -- the place to start is with something over which we have some control (Chapter 09).

Reality Number Twenty-One - We can not add up all the reductionist functions of every subsystem to understand the whole of a naturally evolved system, because at every step we encounter emergent properties (macro-properties/phenotypes, Chapters 04 and 05) that we do not understand (Chapter 09).

Reality Number Twenty-Two - The Facts of LIFE are natural processes that we cannot change. Our long-term survival is not about our tools; our tools cannot change how nature functions. Our survival is mostly about our behaviors; it's about what we do with the tools (technologies). Whether we use them in an effort to dominate the Facts of LIFE and incidentally destroy the balance of LIFE or, holding hands within the community of LIFE itself, use our tools to nourish her healthy abundance (Chapter 09).

Reality Number Twenty-Three - Our world views influence our behaviors; we communicate with our environment primarily with our behaviors, not with our world views. The environment does not "care" about what we are thinking; its primary function is not to care about us, but to sustain itself (see Chapter 04). Therefore, it responds to what we do, but not to why we do it. (Chapter 09)

Reality Number Twenty-Four - The primary requirement of the Biosystem is to balance every part of itself around sustainably regenerating resources of our whole biological system, so that the energy and information of LIFE can flow automatically through its self from high energy/low entropy toward low energy/high entropy (Appendix A). High entropy is the same as chaos.

Reality Number Twenty-Five - Evolution is not about "survival of the fittest." It is about the flow of information and energy through collaborating systems (Appendix A).

Reality Number Twenty-Six - It does not matter how we got here; now that we are here; what matters is how we behave, and how we treat the other sentient beings that already were here (Chapter 11).

"I realized that I had to change
my world view.
But how do I do that?"
(Feldman, 2018)

APPENDIX D

FOURTEEN BIG IDEAS

LIFE is characterized by several traits that we tend to define as separate qualities. They are all connected. They interact. Prominent among them are:

Sustainability = The ability of the individual naturally evolved system to survive without destroying the resources that it requires for its survival. Basically this means the ability of a naturally evolved system to find a suitable niche within its environment that is within the limiting factors the individual requires for its survival, while at the same time it contributes its functions and/or behaviors to the welfare of the whole. The whole is (minimally) itself and its environmental system(s).

Resilience = The ability to survive in changing conditions. Resilience is not possible in the absence of diversity and natural selection, but diversity is not the only necessary element. Other elements are described below.

Balance
    Materials
    Energy

```
Balance
    Materials
    Energy

Naturally evolved systems (04, 05)
    Emergence
    Phenotype

Self Assembly (Chapters 06, 07)
    Energy
    Entropy
    Information
    Complexity

Evolution (Life Codes - Chapter 08, 09)
    Genetics
    Variability
    Natural Selection
```

Balance – As I am using this term, includes the relationships among naturally evolved systems, when all the systems function collaboratively and effectively to sustain the existence and the emergent characteristics of the entire system -- and at the same time maintain the relationships between the recycling of materials of LIFE and the energy that makes the recycling possible. The functions of the natural laws in a viable system is to maintain the balance of the system(s).

Or we could say that naturally evolved systems use the natural laws to maintain their balance.

Naturally evolved systems (see Appendix B under systems and Chapters 04 and 05)
  Emergence
  Phenotype

LIFE is composed of naturally evolved systems. Naturally evolved systems are able to communicate with each other using their emergent properties that are also sometimes referred to as phenotypes or macro-properties. They are able to maintain their balance because they can communicate with each other using the emergence of interacting phenotypes at precisely the right times and places during their own ongoing ontogeny and phylogeny.

Self-Assembly (Chapters 06 and 07)
  Energy
  Entropy
  Information
  Complexity

Naturally evolved systems must sustain themselves in balance between the chaos of entropy and the energy that they require to sustain their complexity.

The complexity helps to sustain these requirements by contributing processes that are elegantly multitasking and inter-connected so that the energy and entropy define the "sweet spot" of every interaction and the sweet spot(s), when they are available determine how the system interacts with other systems to describe the complexity (information) of each interaction and of the whole.

Efficient use of the energy (organic energy carried in organic molecules) of LIFE is much higher than that of non-LIFE (West, 2017)(electromagnetic energy, heat), in part because of the efficiency of the flow of energy through the whole system that is determined by the Codes of LIFE that direct the multitasked processes of every step of the flow of energy through LIFE. The information of LIFE organizes the innate characteristics of non-living components of LIFE to generate the emergence of LIFE.

Evolution (Life Codes - Chapters 08 and 09)
  Genetics
  Variability
  Natural Selection

Diversity/Variability – In the context of evolution, diversity means that every individual within a species (or other naturally evolved system) is usually or often somewhat different from every other, so that some will be better able to survive when changes occur in their environments. Natural selection will tend to preserve those systems that are most successful in passing on their collaborative traits. Evolution then sustains the survivability of naturally evolved systems, using genetics to record and preserve the changes (See evolution and systems) and pass them into the future.

Evolution, including genetics and the Codes of LIFE, including the inheritance of traits and transmission of traits, is responsible for the resilience of LIFE systems and ultimately for their sustainability, because it provides the complex of information that sustains them and at the same time permits them to change in collaboration with their environments.

Evolution is not adaptation; evolution is not reversible. Adaptation is usually reversible.

The above are some of the interacting characteristics of LIFE and of ourselves as living beings. We are naturally evolved systems, living within naturally evolved systems and composed of naturally evolved systems. To survive individually and as a species we must not destroy our internal or external environments. Or the balance among them.

Our choices now determine the environments of our human future.

Death = The absence of the emergent property of LIFE.

APPENDIX E

IN THE BEGINNING

"In the beginning was the word, and the word was with God and the Word was God."
(The Holy Bible, John I:1)

"The matter in the bodies of all life-forms, including, of course, mammals like us, can be traced to the carbon, nitrogen, oxygen and other elements that were made in the supernova explosions of stars." (Margulis and Sagan, 1995)

In the beginning was the Big Bang, and immediately was our universe born. It did not look like this picture, or even like the sun. The universe was and is unimaginable (at least it is for me), even though we can know many facts about it.

Our universe began, so the physicists say, as the explosion perhaps not explosion – perhaps instantaneous conversion into plasma from the most concentrated possible form of pure energy, of a size even smaller than would settle on the palm of a human hand.

For a few nano-seconds after that, the universe was probably a uniform plasma consisting of the most basic building blocks of everything; that is, energy. Smaller than atoms, smaller than atomic nuclei, a quark-gluon plasma* at temperatures unimaginably hot.

All is energy. Energy is, potentially, information, or can be used as information.

The big bang is thought to have occurred about fourteen billion years ago, give or take. (See the time table beginning on page 12 of this chapter.)

The expansion of the new universe, at enormously high temperatures, is thought for a few nanoseconds to have been uniform, but uniform is not random, and is not information. Random variability developed almost immediately as the release of energy led to both movement and cooling. (Hazen, 2001, lecture 30; Gell-Mann, 1994; Lloyd, 2006, 2016; Pang, 2016). And, the physical "forces," the natural laws studied by quantum physics, came into being. From that time until now, the distribution of energy (and mass), the variations in the distribution of formlessness (and form) in the universe have been driven by the physical forces – the force of gravity, the strong and weak nuclear forces, and electromagnetism, and by the natural laws that came into play as higher levels of organization evolved (see chapters 08 and 09 for evolution), which is evidently the primary creative law of nature and so of LIFE and then the Life of Earth. But Earth comes later in this story.

> "Our primeval system in its most primitive state of random uniformity, lacking structure, composed of energy, and formless entropy was nascent information, and this state, according to mathematical models, lasted for some minute fraction of one of our minutes before the uniformity began to take some probably random forms, perhaps aggregations, perhaps swirls and vortices." (L. Pang *et al.* 2016)

This model of the creation of our universe derives from computer simulations that have not so far been convincingly contradicted by other evidence, and thus is interpretation based in the mind of man, rather than the facts of history, but whatever the details, it is very likely there was a big bang, followed by a plasma-gluon uniformity, followed by random or not random aggregations of matter, followed by the natural consequences thereof.

The universe inflated, from less than the size of a pinhead to nearly the entire size of the now universe, in an instant (Sutherland, 2013) and the event began its long future of aggregating information in the form of matter. As it expanded, it cooled, and as it cooled the simplest of energetic systems, the fundamental particles condensed, quarks and leptons, then a vast sea of electrons. About half a million years into its life, the universe had cooled sufficiently that the first very simple atoms formed of protons, neutrons and electrons -- material particles in the universal expanse, and the basic building blocks of atoms and molecules that are necessary components of LIFE

The universe has continued to expand at a rate that depends upon the balance between the force created by the big (unimaginably humongous) bang, and the force of gravity that tends to pull together the mass of the universe that gradually "condenses out" as the universe-system expands and cools.

The interactions among the un-evenly distributed particles of matter invoked the force of gravity, resulting in gravitational systems composed of clouds of material particles, more here and less there as determined by earlier (perhaps random) plasma fluxes.

Gravitational systems, unlike our everyday world, exhibit negative specific energy. This means that matter does not come to equilibrium with its environment in the way that the temperature in a cup of hot coffee will lose heat energy until it matches that of its environment. In a gravitational system, where particles of matter such as the earliest atoms are held together by gravity, whenever an energized particle is lost to infinity, the remaining particles clump more closely together and increase the energy of their motion. Because of this, when the gravitational system loses energy, the system is pulled more tightly together by the force of gravity and the whole system gains kinetic (motion) energy, the particles move faster and faster and pull together more and more closely, getting hotter and hotter. (Seth Lloyd Lecture at Santa Fe Institute, 2016).

And over the next few billions of years, the simpler atoms, hydrogen for example, came together in areas where clouds of atomic dust accumulated, and accumulations of matter gave rise to massive objects that interacted among themselves according to the natural laws. And in areas of very high concentration of matter, as the pressure of its own mass increased, and bore down upon its central core, the first star burst into flame.

> "And God said: 'Let there be light.' And there was light." The Holy Bible, Genesis.

The first stars, and then galaxies, formed at enormous temperatures, about 11 billion years ago, and can be seen today so far away that it has taken that long for the light of their flame to reach us. The light is almost uniformly greenish.

"Some nearby galaxies and nebulae produce a little bit of this hue today. But these early galaxies, seen as they were roughly 11 billion years ago, produce an overwhelming amount." "Everybody was doing it," said Matthew Malkan, an astrophysicist at UCLA. "It seems like all galaxies started this way." _SN: 10/1/16, p. 25_

> "... be not ignorant of this one thing, that one day _is_ with the Lord as a thousand years, and a thousand years as one day." 2 Peter 3.8. Or perhaps a billion years or more; we who have so little sense of God's time.

Stars were born and stars died in great explosions, supernovae, and in the extreme heat and compression of the supernovae were created, various combinations of the smaller atoms such as hydrogen were fused to create larger atoms, the materials of which Life itself was later to be formed. Carbon, nitrogen, oxygen and the rest of the periodic table of elements.

And that is the briefest view of how it came to pass that, between 4 and 5 billions of our years ago, there was an Earth, swinging around a sun as part of our solar system.

> "And God said: 'Let the waters under the heavens be gathered together in one place, and let the dry land appear.' And it was so." (Genesis I-9)

And when the conditions became right, it rained water upon the earth for 10,000 years or more, until water rippled and flowed upon the land and between the continents.

And the universe has been expanding ever since, of course in the process releasing energy that comes to existence in various increasingly complex forms, including LIFE itself.

"We have seen how, when complex adaptive systems establish themselves, they operate through the cycle of variable schemata, accidental circumstances, phenotypic consequences and feedback of selection pressures to the competition among schemata, they tend to explore a huge space of possibilities, with openings to higher levels of complexity and to the generation of new types of complex adaptive system. Over long periods of time, they distill out of their experience remarkable amounts of information, characterized by both complexity and depth." (Gell-Mann, 1994)

In this way the earth gave birth to its own new cycles of information, as the energy and entropy interacted among themselves according to the exponentially increasing numbers of possibilities inherent in the factual information generated by its increasing numbers of integrated complex adaptive systems during its incredible history, based on the multitude of ways in which its subsystems could (or could not) interact among themselves, their sweet spots, in every possible manner – natural selection, symbiosis, emergent properties, even catastrophe -- to generate higher and broader levels of complexity that then again interacted among themselves in an infinitude of ways that were not efficient, and a few ways that were spectacularly well suited to their environments -- and to select/maintain those subsystems that contributed to their common evolution, the Law of The Creation, and further refinement of the available information upon which evolution is based.

Information growing out of information, availing itself of usable energy to generate every possible combination of systems that were available, retain those that were useful to the complex of systems, and thus to grow the complex interactions of the Life of Earth.

And about four and a half billion years ago the Lord said:

"Let there be Life."

And a cell was born, and the Earth gave birth to Life.

"And God saw everything that he had made, and behold, it was very good." (Genesis)

"The information stored in such a system at any one time includes contributions from its entire history. That is true of biological evolution, which has been going on for four billion years or so, and also of the cultural evolution of *Homo sapiens sapiens*, for which the time span is more like a hundred thousand years." (Gell- Mann, 1994)

And the information that has survived this entire history is encoded (see Chapters 06 and 09) in the DNA of our cells, the functions of our physiology, the processes of our modern corposystem, and the world views of our incredible brains that we could be using to survive our current malaise if we would only get it into our heads that the behaviors (including human behaviors) that ARE CAPABLE OF SURVIVAL do not involve our wishes and wants, or especially our efforts, to *dominate* the works of God, but rather those behaviors that *contribute to the ongoing interactive welfare* of the miracle of LIFE within which we are embedded and integrated, and these behaviors are very well described and explained in the very heart and soul of all our major religions that tell us a few of the successful ways that we could survive the millennia by partnering with the rest of the creation, rather than trying to dominate it.

OOOOOOO

---

*Plasma is a physics word that refers to a fourth state (in addition to liquid, solid and gas) in which matter/energy can exist, depending upon conditions. Again, difficult to imagine, but the temperature of the universe at this time was supposed to have been extremely high, and the plasma represented the pure energy from which matter condensed as the universe expanded and cooled. Such conditions of the Creation of the universe would have been highly unusual and un-measurable, and so the related hypotheses are mathematical models based in the observable and testable realities of now.

This Appendix E is dedicated, with great respect, to Dr. Lynn Margulis

History of Biological Systems	Time Frame	Human Population
The Big Bang	13.7 billion ya	0

According to the standard Big Bang model, the universe was born during a period of inflation that began about **13.7 billion years ago**. Like a rapidly expanding balloon, it swelled from a size smaller than an electron to nearly its current size within a tiny fraction of a second.

Atoms and molecules	Small atoms created at the time. Others created through cycles of burning stars, and the same is true of some molecules (water, methane, etc), but not organic molecules that are produced by organisms.	
First generation of stars and galaxies	11 billion years ago	
Earth (non-biological system)	4.4 billion years ago	
LIFE of Earth (prokaryotic) And organic molecules	3.8 billion years ago	
Eukaryotic cells	2.5 billion years ago	
Tissue level (multicellular)	600 – 550 million years ago	
First Forests	350 million years ago	
First true Primates	5.5 million years ago (in Asia) Migration to Africa, diet changed to leaves and fruits	
First hominids	15 million years ago Tool makers, large brain size	
Homo sapiens	100,000-200,000 years ago Talking and thinking	

Out of Africa	70,000 years ago	
Paleolithic partnership style social system	30,000 BCE to a little after 10,000 BCE Population fluctuated around	6 million
Last Ice age	20,000-18,000 years ago Collaborative Style Social System (Eisler, 1987)	6 million
Lascaux Cave Paintings	16.000 years ago	
Invention of agriculture	10,000 years ago	population rise
Domination social system begins	4,300 to 4,200 BCE	
Fall of Crete	3,200 BCE	
Original towns and cities	partnership style social system collapsing	
Modern cities	emerged roughly about 4,000 BCE population doubled or more every millenium	(Newitz, 2016)
Neolithic revolution	Dominator style "co-dependent" social system (Eisler, 1987)	
Sargon – "modern warfare" (Campbell) (Toms, 1990/Campbell)	2,350 BC	27 million
Buddhism	about 2,400 yeas ago	
Roman society in trouble	2000 years ago	over 100 million.
Christianity	modern version About year 400	

Purging of the partnership societies   As late as 12th century
Witchburning and   (Starhawk, 1997)
Church crackdowns

Today   7.5 billion

Looks like a system with a runaway positive feedback loop, perhaps the result of overcoming a limiting factor(s) by means of changed social management styles. Changed, around the time that human social systems invented agriculture – or perhaps about the time that human social systems condensed, from collaborative to dominational, probably with many smaller changes along the way.